Reinventing the Research University

The production and distribution of this book is sponsored by the Hewlett Packard Company in the United States and Europe

Reinventing the Research University

Edited by

Luc E. Weber
and
James J. Duderstadt

⊞ ECONOMICA
London, Paris, Genève

Other Titles in the Series

Governance in Higher Education. The University in a State of Flux
Werner Z. Hirsch and Luc E. Weber, eds.

As the Walls of Academia are Tumbling Down
Werner Z. Hirsch and Luc E. Weber, eds.

Reinventing the Research University
Luc E. Weber and James J. Duderstadt, eds.

To Werner Z. Hirsch
Respected scholar and teacher,
rigorous and independent-minded researcher,
ever inquisitive and creative thinker
and a founder of the Glion Colloquium

his colleagues dedicate this book
with appreciation and admiration.

CONTENTS

PREFACE

The fourth Glion Colloquium was held in Glion, near Montreux, in Switzerland, from June 22 to 24, 2003. The Glion Colloquia were launched in May 1998 by Werner Z. Hirsch, of UCLA, and Luc E. Weber, of the University of Geneva, to bring together university leaders from America and Europe to share their perspectives of the issues facing higher education. The first three colloquia concerned topics such as the global forces driving change in higher education, the governance of the contemporary university and the increasingly permeable boundaries between the university and broader society. Papers presented at each of these colloquia, along with key elements of the ensuing discussion, were then published as books.

The Glion IV Colloquium drew together active university leaders (presidents, rectors, vice-chancellors) along with guests from industry with close ties to academe, to compare perspectives of the future of the research university in America and Europe, as reflected in its title, *Reinventing the Research University*. Although there was considerable discussion about whether it would be more accurate to use other verbs—such as "reforming", "renewing" or "refocusing"—there was general agreement that change would characterize the future of the research university, driven both by powerful social, economic, and technological forces external to academe, as well as by important internal forces such as the changing nature of scholarship and learning.

There was a general recognition that universities have always evolved as integral parts of their societies to meet the challenges of their environments. Indeed, this disposition to change is a basic characteristic and strength of university life, the result of the constant generation of new knowledge through scholarship on campuses that, in turn, changes the education they provide and influences the societies that surround them. In this sense, the research university both drives and is driven by social change. Yet, despite this long tradition of evolution, the forces driving change in higher education are particularly powerful today: the changing needs in education driven by a global, knowledge-dependent economy; demographic change driven by the mobility of populations and the needs of under-served communities; the rapid evolution of information and communications technologies which, in turn, drive the accelerating pace of intellectual change in scholarship and learning; the powerful forces of the marketplace threatening to overwhelm public policy and drive a fundamental restructuring of the higher education enterprise on a global scale; the rising costs of excellence in the face of increasingly limited sources of public funding; and the increasing demands for public accountability driven by an erosion in public trust that constrains both governance and management of our institutions.

These factors raise many complex issues that require serious consideration by the academic community. For example, while the university's traditional mission of creating, maintaining, and diffusing knowledge requires some degree of institutional autonomy and freedom, the increasing dependence of our world on the advancement of scientific and technological knowledge not only expands the mission and roles of the university in addressing social priorities, but it furthermore links the university more tightly to the society it serves. In a similar sense, the increasing complexity and interdisciplinary nature of the problems faced by society will require not only a restructuring of the scientific disciplines, but their further integration with academic disciplines from the humanities, the arts, the social sciences and the professions.

Yet, even as research universities play an ever more central role in identifying and addressing the important problems facing humanity, the erosion of public support suggests that society fails to appreciate the value of these institutions. Here university leaders face the challenge of better explaining to the public the return on investment in research and higher education.

A third challenge involves the nature of the interaction between the university and the wider community (e.g., governments, industry, society at large) as well as within the university itself (e.g., faculty, students, staff, governing bodies). Here again, the forces of change both upon and within our institutions will almost certainly demand a major rethinking, if not a significant restructuring of these linkages.

Yet, despite these challenges, the research university today is more central to contemporary society than ever before. It educates the graduates who sustain commerce, government and professional practice; it performs the research and scholarship so essential to a knowledge-driven global economy;

and it applies this knowledge to meet a diverse array of social needs, including health care, economic development, cultural life, and national security. Hence, while it is clear that universities need to reconsider their future role and mission and seek the resources, autonomy, and freedom that allow them to adapt to a time of change, they must do so in a way that recognizes their public purpose, their responsibility to serve the societies that created, depend upon and sustain them.

While the general nature of these challenges, opportunities and obligations were recognized and shared by all of the participants in the Glion IV Colloquium, it was also clear that they acquired a somewhat different character and required considerably different strategies that were heavily dependent upon particular geopolitical situations. For example, the response to the eroding public support of American universities has stimulated a dramatic increase in student fees (tuition) and private philanthropy, options made difficult in Europe by existing public perceptions and tax policies. The great mobility of students and faculty in America has created a highly competitive university marketplace, a feature only now beginning to appear in the European Union with major policies such as those contained in the 1999 Bologna agreement and the European Research Council proposals.

The papers contained in this book reflect both the consensus and differences in the perspectives of the participants on these issues. In Part I, the papers by Frank Rhodes, Robert Zemsky and James Duderstadt, and Luc Weber and Pavel Zgaga, as well as Sir Howard Newby, set the stage by considering the forces that are likely to change the nature of the research university. In Part II, Roger Downer, James Duderstadt, and Frans van Vught discuss the changing nature of education and scholarship. Part III then continues with papers by Robert Zemsky, Andre Oosterlinck, Nils Hasselmo, Marcel Crochet and Wayne Johnson on the changing nature of the interaction between the research university and broader society. In Part IV, Luc Weber, Marye Anne Fox, Frank Rhodes and Marcel Crochet explore the challenges of financing and governing the contemporary research university. In the concluding chapter an effort is made to pull together these discussions to develop more specific suggestions concerning those issues and strategies that universities should consider as they approach a period of rapid change.

Yet, as Frank Rhodes reminds us in the first paper, despite the powerful forces confronting the contemporary university, we must also bear in mind that this remarkable institution has been one of the most enduring in our society in large part because of its capacity to adapt and evolve to serve a modernizing world while holding fast to its fundamental values and character. Perhaps the real focus of the Glion IV Colloquium and the primary challenge to the research university are a reformation of those fundamental processes that allow and shape institutional adaptation and evolution, while refocusing universities on their most fundamental missions of remaining places of learning where human potential is transformed and shaped, the wisdom of cultures is passed from one generation to the next, and the new knowledge that creates the future is produced.

* *
*

We thank, in Europe, the Higher Education Funding Council for England, and, in Switzerland, the Federal Agency for Education and Science in Bern, the AVINA Foundation in Hurden, the Board of the Swiss Federal Institutes of Technology in Zurich and Lausanne, the University of Geneva and Nestlé in Vevey for their generous financial support, without which the fourth Colloquium would not have been possible. We are also very grateful to Hewlett Packard Corporation in the United States and Europe for sponsoring the production and the distribution of this book.

Finally, we are particularly pleased to thank those who directly or indirectly contributed to the production of this book. We are very grateful to Professor J. F. Grin, from the University of Geneva, and Mr. Gerry Taggart from the Higher Education Funding Council for England who took extensive notes of the debates and made useful proposals for the issues addressed in the conclusion of this book. We also thank very warmly Mr. Edmund Doogue in Geneva, who provided rigorous editorial assistance. Finally, we thank Ms Martina Trucco and Mr. Nicolas Weber for their very kind and efficient help to make the colloquium run smoothly.

James J. Duderstadt   *Luc E. Weber*
University of Michigan   *University of Geneva*

CONTRIBUTORS
AND PARTICIPANTS

CONTRIBUTORS

CROCHET, Marcel

Marcel Crochet holds an electrical and mechanical engineering degree from the Université catholique de Louvain (1961). He pursued his graduate studies at the University of California, Berkeley, where he obtained a Ph.D. in Applied mechanics in 1966. He began his academic career at the University of Louvain in 1966, while he served as a visiting professor in a number of American and European universities. He became rector of the Université catholique de Louvain (Louvain-la-Neuve) in 1995. Marcel Crochet is the author of a book and some 140 scientific publications in the field of rheology; he was awarded the gold medal of the British Society of Rheology in 1995. He was the initiator of a fluid mechanics programme called Polyflow that produced a spin-off company; the programme is now used by a large number of corporate laboratories and universities around the world.

DOWNER, Roger G. H.

Professor Roger Downer was born in Belfast and obtained the degrees of B.Sc. and M.Sc. from the Queen's University Belfast, before moving to Canada where he completed the degree of Ph.D. at the University of Western Ontario. He was later awarded the degree of D.Sc. from Queen's University Belfast and the honorary degree of LL.D. from the same university. Most of Professor Downer's academic career has been spent at the University of Waterloo, Canada, where he served as Professor of Biology and

Chemistry and Vice-President. He is the editor or co-editor of four books, author or co-author of over 160 research publications, an elected Fellow of the Royal Society of Canada and the recipient of several national and international research awards. Professor Downer served as President of the Asian Institute of Technology, an international postgraduate university based in Thailand, from 1996 to 1998. He took up the Presidency and Vice-Chancellorship of the University of Limerick in September 1998, and has served as Chairman of the Council of Heads of Irish Universities and Chair of the Council of Rectors of Ireland.

DUDERSTADT, James J.

Dr. James J. Duderstadt is President Emeritus and University Professor of Science and Engineering at the University of Michigan. His teaching and research interests have spanned a wide range of subjects in science, mathematics and engineering. He currently chairs several major national commissions in areas including federal research policy, higher education, information technology and nuclear energy.

FOX, Marye Anne

Marye Anne Fox, a physical organic chemist, is Chancellor of North Carolina State University and a Distinguished University Professor of Chemistry. She has received many national and international awards for her contributions to science and science policy, and has held more than 50 endowed lectureships at universities around the world. She currently serves on the President's Council of Advisors on Science and Technology, on the National Academy of Sciences Committee on Science and Engineering Public Policy, as co-chair of the National Research Council's Government-University-Industry Research Roundtable, and as a member of the North Carolina Board of Science and Technology.

HASSELMO, Nils

Nils Hasselmo became president of the Association of American Universities in 1998. Founded in 1900, the association now has as members 60 U.S. and two Canadian public and private research universities. From 1989-97, he served as President of the University of Minnesota, and from 1983-88 as senior vice president and Provost of the University of Arizona. Nils Hasselmo received his Ph.D. in linguistics from Harvard University in 1961, after studies at Uppsala University in Sweden. His service to higher education includes the chairmanship of the board of the National Association of State Universities and Land Grant Colleges, and membership of the board of the Carnegie Foundation for the Advancement of Teaching.

JOHNSON, Wayne

Wayne Johnson is Executive Director, University Relations Worldwide, of Hewlett Packard in Palo Alto. During his career, he has gathered significant management experience across a diversified set of business operations including university relations management, engineering management, programme management, international training and logistics, research, international business development and commercial business development mainly with Raytheon in different locations, as well as with Microsoft Research. He has a M.B.A. from Boston College, Caroll School, in Chestnut Hill, MA.

NEWBY, Howard

Sir Howard Newby joined the Higher Education Funding Council for England as Chief Executive in October 2001. Prior to that he was Vice-Chancellor of the University of Southampton from 1994 to 2001. His earlier posts include Chairman and Chief Executive of the Economic and Social Research Council, Professor of Sociology at the University of Essex and Professor of Sociology and Rural Sociology at the University of Wisconsin, Madison. Professor Newby has served on a number of government bodies concerned with the funding of research in the U.K. From 1999 to 2001, he was President of Universities U.K. He was also President of the British Association for the Advancement of Science for 2001-02. Professor Newby was awarded a CBE in 1995 for his services to social science and a knighthood in 2000 for his services to higher education.

OOSTERLINCK, André

André J.J. Oosterlinck received his Ph.D. from the K.U.Leuven in biomedical image processing in 1977 after having worked at a number of American laboratories, including the Jet Propulsion Lab. Full Professor and research manager of the MI2 (Machine Intelligende & Imaging) unit of ESAT (Department of Electrical Engineering, K.U.Leuven), consisting of over 65 researchers active in digital signal and image processing, he became the director of ESAT in 1984 (250 researchers and staff members). He was appointed Vice-President for the Exact Sciences and a member of the board of directors of the University of Leuven in 1990, and President of the Flemish Science Policy Council in 1994. Since August 1995 Prof. Oosterlinck has been Rector and President of the K.U.Leuven (1,500 staff members, including the academic hospital, and more than 28,000 students). André Oosterlinck is also founder and co-founder of several fully international companies such as ICOS Vision Systems (robot vision and automatic visual inspection for the micro-electronic industry), EASICS (a design company for customs ships), ISMC (a company designing software for process control), a member of the board of directors of several institutes and companies and a member of various scientific commissions. His work has been widely published, appearing in more than 250 international publications.

RHODES, Frank H. T.

Frank Rhodes was president of Cornell University for 18 years before retiring in 1995, having previously served as vice president for academic affairs at the University of Michigan. A geologist by training, Frank Rhodes was a member of President Bush's Education Policy Advisory Committee. He has also served as chairman of the National Science Board and chairman of the boards of the American Council on Education, the American Association of Universities, and the Carnegie Foundation for the Advancement of Teaching. He was chairman of the American Council on Education's task force on minority education, which produced the report "One-Third of a Nation", for which former presidents Jimmy Carter and Gerald Ford served as honorary co-chairs. He is currently president of the American Philosophical Society.

Van VUGHT, Frans

Frans van Vught is Rector Magnificus of the University of Twente in the Netherlands. In addition he is member of the Netherlands' Innovation Platform, the Dutch National Social Economic Council, of the Dutch National Council on Education and of the University Grants Committee of Hong Kong. He was the founding director of the Center for Higher Education Policy Studies (CHEPS), the world's largest higher education study centre. He has been published widely on higher education in various languages and has served as a consultant for many international organizations, governments and higher education institutions.

WEBER, Luc E.

Educated in the fields of economics and political science, Luc Weber has been Professor of Public Economics at the University of Geneva since 1975. As an economist, he serves as an adviser to Switzerland's federal government, as well as to cantonal governments, and has been a member of the "Swiss Council of Economic Advisers" for three years. Since 1982, Prof. Weber has been deeply involved in university management and higher education policy, first as vice-rector, then as rector of the University of Geneva, as well as Chairman and, subsequently, Consul for international affairs of the Swiss Rectors' Conference. At present he is vice-president of the Steering Committee for Higher Education and Research of the Council of Europe and of the International Association of Universities (IAU), as well as a member of the board of the European University Association. He is also the co-founder, with Werner Hirsch, of the Glion Colloquium.

ZEMSKY, Robert

Robert Zemsky currently serves as Professor and Chair of The Learning Alliance for Higher Education at the University of Pennsylvania. The Learning Alliance is a broad coalition of organizations assisting universities to implement their agendas for change. Professor Zemsky was the founding Director of the Institute for Research on Higher Education at the University of Pennsylvania. His current research examines how, in a world increasingly dominated by market forces, colleges and universities can remain mission-centred.

ZGAGA, Pavel

Pavel Zgaga is a professor and Dean of the Faculty of Education at University of Ljubljana and Director of its Centre for Education Policy Studies. His research interests are focused on social philosophy, the philosophy of education and education policy. He was State Secretary for Higher Education (1992-1999) and Minister of Education (1999-2000) of the Republic of Slovenia. He was also general rapporteur for the European Education Ministers'conference in Berlin, September 18-19, 2003.

PARTICIPANTS

The following leading academics actively participated in the Fourth Glion colloquium and contributed, with comments and statements, to the revision of the papers collected here and to the conclusion.

Professor Richard ATKINSON, President of the University of California System

Dr. Michel BENARD, HP University Relations, Europe

Professor Robert M. BERDAHL, Chancellor of the University of California at Berkeley

Professor André HURST, Rector of the University of Geneva

Professor Jakob NUESCH, President Emeritus of the Swiss Federal Institute of Technology (ETHZ), Zurich

Professor Christina ULLENIUS, Rector of the University of Karlstad and President of the Swedish Rectors' conference

Professor David WARD, President of the American Council on Education in Washington D.C. and Chancellor Emeritus of the University of Wisconsin-Madison

PART I

•••••••••••••

Setting the Scene

CHAPTER 1

Reinventing the University

Frank H. T. Rhodes

INTRODUCTION

During the course of the next few days we shall examine almost every aspect of the life and the work of the university, asking ourselves the question of what "reinvention" implies. I want, at the outset, to say that I think reinventing the university is at the extreme end of a spectrum of possibilities for changing the institution as we know it. These possibilities go all the way from reinvention – and presumably replacement – through reform, renewal, refocus to retention and reinforcement. Which of these possible changes do we seek? I ask this question, not simply to be pedantic, but to pose the more serious question: Is the university in need of reinvention or renewal?

Reinvention is a radical conception, especially for an institution that has existed for a millennium and is still vigorous, and for which there is no single model or style. And if reinvention implies the replacement of the existing university by some alternative structure, what institution or structure would we propose to respond either to existing needs or to impending needs? "Reinvention" suggests that the existing university is either unwilling or unable to meet those societal needs. Is that really the case?

I propose to limit my comment to the American university. There are in the United States some 3,600 institutions of higher education. That number is doubled or trebled when universities of other nations are considered. The American university, to some extent unlike that of other lands, has no single model, no single membership, no single pattern of organization, no single aim, no single style, no single method of finance, no single method of government. Each of the 3,600 universities and colleges is an individual institution which, although one may identify 8 to 10 institutional categories, has its own distinctive, mission, style and ethos. Though the universities of

3

other nations are less heterogeneous, each of these, in turn, has a distinctive style and a distinctive history. To speak of "reinventing" the university as though the university were a single institutional type is to underestimate the enormous variability of higher education in responding to the broader needs of society.

It is also worth recalling that the university in its long history of a thousand years has proved a remarkably adaptable and flexible institution. Indeed, it might be argued that, apart from the Catholic Church, it is the oldest institution in the Western Hemisphere. Clark Kerr has reminded us that "taking, as a starting point, 1530, when the Lutheran Church was founded, some 66 institutions that existed then still exist today in the western world in recognizable forms: the Catholic Church, the Lutheran Church, the Parliaments of Iceland and the Isle of Man, and 62 universities. They have experienced wars, revolutions, depressions, and industrial transformations, and have come out less changed than almost any other segment of their societies."

In an age of rapid corporate openings and closures and of institutional origins and extinctions it is to be noted that the longevity of the university of the Western world reflects not only its immutability of purpose, but its extraordinary skill in adapting and applying its services to societal needs. That adaptability has sometimes been slow and sometimes begrudging; it has frequently been in response to external pressures and threats; it has proceeded both by nationwide change and by individual institutional change, but it has nevertheless been real and substantial. And it still continues. Current changes are, perhaps, as significant as any in the last 100 years.

Though there is no unity of particular programme, membership, governance, finance, or style in the university, there is, perhaps, a broad unity of function. The typical university combines higher education and advanced research and scholarship so as to serve the public good. The balance between those three activities varies greatly from institution to institution and, to some extent, from country to country and from region to region, but their interconnectedness is what is distinctive about higher education.

In considering the possibility of the reinvention of the university it is also worth recalling that the governments of many Western countries have encouraged a target enrolment pattern of some 45-50 % of their college-age population, 18-22 year olds. This reflects, presumably, the general agreement that university education produces not only personal gain, but also contributes to the public good. This contribution to the public good is of immense significance in the contemporary world. It involves not only general education and cultural enrichment, but also professional training and certification, lifelong education, the inculcation of democratic values, the provision of social mobility, the pursuit of fundamental research, the development of advanced technology, the provision of advanced medical care and public health, support for agricultural development, material resources, conservation and economic development. In each one of these areas the universities play a notable role, some in all these areas, others in a more limited range; but overall the contribution to national wealth and wellbeing provided by the universities is of growing significance in the life of all developed and many developing nations.

What then requires "reinvention"? Is it the university as an institution? Is it the purpose of the university? Is it the performance of the university? Is it the governance of the university? Is it the membership of the university? Is it the balance between its various responsibilities? Is it its responsiveness to public needs and demands, or is it some other aspect of the life of the university? These questions require discussion.

Furthermore, is reinvention and, by implication, replacement, the most responsible method of change for universities? Perhaps a milder form of change involving rethinking, reform, or refocus would be more appropriate. Perhaps we should think of retaining the university, but refinancing its various activities. Perhaps we should think of restoring the universities to the levels of individual support they once enjoyed. Perhaps we should think about reinforcing the university in its role or renewing the ageing facilities of its campus.

All these options are available to us, but only reinvention involves the replacement of the existing broad model of the university by some alternative institutional structure.

Why is it that at this particular time, we face the call for reinvention of the university? It is, I suppose, because societal needs and pressures are now seen by some as so intense that they threaten to overwhelm the structures we have created to respond to them. Let me examine these pressures as they affect the American situation. What, we should ask, lies behind the proposed reinvention of the university? Why is there pressure, or perhaps need, to reinvent the institution?

It seems to me there are four different kinds of pressure, all of them now growing more intense. First, pressures of need and opportunity seem now to be more varied and more intense than those of earlier years. These include not only pressing and growing societal needs, challenges and programmes, but also the scientific, medical and technological opportunities that abound. These latter opportunities exist not simply as mental challenges and intellectual opportunities, but also as direct methods of responding to pressing social needs and contributing to the broader public welfare. Opportunity pressures involve burgeoning society needs, from failing public schools to crumbling physical infrastructures to dysfunctional health-care systems. At the same time, there are growing demands on the expertise of virtually all the major professions and all this in an atmosphere of litigation and complaint. Furthermore, the growing scientific and technological means and opportunities to respond to these needs place heavy professional demands and obligations on the university. Health care and education, for example, on a national level, involve the employment and professional contributions of people trained in the university's laboratories, hospitals and classrooms. Furthermore, success in grasping these opportunities now results in intense inter-institutional competition, with all the pressures that accompany it because some of these challenges exist on such a scale that smaller institutions are incapable of undertaking the educational and scholarly work required. Only institutions with major resources and facilities can provide the necessary contributions.

Financial pressures are also extreme, both for public and for private universities. For public universities, the budgetary shortfalls being experienced in virtually all the states have led to severe curtailment of state support for higher education. In some cases, the reductions range from 10 % to 20 %, but few institutions have been spared some significant financial loss. In some cases, these reductions have been imposed in the middle of the academic year.

For private institutions, the declining levels of institutional endowments have forced significant reductions in operating budgets. Since most operating budgets are based on the three-year rolling average of the returns on investment, the most severe operating budget reductions are only now beginning to take effect, but they are, in many cases, as severe as those being experienced by public universities. For both public and private universities, the burdens of federal requirements and reporting are also severe, and the general deterioration in the economic and fiscal environment poses significant long-term problems for the funding of higher education. There is also the added complication that federal tax policies that are needed to stimulate the economy, may, or may not, benefit higher education. Congress has still to re-authorize the higher education act that regulates federal student financial aid programmes. The level of support for this legislation is of critical interest to the universities.

In the midst of these pressures, the level of support from donors, sponsors and foundations has also declined, largely as a result of the same reversals in the stock market that have impacted institutional endowment support. Many foundations have now cut back significantly in their support for higher education, and gift levels to universities, though steady in a few cases, are in most cases showing declines.

The impact of these various financial pressures has resulted in two other kinds of secondary financial pressures on the universities. First, demand for student financial aid has shown sharp increases, as the families of undergraduates have themselves been exposed to financial pressures. Second, local community needs have increased sharply, as a result of lost tax revenues and declining employment, and have placed added demands on the university for local contributions and support.

Accessibility pressures are also playing a part in leading some to demand reinvention of the university. Overall enrolments over the last few decades have increased steadily and the composition of each entering class shows increasing social diversity in the presence of non-traditional undergraduates and of those from previously under-represented communities. This creates two distinct challenges. On the one hand, the increasing numbers of both non-traditional and previously under-represented students means that there are some who, not having enjoyed the benefit of a superior high-school education, are less well prepared than others. On the other hand, there is now a major challenge before the Supreme Court to the University of Michigan's admissions programmes, both at the undergraduate level and in the Law School. The whole future of affirmative action is at present unclear, but the issue is not likely to go away.

The other enrolment pressure involves not admission, but retention and graduation. There is widespread concern at the dropout rate of individuals of all groups before graduating. This is a conspicuous statistic and is widely seen by the public as an example of either instructional inefficiency or academic waste, or both.

Accountability pressures are also a matter of increasing importance. These involve funding-agency pressures, not all of them governmental, pressures for economy in the use of resources and efficiency in the achievement of results. Nowhere are the pressures for accountability more conspicuous than in areas of quality assessment. Traditionally, the universities have enjoyed the privilege of self-regulation, but some are now confronted with the threat of standardized tests imposed by the states, sometimes on graduating seniors, to assure the quality of their product. In contrast to earlier voluntary accreditation, some public institutions are now confronting the prospect of state validation, authorization, regulation and prescription in the award of degrees. Republican leaders of the U.S. House of Representatives are reported to be looking "for ways to hold colleges more accountable for the performance of their students and to curb increases in the institutions' prices." (Chronicle 2003). This would represent a fundamental change in institutional autonomy and one that has the potential for serious damage.

Added to the pressures for economy and efficiency, there is also the pressure, both internal and external, for relevance. One sees, for example, the decline in applicants for admission to courses in science and engineering, both in North America and in the U.K. One sees the same call for relevance in the case of those who argue for less emphasis on the traditional liberal arts and more on "relevant training". Even strong departments with established reputations are now facing a lack of sustainability because of a lack of student numbers. The debate concerning targeted research, as opposed to speculative research, is also becoming more sharply defined.

In all these areas the question of balance becomes fundamentally important and this is rarely achieved by external imposition. It tends to be achieved rather by refined and sensitive internal adjustments, and it is these that may be threatened by excessive external control. This is as true in the instructional area as it is in research and development.

One particular area of both public and internal discontent is the subject of inter-collegiate athletics. With increasing frequency, universities, both large and small, have been accused of serious lapses of moral and financial responsibility in pursuing athletic competition. Unless universities show more responsibility in self-regulation, it seems increasingly likely that increased external regulation may be imposed.

In the area of research and development, three particular pressures have recently emerged. The first concerns ethical issues involved, for example, in stem-cell research. The realization that the number of stem-cell lines available for biomedical research is now significantly smaller under federal regulations than was originally supposed, will create increasing ethical issues on many campuses. Furthermore, the whole question of commercialization, not only of research and development, but of such university services as distance learning, imposes both potential hazards and potential benefits. The use of human subjects has also become a matter of public concern in both research and development and in the broader area of patient care, clinical trials and public-health studies. Well-publicized lapses in these areas are likely to bring growing external pressure for reform.

Added to all these issues is that of homeland security. Colleges and universities are now required to implement three significant acts, the U.S.A. Patriot Act, the Border Security Act and the Bio-Terrorism Preparedness and Response Act, each of which has the potential to intrude into areas of traditional campus responsibility. The latter act, for example, strengthens federal oversight over bio-hazardous materials.

It is, presumably, the sum total of these pressures which leads some to call for the "reinvention" of the university.

AREAS OF POTENTIAL CHANGE

As one looks at both these pressures and at the external and internal critiques of the university, it becomes clear that there are at least four major areas of concern: the mission, goals and scale of individual universities, performance, costs and outreach. Let me refer to each of these in turn.

It is now clear that, while each nation and each state has a broad series of goals and aims for its universities, any reinvention of the American university is likely to proceed largely on an institution-by-institution basis. This is notwithstanding the fact that the performance of individual institutions will be greatly influenced by national, state, and even local policies and support. It becomes essential, therefore, for each institution to develop an unambiguous statement of its mission, goals, broad programmes and scale. This statement will require agreement between the institution, its governors, its faculty, and its external constituents, whether those represented by a state legislature, on the one hand, or the major donors who support institutional ventures, on the other. Only by developing clearly articulated and broadly acceptable statements of mission, goals and programmes, can there be any meaningful discussion of the effectiveness of individual institutions. Do those various missions and goals require "reinvention" and, if so, why?

Institutional performance is clearly the focus of many concerns and criticisms that now confront the universities. There is widespread public concern that commitment to research may become less a foundation than a distraction from undergraduate teaching. There is some scepticism that an expensive education at a major research institution is more effective for the undergraduate than the experience at some less prestigious liberal arts institution. Whatever the merits of these questions, there is clearly a need within the universities for sustained attention to the nature and quality of undergraduate education, in which all long-standing dogmas are scrutinized and justified.

The same is true of graduate education which, at the doctorate level, is still chiefly focused on the production of scholars and professorial teachers. At the master's level the situation is rather healthier, but the whole question of graduate education, its duration, its purpose and its costs, needs serious study, as does its articulation to undergraduate education.

Professional education requires, perhaps, the most scrutiny of all. To take but one basic question. How do we justify four years of undergraduate preparation for, say, business, medical, dental or legal training in the United States when our European colleagues, almost without exception, begin these studies at the undergraduate level? Is there a cultural assumption here, or are the educational differences between the high school experiences so great that the difference in professional training is justified? Furthermore, what evidence can we produce that one system or another better prepares practitioners and professionals?

Maintaining integrity in teaching, research and commercialization is a lurking problem for us on the campuses, but emerges, from time to time, with stories of scientific fraud, or lack of balance in teaching or lack of due process in appeals. The university lives or dies by its integrity and we need to take these concerns seriously, dealing with them promptly as they occur.

Faculty appointments are seen by some informed external observers as particularly indulgent sinecures. Tenure is under attack by some as a shelter for the incompetent or the unconcerned. Do we need to continue to employ and defend tenure? Is a five-year rolling contract something whose time has come?

The third area concerns costs and is related, not only to the quality of product, whether represented by the skills of a recent graduate or the value of a research contribution, but also to the whole question of the roles of state and federal governments in meeting the differing costs of higher education. The role of state governments in financing public universities has declined steadily over the last three decades as a proportion of the total income of the institutions involved. I see no short-term likelihood that this trend will be reversed and some indications that it will not. Coupled to this has been the steady and rapid increase in tuition fees at both private and public universities. At the better private universities and colleges, tuition, room and board now run from $35,000- $40,000 a year. Multiplying that by four years, it is clear that even wealthy families face a formidable burden in providing education for their children. For lower-income families, financial aid is available on a substantial scale, but we need to rethink the whole question of tuition and fees in relation to financial aid and public support. Many upper-middle-income or wealthy parents now receive the benefit of state subsidies at public institutions. There is nothing inherently wrong with this, but we need to inquire whether there are better ways of employing public support for higher education.

Linked to the question of the responsibility for financial support is the question of effectiveness of internal management. The revolt of a significant number of Harvard alumni in recent months over what they regarded as inadequate purchasing practices at the university has highlighted what many external critics see as inadequate management within the academy. Because we profess to teach effective management in our business schools, we must also exemplify it in our own practices.

A not insignificant question that continues to arise is the responsibility for supporting R & D on the campus. Although the federal government, foundations, corporations and others provide generous support here, there is still concern that some of the costs of R & D are offset as a portion of the tuition payments. The clarification of funding of research would facilitate the broader debate over higher educational costs.

Outreach is a fourth area that calls for significant review. It has been argued that the problems of contemporary society are such that they call for the development of a newly designed land-grant programme, which would embrace the range of societal and technological problems in much the same way that the earlier land-grant programme embraced the agricultural problems of the nation. This is clearly a matter of huge significance and involves the question of partnerships between the academy and its neighbouring communities on a significant scale. It may be argued that the creation of broader partnerships will dilute the independence and integrity of the university, but the century-and-a-half of the existence of the land-grant programme scarcely supports such a thesis. Whether or not one accepts the possibility of expanding the land-grant programme itself, the pressing problem remains of how best to harness the expertise and experience of the universities in addressing the myriad social challenges that now confront us, ranging from the deplorable state of the nation's public schools to the inadequate provision of health care in poorer communities.

The nation's universities have already been harnessed in the areas of science and technology, but there is no comparable programme for linking their skills in areas of broader societal need. I believe this is, perhaps, the most urgent priority confronting the universities.

WHAT SHOULD NOT CHANGE?

If we are serious about the need to "reinvent", or at least refocus the university, we should, I think, be careful to ask ourselves what should not change. Alfred North Whitehead once declared that the art of progress is to preserve order amid change and to preserve change amid order. What, then, should not change as we contemplate reinvention of the university? It seems to me that there are five fundamental powers of the university that should not be eliminated, modified or reduced. These include the power to select, admit, instruct and certify or graduate students in fields that are represented by the institution, power to select what to teach and how to teach, the freedom to study, explore and publish on any topic, the power to accept funds and create partnerships and the autonomy of the institution and the independence of its governance.

Any erosion of any one of those responsibilities seems to me to threaten the idea of the university. This is a topic worth discussion for, although there are clear limits to some of the powers I am describing – for example, the power to accept funds from donors deemed dishonest, or the power to create partnerships with destructive organizations – in broad principle each of those powers defines the identity of the university.

IS SIGNIFICANT REFORM POSSIBLE?

We have analysed the pressures for reform, examined the areas of possible reform and described those powers that should not be reformed. A further question remains. Is reform possible? Historically, we may take some comfort from the fact that, in addition to the constant internal renewal and reform that universities have shown over the centuries of their existence, public pressures and needs have led to major changes. The Land Grant Act signed by Abraham Lincoln in 1862 changed forever the role of the nation's great public institutions. The G.I. Bill of 1945 changed forever the accessibility of America's universities and colleges. The Vannevar Bush report to President Roosevelt of 1945 changed forever the relationship between science in the academy and sponsorship by the federal government. In more recent years, affirmative-action legislation and the Dole Baye Act had comparable effects. There is no lack of evidence that universities are capable of adaptation in the face of emerging national needs and are responsive to societal programmes.

In our present world, it seems to me that the most fundamental needs of nations and groups of nations depend on the provision of six qualities and services, in each of which the university plays a significant role. A healthy nation requires an educated workforce, effective professional services, economic self-sufficiency, sustainable development, effective health and nutritional programmes, wise governance and national security. In each of these, the university has a role to play, especially in the first five. Indeed, the work of the university is inseparable from the creation of an educated workforce and the provision of effective professional services. Economic self-sufficiency flows from the effectiveness of those two groups and sustainable development and conservation depend, in part, on programmes developed largely within the campus. The same is true for health and nutrition. It seems unlikely, therefore, that the functions of a university will soon be in need of replacement. One might argue, in fact, that they become more urgent as one looks at the future.

Could the university serve society better in performing those functions? Surely it could, though not perhaps when many individual universities are themselves severely underfunded.

The question, therefore, is likely to be one of balance. Balance between the external demand for performance and progress and internal priorities and inertia. Balance between the view of undergraduates as consumers and of the view of them as students. Balance between accountability and autonomy. Balance between knowledge as power and knowledge as enlightenment. Balance between public prescription and the public good.

All this argues for me, at least, that there is not a case for reinventing the university, but rather a case for refocusing and reforming it. The university itself is the greatest invention of the second millennium. It is the most effective institution yet devised for the maintenance of human culture, the advancement of knowledge and the humane service of society. If it is to play a more constructive role in humanity's future, it requires not "reinvention" but renewal. That will require internal courage and external support. As Lord Chesterfield once said: "No man should tamper with a university who does not know and love it well." This is a useful caution as we employ terms such as "reinventing" the university.

REFERENCES

Chronicle (2003). *http://chronicle.com/daily/2003/05/2003051401u.htm*

CHAPTER 2

Reinventing the Research University: An American Perspective

Robert Zemsky and James J. Duderstadt

INTRODUCTION

F rank Rhodes is right to remind us that our most pressing task may not be imagining how to reinvent the research university. Over the span of a thousand years universities have largely resisted being reinvented and have instead adapted and evolved in profound ways to serve a modernizing world. Perhaps what is really being asked of universities today is a reformation of processes that have become detached and hence unwieldy, on the one hand, and, on the other, a refocusing on mission and strategy such that universities more effectively invest their resources.

It may also be the case that "reinventing" is the wrong verb simply because the pace of university change is being driven by social, economic and technological forces largely external to the academy. Today universities, as institutions, are much more likely to respond to rather than initiate change – and in that sense, universities are being remade rather than reinvented.

Among those forces perhaps the most dramatic, though to the public not always the most visible, is a knowledge base that is expanding exponentially while, at best, resources are growing linearly. It is the point Donald Kennedy, then president of Stanford University, made when he asked: "How can we look so rich and feel so poor?" (Kennedy, 1997). His answer was that universities were much better at getting new things started than at finding the necessary funds to sustain them. To this dilemma has been added the challenge of massification and the very real question of who is to pay for making higher education both broadly available and broadly affordable. The lesson learned more than two decades ago by public universities in the United States – that no government has sufficient tax receipts to provide a higher education to all who seek it at little or no cost to the seeker – is now being absorbed by universities across Europe and Asia. Universities everywhere are "going to market" to raise the kind of revenues that are required to sustain quality and insure stability – even as they protest at what they see as the erosion of public support.

This push to market is having a host of consequences, not the least of which is the commercialization of much of what universities produce. Students have become "customers" demanding that they get their money's worth. The higher the tuition bill, the louder the cries that a university education needs to be "relevant", culminating in the kind of job that a graduate needs to recoup the costs of enrolment. At the same time, the agencies that provide external funding for research – government bureaus, foundations, and, increasingly, for-profit corporations – now see themselves as the universities' customers as well. What they want back are the "deliverables" they contracted for, somehow leaving to others the cost of the kind of basic research that has little or no immediate applicability. Universities have added their own momentum toward commercialization as they have sought to capture and exploit the value of the intellectual property produced through their research – ironically behaving much as they have for decades in exploiting the commercial entertainment value of college sports.

Then there are the changing educational needs of knowledge-driven economies that are becoming increasingly interdependent as globalization recasts the nature of commerce and the meaning of culture. Technologies, largely invented at universities, are redefining the boundaries of individual disciplines while simultaneously creating research communities that are global, that easily include researchers outside the academy, and that, as a consequence, often come to see universities and their constraints from academic values and government accountability more as hurdles to be overcome than as institutions that add more than funds to the research process.

THE FORCES REMAKING THE RESEARCH UNIVERSITY

How, when and where these forces interact to reshape individual universities largely reflect national circumstances and proclivities.

Diminishing Public Appropriations

In the United States today the most pressing concern is funding. Most public universities are facing devastating cuts in their appropriations from tax dollars – a function of the crushing budget deficits confronting most states.

Private universities and the best endowed public universities face a parallel erosion of private support from gifts and endowment income – a function of a weakened economy and a sense on the part of many traditional donors that higher education no longer needs or merits the same level of philanthropy as before.

The optimists among us will want to argue that today's troubles are just part of the ebb and flow of an economic cycle that gives as well as takes. In bad times, state governments and donors cut back support, and then restore their largesse once good times return. Now some are not so sure. As one state budget officer noted: "College leaders are fooling themselves if they think the end of this recession will be like all the others. What we're seeing is a systematic, careless withdrawal of concern and support for advanced education in this country at exactly the wrong time" (Selengo, 2003).

Today, the priorities of both the electorate and the makers of public policy are heath care, prisons, homeland security and reduced tax burdens for the near term rather than investment in the education of the next generation and in the future. This situation is being exacerbated by the circumstances of those needs that, on the state level, compete directly with higher education for taxpayer support – public schools, prisons, highways and medical care for an ageing population no longer able to bear the full cost of health care. The problem is that public primary and secondary schools cannot charge tuition; prisons cannot charge rent; highways in the United States seldom charge tolls; and the nation's politically active elders have made clear they do not want to be charged for anything. But universities can and do charge tuitions; each time there is a downturn in the economy and a reduction in tax revenues, most universities make up for the loss in public funds by increasing the prices they charge their students. The result is that most public and all private universities in the United States are creatures of an increasingly competitive market for student enrolments as well as for research grants and private donations.

It is the market that calls the tune in the United States, and it is a market that is becoming increasingly segmented with those at the top the top of the pyramid – the nation's medallion and name-brand universities – getting stronger, while those in the middle and bottom continue to lose ground. It is not hard to imagine higher education in the United States, a decade from now, being dominated by 20 or so super – as well as super-rich universities, while the balance struggle to maintain programmes and preserve quality.

Changing Student Demands

At the same time universities are being asked to do more – becoming in the process more open, more flexible, and above all more responsive to student concerns about their employability after graduation. Today, a college degree has become a necessity for most careers, and graduate education desirable for an increasing number. The fact that the population as a whole is growing will yield at a minimum growth rates in the 10-15 % range over the next decade for that portion of American higher education that serves traditional college-age students. In some states, particularly those in the American southwest such as California, Arizona and Texas, the rate of growth will be considerably greater. Expanding demands for adult education at the collegiate level will further strain higher education's capacity to serve those seeking jobs in high-performance workplaces. It is now estimated that by 2010 over 50 % of all university students will be working adults over the age of 25 (Almanac Issue, Chronicle of Higher Education, 2003).

Accompanying this increase in demand will be a marked shift in the kind of learning experiences most students have come to expect. What the digital- and media-savvy young as well as their adult counterparts and adult learners will increasingly demand are interactive, collaborative learning experiences, provided when and where the student needs the knowledge and skills. The continued blurring of the various stages of learning throughout one's lifetime – primary, secondary, undergraduate, graduate, professional, job training, career shifting, lifelong enrichment – will require a far greater coordination and perhaps even a merger of various elements of the nation's educational infrastructure – with the result being an infrastructure that sees its students as active learners in search of consumer-friendly educational services.

It is a utilitarian view of higher education that is having a marked – some would say, a profound – impact on American public policy. The National Governors Association notes that: "The driving force behind the 21st-entury economy is knowledge, and developing human capital is the best way to ensure prosperity." (National Governors Association, 2001) The telltales of the knowledge economy are everywhere. The pay gap between high school and college graduates continues to widen, doubling from a 50 % premium in 1980 to 111 % today. Not so well known is an even larger earnings gap between baccalaureate degree holders and those with graduate degrees. In the knowledge economy, the key asset driving corporate value is no longer physical capital or unskilled labour. Instead it is intellectual and human know-how.

The Politics of Diversity

Education is also becoming a powerful political force. Just as the space race of the 1960s stimulated major investments in research and education, there are early signs that the skills race of the 21st century may soon be recognized as the dominant domestic policy issue facing the United States. But there is an important difference here. The space race galvanized public concern and concentrated national attention on educating "the best and brightest", the nation's elite of tomorrow. The skills race of the 21st century will value instead the skills and knowledge of the entire workforce as a key to economic prosperity, national security and social well-being.

In this regard, the increasing diversity of the American population with respect to race, ethnicity, gender and nationality is both one of the United States' greatest strengths and most serious challenges. Far from evolving toward one America, the United States remains hindered by the segregation and non-assimilation of minority cultures. Nor is it clear that the consensus forged in the 1960s as part of the civil rights' movement still holds the political high ground. Instead a variety of groups, often centred in some of the nation's most advantaged communities, are effectively challenging long-accepted programmes of affirmative action and equal opportunity put in place to expand access to higher education to under-represented communities.

In this struggle American universities have become a major battleground as affirmative action's opponents have sought to limit, if not actually eliminate their ability to consider race as a factor in deciding which applicants to admit. As a reflection of that society, the nation's universities have a unique as well as a special responsibility to be effective multicultural communities. They also need to make affirmative action work, yielding new levels of understanding, tolerance and mutual fulfilment for peoples of diverse racial and cultural backgrounds. They need to move beyond simple questions of access to the tougher challenge of making more certain that those admitted through programmes of affirmative action achieve the same educational advantages that majority students achieve.

It is a struggle that has become all the more difficult as the nation's leading universities have become the target of a sophisticated political and legal campaign to limit programmes of affirmative action. What the future holds is more of the same – more court cases, more voting initiatives designed to curtail the universities' political autonomy and more internal debates as to the appropriateness of making the defence of affirmative action a major institutional priority. As the largely successful battle the University of Michigan waged in defence of its race-sensitive admissions policies demonstrated, universities can be successful in this struggle, preserving their ability to insure ethnically diverse student bodies. The salient and troubling question then becomes, at what cost in terms of dollars spent, energy invested and political capital expended?

The Push-Pull of Technology

Today's world is being transformed by a digital technology (computers, networks, wireless devices) that is evolving at an exponential pace. Capacity per unit price – whether measured in terms of computing speed, memory, or network transmissions – is increasing by a factor of 100 to 1000 every decade. A recent National Academy of Sciences study group concluded that the extraordinary evolutionary pace of information technology is not only likely to continue for the foreseeable future, but it could well accelerate on a super-exponential slope. For American universities, the best planning assumption holds that by the end of the decade both scholars and students will have available infinite bandwidth and infinite processing power (at least compared to current capabilities). The world will denominate the number of computer servers in the billions, digital sensors in the tens of billions and software agents in the trillions. The number of people linked together by digital technology will grow from millions to billions as they proceed from e-commerce, e-government and e-learning to e-everything. The impact of these technologies on the university will be profound, rapid and discontinuous – just as it has been and will continue to be for the economy as a whole and the full range of institutions that comprise a nation's civil society.

It for this reason that Clayton Christensen writes about the digital revolution as the initiator of a disruptive technology (Christensen, 1997), one that will ultimately redefine the core activities of most universities (their teaching and research), their form of organization (academic structure, faculty culture, financing and management) and their links to the broader community (their outreach to the communities that host them, the governments that support them, and the corporations that hire their graduates and provide a critical portion of their research funding). It is a world that will require universities to anticipate as well as to react, in the process developing effective strategies and making focused investments in an increasingly uncertain future (Duderstadt, Atkins & Van Houweling, 2002).

Some of the world's leading universities are also learning what happens when the promise of these digital technologies is misjudged, leading to risky investments that fail to deliver the expected dividends. A decade ago, the promise of e-learning seemed irresistible – faculty would teach differently, students would learn at their own pace and in their own way, electronic learning would make a university education available to everyone by offering electronic instruction any-time-any-where. Respected agencies predicted the rapid expansion of the market for e-learning to embrace millions of students and billions of dollars. Universities would be able to replenish their coffers from the profits their new e-learning enterprises earned. And, to be sure, efforts such as the Sloan Foundation's Asynchronous Learning Network project and Carnegie Mellon University's cognitive tutor software demonstrated that such technology could create effective learning environments.

With that level of market anticipation at hand, a uniquely American stampede toward exploiting the commercial potential of instructional technology was ensured. Columbia University launched Fathom; New York University nearly matched those efforts with NYU.online. Cardean University became the model of a for-profit/not-for-profit collaboration in which some of this country's and Europe's best-known universities partnered with Unext to launch a high cost-high prestige programme of international business education. Individual states made similar investments, choosing to focus instead on providing low-cost, but ready access to the educational assets already available on publicly funded university campuses. California's brief fling with its own electronic university and the better known Western Governors University were probably the two best-known examples, though efforts in Massachusetts, Maryland, and Michigan in the end demonstrated more staying power.

Not surprisingly, perhaps, the reality never matched the promise. There has been no pedagogical revolution – most faculty who use the new technologies have not changed how or what they teach. Most of the commercial e-learning enterprises founded by major universities have closed. There has been no real burgeoning of distance education – the limited number of successes owe more to their past market triumphs – as in the case of both University of Maryland's University College and the University of Phoenix – than to the effectiveness of the new technologies.

Through it all, the new educational technologies have retained a core of true believers who argue, still forcefully and at times persuasively, that a revolution is at hand – that the computer will do for learning today what printing did for scholarship in the 15th century. Don't be fooled by the failures and false steps, they proclaim, the best is yet to come. More quiet and also more numerous are the pragmatists in the middle. They point out that e-learning is alive and well and has in fact spurred a host of important educational changes probably best symbolized by the widespread adoption of course management tools like Black Board and WebCT. Money is being spent, smart classrooms are being built everywhere, and university faculty are successfully integrating electronically mediated learning into literally thousands of courses focusing on both traditional and non-traditional subjects.

What is clear is that the story is still unfolding. The underlying information technologies on which e-learning depends are themselves too ubiquitous and the people attracted to having them serve as learning platforms are too smart for universities not to take seriously the prospect that major changes will flow from their efforts. The best guess is that the decade ahead will be one of continued experimentation as universities and their faculties get better at anticipating how the new technologies will impact their basic operations, both within and without the classroom. The danger is that universities will be inclined to delay, deciding to wait and see how e-learning involves before making further investments.

The Changing Nature of Research

Although the changing needs and nature of society have been important factors in the making of the university, so too has been the changing nature of research and scholarship. Intellectual transformations will in the future, just as they have in the past, play a major role in defining the nature of the university. One way to track those changes is to note the continuing modification of the disciplines that collectively define the structure of scholarship for any given age. What are too often regarded as entrenched and fixed are in fact constantly changing, combining and splitting in a continuous process of constant discovery and invention. Just as a century ago, Einstein's theory of relativity and the introduction of quantum mechanics revolutionized physical concepts, today speculation about dark matter and quantum entanglement suggests that yet another revolution in the physical sciences may be at hand. The articulation of the molecular foundations of life is having the same transformative impact on the biomedical sciences. What most scholars now understand is that 21st-century science will be marked by increasing complexities that will overwhelm the reductionist approach on which disciplinary definitions and boundaries have traditionally depended.

At the same time the process of creating new knowledge is evolving rapidly away from the solitary scholar to teams of scholars, often spread over a number of disciplines at a variety of universities. This push to collaboration is in part a function of the enormous expense of major experimental facilities, and in part driven by the complexity of contemporary research topics. To study issues ranging from protein functions to global change to the harnessing of the new nano-technologies requires evolving teams of scholars drawn from a wide variety of disciplines.

In science and engineering education a new age is dawning, pushed by continuing progress in computing, information and communication technology, and pulled by the expanding complexity, scope and scale of today's challenges. The capacity of this technology has crossed thresholds that now make possible a comprehensive cyber-infrastructure on which to build new types of knowledge environments and organizations and to pursue research in new ways and with increased efficiency. The emerging vision holds that a rapidly expanding cyber-infrastructure (Atkins, 2003) will yield more ubiquitous as well as comprehensive digital environments that become interactive and functionally complete for research communities drawing together people, data, information, tools and instruments, all operating at unprecedented levels of computational speed, storage and data-transfer capacities.

The Dominance of Markets

The nation's research universities are similarly being changed by strong economic forces triggered by increasing competition and the government's reliance on market mechanisms to distribute public subsidies. One result could be the same kind of massive restructuring experienced by other sectors of the economy – for example, health care, transportation, communications and energy, to name just four. More generally, what the modern university may be experiencing are the early stages of a process whose logical outcome is the emergence of a global knowledge and learning industry, in which the activities of traditional academic institutions converge with other knowledge-intensive organizations such as telecommunications, entertainment, and information service companies (Peterson & Dill, 1997).

One of the principal drivers of this process is the worldwide movement toward revenue-driven, market-responsive systems of higher education. In large part, this emphasis on raising revenues (as opposed to controlling costs) is the recognition that taxed-based revenues cannot support the massification of higher education required by knowledge-driven economies, on the one hand, and, on the other, the demands of an ever-increasing proportion of the population for a university degree. Among many of higher education's key supporters and funders there is also a growing recognition that the conventional model of public funding for universities, with its emphasis on high public subsidies coupled with low student tuitions, is in itself highly regressive, amounting to a subsidy of education for the rich by the tax dollars paid by the poor.

Some might argue that this emphasis on the pursuit of market revenues in lieu of public appropriations need only be temporary. A decade or two down the road a new generation of citizens will restore a more appropriate balance between the consumption needs of an ageing population and the educational needs of the young. The problem is that, while it is relatively easy to start markets, it is very hard to stop them. The world of higher education is at a point where resistance to market forces no longer yields resilience – instead the discipline of the market virtually guarantees a Darwinian process in which only the financially fit will survive.

WARNING SIGNS

The sum of these forces – the dominance of the market, the changing nature of research, the push-pull of the new electronic technologies, the politics of diversity, and the changing nature of student demands – suggest that what way may be at hand is a fundamental remaking of universities, not just in the United States but world-wide. The danger is that universities will want to believe they remain largely immutable. The university, after all, is one of but a handful of social institutions to survive in recognizable form for a thousand years and more. Who is to say it would not endure in much its present form for another millennium?

We are not so sure. From our perspective, the ideal of a research-intensive university is now at a tipping point. Once the forces of change carry universities beyond that point, they will have entered a different era. More than that, they will become fundamentally different institutions no longer in control of their own destinies. The warning signs are clear and present – to ignore them will likely lead to universities that are no longer all that they should be.

Warning Sign 1: Darwinian Competition

The often corrosive effects of often unbridled competition are increasingly being reflected in the market focus of a growing number of universities. It is an arms race that escalates yearly, as institutions of every stripe compete ever more aggressively for better students, better faculty, government grants, private gifts, prestige, winning athletic programmes, and commercial market dominance. This competition for the resources necessary to achieve a competitive advantage is being aggravated by the vast wealth being accumulated by a handful of elite private universities that allows them to buy "the best and brightest" students through generous programmes of student financial aid (including a growing number that award aid based on merit rather than need). At the same time the growing gap between faculty salaries characterizing private and public research universities is creating a Darwinian ecosystem in which wealthy elite universities have become predators feeding on the faculties of their less well-endowed prey, causing immense damage to the quality of the latter's programmes by luring away their top faculty with offers they are unable to match.

Warning Sign 2: Commercialization of the Academy

A second warning sign is reflected in the efforts of universities and faculty members to capture and exploit the soaring commercial value of the intellectual property created by their research and instructional activities. As in the dot-com-inspired investments in e-learning enterprises, research universities are focusing increasingly on for-profit ventures intended to provide the sponsoring institution with robust and stable sources of revenue. This pursuit of profits is proving both infectious and diverting. To be competitive in this changing environment requires major investments in technology transfer staff, the placing of limits on the open sharing of research results and, not least, the hiring of teams of lawyers to defend an institution's ownership of the intellectual property derived from its research and instruction. In the near term, universities and their faculty members are likely to find themselves setting aside fundamental values such as openness, academic freedom, and a willingness to challenge the status quo in order to accommodate this growing commercial role of the research university (Press & Washburn, 2000).

Warning Sign 3: From Public Good to Private Benefit

There is a deeper issue here. The American research university has been seen as an important social institution, created by, supported by and accountable to society at large. The key social principle sustaining the university has been the perception of education as a public good – that is, the university was established to benefit all of society. Like other institutions such as parks and police, it was felt that individual choice alone would not sustain an institution serving the broad range of society's education needs. Hence public policy dictated that the university merited the broad support of all of society, rather just the patronage of those who benefited individually from its instruction. And public finance made certain that these institutions, both public and private, received direct appropriations and were the beneficiaries of a host of tax-subsidies, both direct and indirect, thus allowing them to discharge their public obligations.

The irony is that today, even as the needs of society for post-secondary education intensifies, there has been a visible erosion in the notion that universities provide a public good deserving of strong societal support (Zemsky, 1997). State and federal programmes have shifted from investment in the higher-education enterprise (largely in the form of appropriations to institutions for the benefit of students) to investment in the marketplace for higher-education services (most often through direct grants, access to capital and indirect tax benefits to students and parents). Whether a deliberate or involuntary response to the tightening constraints and changing priorities for public funds, the new message is that education has become a private good that should be paid for by the individuals who benefit most directly, the students. Government policies that not only enable but intensify the capacity of universities to capture and market the commercial value of the intellectual products of research and instruction represent additional steps down this slippery slope.

This shift from the perception of higher education as a public good to one that can best be described as an individual benefit has yet another implication. To the degree that higher education was a public good, benefiting all (through sustaining democratic values, providing public services), one could justify its support through taxation of the entire population. But viewed as an individual benefit, public higher education is, in fact, a highly regressive social construct since, in essence, the poor subsidize the education of the rich, largely at the expense of their own opportunities.

The implications are that the marketplace coupled with a commitment to provide educational opportunities to all, regardless of economic ability, will increasingly drive many of the best public universities toward high-tuition, high financial aid policies in which state support becomes correctly viewed as a tax-supported discount of the price of education. Reputations earned using public funds become the key to winning a fair share of the revenues the market is now expected to provide: student tuitions and government grants along with the philanthropic largesse of foundations, corporations and individuals of substantial wealth. The consequence is the rise in the number of public "flagship" universities that now seek to become privately financed all at the expense of their once dominant public characters.

Warning Sign 4: The Loss of Public Purpose

In this process of responding to the marketplace by privatizing public higher education, the nation is in the process of diminishing the importance of the university as a place of public purpose. History demonstrates that markets are inexorable; it is both fruitless and dangerous to pretend they are not. At best, markets can be shaped by informed consumers and guided by government regulation meant to constrain the most egregious effects of unchecked competition. At the moment higher education in the United States has few informed consumers – what most students and their families seek is a competitive edge for themselves and their children, an outcome that can best be secured by focusing on institutional prestige rather than educational quality. Nor have governments demonstrated either the skill or inclination to enter the arena as regulators – in part because most public officials have been persuaded that universities are complex enterprises that, for the most part, can only be understood by those steeped in the traditions of the academy; and in part because these same public officials now have a vested interest in having public institutions succeed as market enterprises.

What is at stake are those core values and traditions that have afforded the research university its historic standing. Will the university retain its special role and responsibilities, its privileged position in society? Will it continue to prepare young students for roles as responsible citizens? Will it provide social mobility through access to education? Will its scholarship in pursuit of truth and openness continue to challenge society? Or will the university become, both in perception and reality, just another interest group defined largely by market forces?

A FINAL OBSERVATION

For American universities there is at least one more warning sign: the unforeseen and too often unrecognized rise of the European university as an important competitor. The events that created the American research university of today largely occurred in years following the Second World War, spurred by Vannevar Bush's *Science, The Endless Frontier* which called on the federal government to make a massive and sustaining investment in basic scientific research (1990). The agency of that research, Bush argued, should be the American research university, in part because of the role it had played in the war effort, but mostly because only a university and its research faculty were capable of achieving what the nation required. Most of what Bush recommended, including the chartering of a National Science Foundation, became federal policy, making the federal government the principal funder of a scientific revolution that gave science and science departments an often dominant voice in the ordering of their universities.

Today European universities are on the edge of a parallel breakthrough. The European Union has laid out an ambitious plan of scientific investment that has at its core a pledge to create annual investment funds equal 3.5 % of the E.U.'s gross domestic product (GDP). The Bologna Process and the newly established European Research Council hold out the promise of a re-invigorated set of universities with greater flexibility, more attention to market forces and more willingness to invest in the entrepreneurial instincts of their faculty. The only remaining stumbling block is the resistance by many to the concentration of resources in 50 or so research-intensive universities. But that too is likely to change under the pressure of budget constraints and market competition.

Three possibilities describe the likely future of research universities on either side of the Atlantic. The least attractive is an era of unbridled competition, spurred in part by Europe's search for greater independence and the United States' pursuit of continued hegemony. The least likely future is an era of cooperation in which is there is a pooling of expertise and ambition made possible by a conscious political as well as academic decision to forgo the pursuit of competitive advantage. The middle path is one of competition mediated by cooperation. It is a path that would allow universities to shape, but not control, their own futures. But it is also a path that begins with a frank recognition of the current centrality of market forces and then moves with forthrightness to address the questions of the changing nature of research, the push-pull of technology, the politics of diversity and the shifting nature of student demands. Done right, it is a future that promises universities that are being remade in their own image.

REFERENCES

Almanac Issue, 2003-2004, *Chronicle of Higher Education*, Vol. XLIX, No. 1 (August 31, 2003).

Atkins, D. (Chair), (2003). *Revolutionizing Science and Engineering Through Cyberinfrastructure*, Report of the National Science Foundation Blue-Ribbon Advisory Panel on Cyberinfrastructure. National Science Foundation, Washington, D.C.

Bush, V. (1990). *Science, the Endless Frontier*, Report to the President on a Program for Postwar Scientific Research. National Science Foundation, Washington, D.C.

Christensen, C. (1997). *The Innovator's Dilemma: When New Technologies Cause Great Firms to Fail*. Harvard Business School Press, Boston, MA.

Duderstadt, J., Atkins, D. & Van Houweling, D. (2002). *Higher Education in the Digital Age: Technology Issues and Strategies for American Colleges and Universities*. Greenwood Press, Westport, CN.

Kennedy, D. (1997). *Academic Duty*. Harvard University Press, Cambridge, MA.

National Governors Association (2001), Postsecondary Education Policy, National Governors Policy Statement HR-44, Washington, D.C.

Peterson, M. & Dill, D. (1997). "Understanding the Competitive Environment of the Postsecondary Knowledge Industry." In *Planning and Management for a Changing Environment*. Jossey-Bass Publishers, San Francisco, pp. 3-29.

Press, E. & Washburn, J., (March, 2000). "The Kept University," *The Atlantic Monthly*, 285(3), pp. 39-54.

Selengo, J. (February, 2003), "The Disappearing State in Public Education", *Chronicle of Higher Education*, A22-A24.

The Knight Higher Education Collaborative, (1997). "*Rumbling*," *Policy Perspectives*. Pew Higher Education Roundtable.

CHAPTER 3

Reinventing the European Higher Education and Research sector: the Challenge for Research Universities

Luc E. Weber and Pavel Zgaga

INTRODUCTION

The European higher education and research sector, as well as the European research universities, are facing issues and challenges that are sometimes different in magnitude and more often quite different in nature from those in North America. In any case, the continuous transformation of the European higher education and research sector has been subject to a strong acceleration over the last five years, which will provoke deep changes in the coming decade.

By far the main consequence of these significant changes is the fact that the environment in which European universities function will become more transparent and competitive. All universities will therefore have to take initiatives and implement clear strategies to better position themselves. This will clearly require major transformations. The question of whether institutions should really "reinvent" themselves depends on the definition we give to this word. In any case, it is certain that universities will have to change more over the next 10 years than they have over the last 50 years, during which they had to adapt to the massification of higher education. During this latter period, they faced the major challenge of boosting their capacity to absorb additional students. But few changes were made regarding their missions, structure and decision-making processes. Today's environment requires

strategic decisions affecting the missions and the structure of each institution, that is measures and decisions which are much more difficult to make
and implement.

In this second introductory chapter, we shall mainly describe and comment on the main policy developments in Europe, and briefly analyse how
they will affect research universities.

THE TRANSFORMATION OF THE EUROPEAN HIGHER EDUCATION AND RESEARCH SECTOR

Introduction

Both Europe, as a continent, and its higher education and research sector
have entered a period of rapid and deep change. The European integration
launched in 1957, with six countries deciding to create the European Economic Community, entered into a new phase at the turn of the millennium
with the creation of a single currency for 12 countries – the Euro – and with
the forthcoming integration of ten additional states from Central and
Eastern Europe, enlarging the European Union to 25 countries in May 2004.

The European higher education and research sector itself has been shaken,
in particular, by two political initiatives. The first one, launched in 1998 at
the Sorbonne in Paris and confirmed in 1999 in Bologna, aims at creating a
"European Higher Education Area" (EHEA)[1] without borders by 2010. The
declaration signed in Bologna (1999) stressed the "central role of universities
in developing European cultural dimensions", and "it emphasized the
creation of the European area of higher education as a key way to promote
citizens' mobility and employability and the continent's overall development". We shall later refer to this initiative as "the Bologna process" or
EHEA.

The second initiative was taken in 2000 by the Council of Ministers of the
European Union. It aims at creating a "European Research Area" (ERA),
with the explicit ambition that Europe becomes "the most competitive and
dynamic knowledge-based economy in the world, capable of sustainable economic growth with more and better jobs and greater social cohesion" (Lisbon
European Council 2000).

The political, economic and social changes, as well as these two initia-
tives, are giving rise to a series of reforms, some with profound consequences.
These reforms were generally initiated by national governments and by the
European Union, but diverse university organizations and individual univer-

---

1 In order to shorten the text, several abbreviations are used. A list is available at the end
of the chapter, after the references.

sities, as well as the Council of Europe, subsequently took a proactive role. The clear political objective is to improve the competitiveness of the European economy thanks to the promotion of knowledge creation and transfer, and to the improved efficiency of the higher education and research sector, globally and at the level of each institution. Universities themselves are using this opportunity to reaffirm their central role in the creation of new knowledge and in the training of researchers, as well as to reinforce arguments for their autonomy.

Characteristics of the European higher education and research sector

When considering anything happening in Europe on the political as well as the higher education front, it is essential to realize that Europe is a conglomerate of 50 countries, 45 of them members of its largest governmental organization, the Council of Europe (2003), with a total population of 800 million people. Some countries are geographically large, like the Russian Federation and Germany, some very small, like Liechtenstein, Estonia, Luxembourg and Slovenia. Europe is moreover characterized by a broad cultural diversity of language, history, political system, economic development, attitude to work and studies, social aspiration and religious background and faith.

Therefore, it is not surprising that the European higher education and research system is also extremely diversified. Each country has its own system and there are even differences within federal states. In particular, some countries have a binary system, with a relatively clear division of tasks between the universities and the mostly teaching and vocational institutions, whereas the system is unified in other countries, which does not, however, mean that all institutions are alike. In some countries, basic research is done exclusively within universities, whereas, in other countries, part or most of the research is done in separate laboratories or centres.

Traditionally, European universities are public. This means that they are mainly financed and controlled by the state, which however grants them a more or less large degree of autonomy. However, the political "earthquake" provoked by the fall of the Berlin Wall in November 1989 was followed in East and Central Europe by the creation of well above 1,000 private universities, most of them focused on teaching and highly dependent on teachers employed in the public sector. Another characteristic is that the size of the European institutions varies enormously, from 100 to more than 100,000 students! Moreover, the huge majority of the approximately 1,000 public universities purport to do basic research, although few ask themselves whether the research they are doing is contributing to new knowledge or to solving important societal problems. This also explains why the average size of research universities is clearly smaller in Europe than in the United States. Moreover, the geographical division of quality research is quite unbalanced, as most of the top research universities are concentrated in the north-west quadrant of the European continent. Finally, the lion's share of teaching is carried out in the language(s) spoken in the country, which means on the whole more than 20 different languages are used! Last but not least, it is not surprising that, with approximately 50 sovereign states, there are all sorts of barriers to mobility, of a political as well as of an administrative nature.

Towards a European Higher Education Area (EHEA): The Bologna process

By far the most discussed topic in higher education is the implementation of the "Bologna Process", which aims to create a European higher education area without borders – internal or external. The objective is to improve the quality of education and to develop the sense of a European community thanks to the mobility of students and teachers, and to make the European higher education system more understandable and therefore more attractive to overseas students. Launched in May 1998 by France, Germany, Italy and the United Kingdom – independently of the European Union – this initiative was adopted by 29 countries a year later in Bologna (city of the most ancient European University) (Bologna declaration, 1999). Realizing that the European higher education system was anything but transparent, and that there are numerous barriers to the mobility of students between countries, the ministers of education pledged to take the necessary measures to overcome these difficulties.

The central idea of the Bologna process is built on four pillars:

- Each country adopts a system articulated around "Bachelors" and "Masters" degrees. The first cycle, the "Bachelor", should be conceived as a first period of education, which should also facilitate the entry of students to employment: basic skills are transmitted alongside scientific knowledge and methodologies. The second cycle, the "Master", should allow students to deepen their knowledge, either by specializing in a discipline or by embracing a multidisciplinary or interdisciplinary approach.
- The development of the European Union students' mobility programmes *Erasmus* and *Socrates* encouraged the introduction of the European Credit Transfer System (ECTS), which attributes to each course (or other learning activity) a number of credits corresponding to the effort required (ECTS, 2003). This is a very useful tool for validating credits obtained during a semester or a year spent abroad and for taking them into account towards obtaining a degree in one uni-

versity. The new system, which has yet to be put in place, is more ambitious as it should allow the accumulation of credits by students who would like to study at two or more universities, taking their degree from the final one.

• Obviously, an institution with high academic requirements will not accept students who have accumulated any number of credits if they have been acquired at an institution that they do not consider of a relatively equivalent level. Therefore, the quality of each institution is going to play an increasing role in the success of the process. In this respect, the three key words are accreditation, which means that a formal process assesses whether an institution has reached a standard of quality which can be considered as sufficient; quality assurance, which means that universities should pay greater attention to improving their quality in teaching and research; and recognition of degrees or years accomplished. We shall consider accreditation and quality assurance later. The issue of recognition of knowledge acquired has been considered earlier and independently of the Bologna process. The Council of Europe and UNESCO jointly developed a convention of mutual recognition of years of studies based on a set of principles accepted by all countries signatory to the convention (1997). Moreover, the Commission of the European Union, the Council of Europe and UNESCO developed the idea of the "Diploma supplement", that is a standardized document annexed to a final diploma, where the programme of studies is described in some detail. Developed first of all to respond to the needs of employers, these "Diploma supplements", if used on a broad base, might become another instrument to build trust and transparency between institutions.

The first phase of implementation of the Bologna principles has been rather chaotic: in some countries, governments have passed laws; in others, the universities or their national organization have been allowed to conceive their strategy. Hence, it appears obvious that the system, which will eventually work, will remain quite diversified, but will be more competitive: each institution will be forced to develop Bachelors and Masters where they are best in order to attract students.

The Bologna Declaration has foreseen a follow-up procedure and the ministers agreed in Bologna to meet again within two years in order to assess the progress achieved and the new steps to be taken. In May 2001 the ministers meeting was organized in Prague. A progress report was presented (Lourtie, 2001), together with a survey of trends in learning structures in higher education – Trends II (Haug & Tauch, 2001). The ministers acknowledged that the goals laid down in the Bologna Declaration have been widely accepted and are used as a basis for the development of higher education in most signatory countries. Four additional countries have been accepted to join the process, thus enlarging it to 33 members.

The Prague meeting confirmed the six objectives from the Bologna Declaration – synthesized above as four pillars – adding three additional points: lifelong learning in higher education, the involvement of higher education and student organizations into the process to secure its "social dimension", and the promotion of the attractiveness of the European Higher Education Area (Prague Communiqué, 2001). Finally, the ministers encouraged the follow-up group to arrange a series of thematic seminars during the next two years and decided to meet again in Berlin in 2003.

Thus, the central activity of the follow-up period 2001-2003 was organized around "official Bologna seminars", focused on six problem areas: quality assurance and accreditation, recognition issues and the use of credits, development of joint degrees, degree and qualification structure, social dimensions of the Bologna process and lifelong learning. Moreover, the European University Association (EUA) and the National Union of Students in Europe (ESIB) organized important conventions.

THE EUROPEAN RESEARCH AREA (ERA)

Observing the continuous rapid growth of the U.S. economy during more than a decade, Europe realized that this success was in large part due to the fact that knowledge was becoming a production factor as important as labour and capital, and that information technologies were becoming a crucial tool of development. The European Council, that is the Council of Heads of States of member countries of the European Union (2000), decided in 2000 in Lisbon that the European Union should increase its investments in research and technology development in order to become "the most competitive and dynamic knowledge-based economy in the world" (Lisbon European Council – President's conclusion, 2000). The basic strategy proposed was to create the "European Research Area" (ERA) (COM, (2000) 6 and (2000) 612 final).

The belief is that, in order to unleash the great potential of European research, it is essential to better integrate national efforts by encouraging researchers to work better together at the European Union level, by promoting cooperation between university and industry and by lowering administrative and political barriers to that cooperation.

The tools enacted or considered to reach this target are manifold:

• To introduce new tools in the traditional "European research programmes", starting with the sixth framework programme 2002-2006

(2002). These are first the *networks of excellence*, which aim at pooling a critical mass of competence and skills in order to advance knowledge on a defined theme and, second, the *integrated projects* created to reinforce European competitiveness or to contribute to the solution of important societal problems through the mobilization of a critical mass of research and technological development resources and skills.

- To integrate, at least partially, the European Union and the national research programmes in order to break the tendencies to protectionism of the national programmes. This remains a long-term target. However, the creation of a "European Research Council", which is currently on the agenda, could contribute to reaching this target. This Council would act as an international research funding body at the European level to finance European projects, essentially in basic and curiosity-driven research. If the leading research countries are generally favourable to this project, there is opposition from those countries that do not expect to gain much from it; therefore, it will be necessary to conceive accompanying measures for the latter to secure its implementation.

- Very recently, the European Commission issued a communication "More Research for Europe, Towards 3 % of GDP" (2002), stating that the only way to reach the ambitious target set up in 2000 was to increase the general effort made in research to reach 3 % of gross domestic product (GDP) and that a great part of the additional effort should be made by the private sector. An implementation plan has just been published (2003).

The creation of the European research area focuses not only on questions of organization and funding. It tries also to address the European paradox in that the excellent level of basic research – probably as good as in the United States – does not translate into new applications as well as in the United States. This is partly due to the division of Europe into numerous sovereign countries. This requires that Europe – but it means in most cases each European country – takes many political and administrative measures to:

- Reduce the barriers to the mobility of researchers,
- Promote the transfer of knowledge, e.g. in creating a European patent,
- Find new ways to finance research,
- Develop a set of rules to secure fair university-industry collaboration,
- Clarify the ownership of the intellectual property rights,
- Attract the best researchers worldwide,

- Avoid bureaucratic behaviour, which is consuming too much of the best researchers' time.

Berlin Summit 2003: connecting the two pillars of the knowledge-based society

On September 18-19, 2003, the ministers responsible for higher education from countries that are participating in the Bologna process met in Berlin for the third time to assess the progress and to trace future developments. A progress report was presented (Zgaga, 2001) together with a survey of trends in learning structures in higher education – Trends III (Reichert & Tauch, 2003). The summit reaffirmed the nine action lines from the two former meetings and took some important new decisions, in particular the politically sensitive decision to further enlarge the process to Andorra and the Holy See, four countries of South East Europe (Bosnia and Herzegovina, Serbia and Montenegro, Macedonia and Albania) and, last but not least, to the Russian Federation. The Bologna process now encompasses 40 European countries and, even after the enlargement of the European Union to 25 members in May 2004, the process will still include 15 members more than those concerned by the E.U. framework and agenda. The next summit will be in Bergen (Norway) in May 2005.

The real issue of the follow-up period 2003-2005 will be the decision to speed up the process. In the Berlin Communiqué (2003), the ministers stressed the need to intensify the efforts at institutional, national and European level, and committed themselves to three intermediate priorities for the next two years: promotion of effective quality assurance systems, effective use of the system based on two cycles and improvement of recognition system of degrees and periods of study.

Even more important, the Berlin Communiqué brought about a 10th "Bologna objective": to connect the European Higher Education Area and the European Research Area, as the two most important "pillars of the knowledge-based society". Criticisms had often been made that the Bologna process concentrates predominantly on "mass higher education" at undergraduate level and did not consider seriously the role of doctoral degrees in the emerging EHEA. The necessity of linking higher education and research on a broad European level had been stressed at various occasions before the Berlin summit, in particular among the academic community and in particular by the EUA. Therefore, it was good news for universities to learn that the ministers consider it necessary to go beyond the present focus of two main cycles of higher education to include the doctoral level as the third cycle in the Bologna Process. (Berlin Communiqué, 2003). In other words, ways have been found to bridge the gap between the EHEA as a European intergovernmental process and the ERA, as a European Union process. These new developments are obviously of direct concern to the research-led universities, which could see with some anxiety that all the attention was focused on the teaching part or their mission.

RELATED OR ONGOING CHALLENGES

If there is no doubt that the discussion around higher education and research in Europe is at present largely dominated by the Bologna process and the creation of the ERA, many other issues – related or ongoing – deserve as much attention. This is in particular the case regarding financing, quality, university autonomy, governance and management, and the negotiations of the general agreement on trade in services (GATS).

Under-funding of the higher education and research sector

Financing higher education and research is obviously an ongoing issue in Europe, but apparently not of the same magnitude as at present in the United States. However, some countries and the European Union (2002) are now recognizing that the funding of universities and research is globally too low. The large increase in the number of students over the last 30 years was never matched with an equivalent increase in funding. Therefore, over the years public subsidies have been more or less stagnating or even decreasing per student in many countries, and industry support, mainly to research, although slightly increasing, has not compensated for the diminishing public input. Recent willingness expressed by the European Union and some countries to significantly increase financial support to universities and research is today threatened by the sluggish or stagnant economy. This explains why one of the most sensitive issues in Europe is the determination of an increasing number of political or university leaders to introduce – or to significantly increase – student fees (see chapter 13).

It is worth noting that in its communication *Towards the European research area* (2000) the European commission did not mention even once the role of universities, which prompted strong reactions from the university community. The crucial role of universities in the training of researchers and the development of new knowledge was recognized in further communications and in particular in the communication mentioned above: *The role of Universities in the Europe of knowledge* (2003). Supporting the creation of the ERA, the Communication openly stresses in its introductory part that "the European universities are not at present globally competitive with those of our major partners, even though they produce high-quality scientific publications". One of the main reasons is that there are "insufficient means" for their complex activities. Considering the critical need to adapt and adjust to a whole series of profound changes, it is crucial that European universities have sufficient and sustainable resources. The Communication tries to iden-tify possible points of increasing and diversifying universities' income and using the available financial resources more effectively. Moreover, it also stresses the need to apply scientific research results more effectively, to create the right conditions for achieving excellence and to develop European cen-tres and networks of excellence. It concludes that "if it is to achieve its ambi-tion of becoming the world's most competitive and dynamic knowledge-based economy and society, Europe simply must have a first-class university system – with universities recognised internationally as the best in the various fields of activities and areas in which they are involved."

Necessity to promote a culture of quality assurance

The quality of teaching and research has become one of the most important issues at governmental, as well as at institutional levels. This is a direct con-sequence of the increasingly competitive environment, and a necessity for the success of the Bologna process. The debate is presently concentrated around different issues and tensions.

One of the tensions concerns who should be responsible for evaluation. Many governments are setting up accreditation or evaluation agencies to audit and control the universities. There is clearly mistrust about the ability of universities to take quality assurance seriously.

Another tension concerns what should be done – accreditation or pro-mote quality assurance procedures – and how? In this context, different ini-tiatives deserve mentioning. Established on the basis of the European Coun-cil Recommendation of 1998, the European Network for Quality Assurance (ENQA) is a network of quality assurance agencies set up to disseminate information, experience, good practices and new developments in quality assessment and quality assurance in higher education. To this end, it ini-tiated, among other measures, a useful survey (The Danish Evaluation Insti-tute, 2003) to identify shared protocols of quality assurance among European countries.

The experience in countries which put great hopes into very comprehen-sive approaches shows that these efforts are extremely costly and do not bring the expected results with respect to improving the quality of teaching and research, and even induce negative strategic behaviours. This situation encouraged England, for example, to abandon its ambitious evaluation pro-cedures and to envisage replacing it with a system of institutional evaluation. This is also why the EUA is firmly advocating the adoption of a system of quality assurance which takes into account the fundamental characteristics of universities, in particular their autonomy and the high quality of their human resources. At its Graz convention in May 2003, the EUA adopted a position paper stating that any evaluation system should be based on the following principles (EUA, 2003):

- Autonomy: the institution's autonomy must be respected and promoted. It is also the responsibility of an autonomous institution to continuously enhance quality,
- Trust: if the State considers that universities must be autonomous, it must trust them to be able to take the necessary measures to improve their quality. However, trust does not mean absence of control; control must be *a posteriori* and limited to the institution,
- Subsidiarity: the responsibility should always be left at the lowest level possible. Consequently, universities are best placed to control quality within, and evaluation agencies should control that they are doing it correctly. Obviously, the latter should also be evaluated,
- Pay due respect to the complexity of the teaching and research missions of a university: the quality of a university cannot be reduced to a couple of tangible criteria,
- Avoid bureaucracy: it has a high cost, without contributing to value (to better teaching and research).

At their Berlin meeting the ministers stressed also that "the primary responsibility for quality assurance lies with each institution itself", and confirmed their call made in Prague (2001) to the different university and quality assurance organizations to develop until 2005 an agreed set of standards, procedures and guidelines on quality assurance" (Berlin Communiqué, 2003).

This decentralized strategy is certainly valid for established institutions whose main concern should be to enhance quality. However, we consider that the new institutions (public or private, national or foreign) have to be accredited to guarantee that they reach a minimum standard of quality in the interest of the protection of the students-consumers. In other words, it is important to make sure that only institutions which guarantee a satisfactory level of quality can call themselves a "University". In order to support this aim, the representatives of 13 accreditation organizations from eight countries (Austria, Belgium/Flanders, Germany, Ireland, Norway, Spain, Switzerland, the Netherlands) met in June and November 2003 to create the European Consortium for Accreditation (ECA) in order to contribute to the development of a concept of accreditation that serves not only national needs, but also the needs of the emerging EHEA. As the ultimate objective, participants aim at a mutual recognition of accreditation, either bilaterally or multilaterally.

All these initiatives – to which should now be added the decision of the Steering Committee for Higher Education and Research of the Council of

Europe, taken on October 10, 2003, to put "quality" in its agenda for the forthcoming years, next to the ongoing recognition agenda – show how important these issues are for the future EHEA and how difficult it is to link systems of different traditions and to negotiate commonly agreed standards.

Autonomy, governance and management

The topic of university autonomy, governance and management is also receiving increasing attention in Europe. The main reason is that the fast-changing environment and permanent budget shortages are revealing the limits of the present decision-making mechanisms. University decision-making mechanisms have always been complicated and heavy due to the willingness to apply a system of shared governance, mainly between university professors. Things became even more complicated – not to say more cumbersome – in the 1970s when many European universities introduced the participation of other stakeholders, in particular the students. At present a move backwards can be observed, aimed at streamlining the decision process to make it more hierarchical and hopefully more favourable to decision-making, in particular unpopular ones.

This situation has led to increasing dissatisfaction on the part of the political authorities, which complain ever more frequently that university decisions are not transparent or even that universities are unable to make decisions. This has led to increasing pressure for better accountability and to a clear tendency to political micro-management.

General agreement on trade in services (GATS)

The new round of negotiations to liberalize trade in services will cover education and higher education, as many countries have requested. It is a fact that higher education and research are becoming more and more international and this internationalization can take many forms:

- Cross-border supply with distance education and virtual universities,
- Consumption abroad with students studying in another country,
- Commercial presence with branch campuses and franchises.

However, the higher education community in Europe as well as in North America stresses that higher education and research are a pubic responsibility and therefore fears that a greater "commercialization" of higher education will in particular neglect some fundamental aspects like equal access to all those who have the capacity, and will lower the diversity and quality of higher education, and even threaten governmental support to higher education.

Other issues of lesser concern

Although the present discussion in Europe is dominated by the Bologna process, the ERA, quality, governance and management, as well as financing and international issues, many other questions are on the agenda in different countries or in different institutions. Let us briefly state some of them:

- Promotion of learning: many universities do not realize that the implementation of the Bologna process is a fantastic opportunity to revise and improve the pedagogy, globally at the level of programmes and individually at the level of teachers. It offers in particular an opportunity to promote an education process focused on learning instead of teaching.
- Use of information technologies in teaching and distance learning: European institutions are aware of the potential and limits of the use of new technologies in teaching. However, apart from dedicated organizations like the Open University in England, the range of courseware available at distance or within institutions is still not very large. A great number of scattered initiatives can be observed at the level of teachers, departments, institutions or even countries, but most have an exploratory character or are of rather local use.
- Lifelong learning: the situation regarding lifelong learning is rather similar to that regarding the use of information technologies in teaching and distance learning. There are many local initiatives within universities, but it does not appear that the universities will gain a position in this market as important as with the traditional students. These initiatives are often hindered by inflexible, traditional higher education structures (enrolment, part-time study, financing, etc.).
- Under-representation of low-income social classes: in most countries, universities are open to any student with a high school certificate and are extremely cheap (less than $1,000 a year). Therefore, the financial barriers to entry are still relatively low. This does not mean, however, that the situation is satisfactory. There is an obvious under-representation of students of low-income parents or living in remote places. Encouragement policies based on free – or quasi free – access to university have not brought the expected results. This raises two issues. First, should European governments take proactive measures to encourage children of low-income parents to go to high school and then to the university? It appears that Europe is not yet ready for proactive measures. Secondly, we could argue that if free access has not served its purposes, this should be abandoned as it has many drawbacks (see chapter 13).

- A particular problem has appeared in many countries of Central and Eastern Europe where the former "socialist model" with no fees (but limited enrolment) has been widely substituted by a "transitional model", where students are divided into two groups. The first group is selected on basis of their former academic achievements (e.g. final examination results in high school, entrance examination, etc.) and do not pay fees, while the second group of students, with lower achievements, have to pay. Obviously, this change was influenced by severe budget restrictions, but it produces huge problems in access and equity issues.

- Quality of pre-college education: this is an issue, but the real facts are difficult to appreciate. There is a general feeling that the quality of pre-college education is decreasing in Europe, but this is very difficult to prove.

- Relationship and responsibility of universities to their community: this is also a source of increasing pressures; universities must develop their "third mission", service to the community, which is often a costly and/or time-consuming additional responsibility. In some countries, some new "regional" universities have been also established.

- Political correctness: this is not really a subject of discussion in Europe. However, it does not mean that the university community is totally independent of external pressures or that it is easy to take firm positions opposing the views of governments or criticizing the economy on delicate societal issues. Many professors therefore prefer to write or speak for their colleagues rather than participate in political debate.

- Replacement of the teachers who are leaving: most of European universities are subject to mandatory retirement, most frequently at the age of 65. The increasing number of professorial positions currently falling vacant is becoming a real challenge as it is not always easy to find highly qualified people to fill them. This should encourage universities to recruit internationally, but in many countries this is not the tradition. Moreover, the salary and working conditions may often not be attractive enough. In the future, however, the difficulties faced by pension funds and an ageing population may force postponing the legal retirement age by 2-5 years. For special reasons, this is already occurring in some Central European countries. However, it opens another issue: the problem of obstacles to the renewal of faculty members in higher education institutions.

A PROVISORY CONCLUSION: CONSEQUENCES FOR THE EUROPEAN RESEARCH UNIVERSITIES

It is obvious that the European higher education and research sector has entered a period of profound changes that will deeply transform it within a decade. This has obvious consequences for institutions, national systems and even for European higher education and research. The aim of this book drawn from the Fourth Glion colloquium is to identify the challenges facing research universities and to propose lines of action for them. Herewith, we shall very briefly identify the main consequences, as well as the main lines of action. The latter will nevertheless form the core of the book (chapters 4 to 16) and the concluding chapter of the book will try to identify more precisely which strategies research universities should pursue to maintain their leading position as research-led universities.

Identification of the most important challenges

Our reading of the recent and expected developments is that the challenges for the next ten years will be concentrated mainly around the three following issues:

- Increasing competition: Globalization and the move towards the creation of the EHEA and ERA will create more transparency and therefore increase competition between institutions and national systems. This will force each institution to better profile and position itself in order to become more visible and attractive. This means in particular strengthening strong points and abandoning weaker ones, as well as searching for broad domains of activity or niches in order to exploit comparative advantages.
- Secure enough funding: quality research and teaching in a competitive world will continue to become increasingly expensive. Research requires more and more expensive scientific equipment or investigations as well as bigger teams, as it becomes more complex and interdisciplinary. Quality teaching and in particular teaching at an advanced level, and teaching focused on the promotion of a learning culture will remain labour intensive and therefore increasingly costly. The preparation of material for distance learning is also very costly, even if the work is spread over large teams. At the same time, state budgets are under increasing stress due in particular to the ageing population and the heritage of a non-sustainable social security system.
- Regaining trust from the public authorities and the population: universities no longer enjoy unlimited trust from the public authorities

and the population. The climate of increased competition in the private sector and induced by tight public budgets, the lack of transparency of their decisions, their great difficulty making decisions and the increasing sophistication and societal impact of science are provoking increasing mistrust in universities and in science. To guarantee the autonomy essential to their creativity, universities must therefore do their utmost to regain this trust.

Promising alternative strategies

This new environment is obviously seriously challenging the European research universities. The fact that the climate of increased competition will encourage universities to specialize more in what they are doing best and even aim at being excellent in specific niches will clearly affect also the research universities. They could lose students to those institutions – even small, but specialized ones – that pay greater attention to the adaptation of their programmes to the short-term requirements of the labour market and to the right balance and coherence of their programmes. The Bologna process will also challenge them, as they will not be able – for quality reasons – to accept in their masters and doctorate programmes all students with a bachelor degree, whatever institution they come from. As they are active in basic research and postgraduate studies, they are expensive institutions that require ample funding. The present mistrust of science and basic research also affects them directly as they are principally active in research at the frontier of human knowledge; in other words, in a type of research which is particularly difficult to explain and justify to broad circles of the public. Below is a non-exhaustive shortlist of the main strategic questions research universities must consider:

- Revising the missions of research universities: research universities should revise the way they fulfil their most important missions, that is to produce new knowledge and to transmit knowledge. To us, these two missions, in particular the teaching mission, as well as part of the research mission, should not only be conceived as aims for the universities themselves, but as aims which should serve society. The right balance between curiosity-driven research, that may or may not serve society in the long run, and research that tries to be useful to society appears to be the main point of misunderstanding between universities and society. (This is also partly true of teaching). This may explain to some extent why external stakeholders are forever trying to intervene in university choices.
- Better profiling and positioning (strategic thinking): the European system is probably weakened by the fact that there are too many

institutions trying to do more or less the same thing (being universal institutions, covering most traditional disciplines) and that too few are really strong in most disciplines or in a selection of disciplines. This is a very serious academic and political issue, but Europe and the European countries cannot hide the question for much longer! It appears also that most of the present top research universities have not really been following strict voluntary strategies to position themselves. Their success can be attributed to a comparatively favourable environment regarding funding and autonomy from the state, and, indeed, to their recruitment policy. All these factors secured them an excellent position in the competitive search for research funding. In other words, they benefited from a "virtuous circle". The most challenging question today is to know if such an attitude of "laissez-faire" at the level of the leadership of the institution will be sufficient in the decade to come. Our belief is that it will not, as the changes are of a much deeper nature than those of the past. These universities will be increasingly challenged by other institutions trying to better profile or position themselves to meet increased competition.

- Better leadership, governance and management: better profiling or positioning a university implies that the leadership can initiate the analysis and, more importantly, make decisions and implement them, which often signifies making structural changes that affect people. The observation shows unambiguously that this cannot be done without strong leadership and that these conditions are not currently satisfied in the overwhelming majority of European universities. However, the ideal solution is not easy to conceive. One cannot simply give greater powers of decision to the rector or president because in universities, as in no other institutions, there is a lot of knowledge at the bottom of the hierarchy (Weber, 2001). Therefore, there is a very serious trade-off between the creation of a streamlined as well as a more hierarchical process and counting on a more democratic system, which is necessarily heavy and cumbersome, but allows for the participation of all those who can make a contribution to the improvement of the institution. University activities – like all human activities – are becoming more and more complex. Moreover, human resources, representing almost 80 % of total expenditures, are so costly that their action must be better supported. This is why good management counts.

- Another crucial issue in Europe are the mechanisms of control and influence by the government: as has already been mentioned, the institutional autonomy of public universities is most often limited or threatened. One solution both public authorities and universities are exploring to solve the problem is to create an administrative board between the state and the institution, and give it real decision-making power. This would allow for a clear separation between the bodies that propose a decision, make it and control it.

- Develop a culture of quality: it is also paradoxical that research-intensive universities are generally slow in introducing measures of quality assurance. This is partly due to the position of the researchers who get their scientific reputation outside the institution in their discipline; therefore, they tend to expect as much support as possible from their institution, but are not always as conscientious in serving the institution. This is also partly due to the broad autonomy given to the researchers to choose their field of research. However, even if research-intensive universities can be satisfied with being known in research circles, they should realize that they could improve their global performance by developing an effective culture of quality.

- Secure the necessary financial resources: last but not least, another topic of crucial importance is the funding issue. Even if the new university will be better positioned, therefore, better focused, it will continuously need more financial resources to develop the research infrastructure and to offer better learning opportunities, in particular at the postgraduate level.

- Recruitment policy: paradoxically, it appears to us that the most important action ambitious universities must take is to continue to apply with great rigour one policy that has been key to their success up until now, that is a very strict recruitment policy. More than any other institution, the quality of a university depends on the quality of its human resources. In particular, there is no doubt that to be among the best, a university must be able to keep or attract the best researchers and professors, those able to innovate or to offer solutions at a high level of complexity.

- Attracting the best students: this means also that top research universities must be able to attract some of the best students. To make this possible, the institutions must be visible and attractive. This implies also a selection process at the entry to different stages of a course of study, and, every year, at different levels.

REFERENCES

Barcelona European Council (2002), *Presidency Conclusions*,
    http://ue.eu.int/newsroom/makeFrame.asp?MAX=&BID=76&DID=
    69871&LANG=1&File=/pressData/en/ec/69871.pdf&Picture=0

Berlin Communiqué (2003).
   http://www.bologna-berlin2003.de/pdf/Communique1.pdf
Bologna declaration (1999).
   http://www.bologna-berlin2003.de/pdf/bologna_declaration.pdf.
Campbell, C. & Rosznay, C. (2003). *Quality Assurance and Development of Course Programmes*, Unesco-Cepes, Bucharest.
Capucci, S., Finocchietti, C., Sticchi Damiani, M. & Testuzza, V. (ed.) (2003). *Joint Degrees. The Italian Experience in the European Context*, Cimea, Fondazione RUI, Rome.
Communication from the Commission to the Council, the European Parliament, the Economic and Social Committee and the Committee of the Regions (2000). *Towards a European research area* – COM (2000) 6 – 18 January 2000, http://europa.eu.int/eur-lex/en/com/cnc/2000/com²000_0006en01.pdf.
Communication from the Commission to the Council, the European Parliament, the Economic and Social Committee and the Committee of the Regions (2000). *Making a reality of The European Research Area: Guidelines for EU research activities (2002-2006)* – COM (2000) 612, 4 October 2000, http://europa.eu.int/eur-lex/en/com/cnc/2000/com²000_0612en01.pdf.
Council of Europe/Unesco (1997). *Convention on the recognition of qualifications concerning higher education in the European Region*, http://conventions.coe.int/Treaty/EN/cadreprincipal.htm.
Council of Europe Cultural convention (2003), http://www.coe.int/T/E/Communication_and_Research/Contacts_with_the_public/About_Council_of_Europe/CoE_Map_&_Members/.
Diploma supplement (2003). http://europa.eu.int/comm/education/recognition/diploma.html.
ECTS (2003). http://europa.eu.int/comm/education/socrates/ects.html.
Council of Head of States of countries member of the European Union (2000). http://europa.eu.int/comm/lisbon_strategy/pdf/79_en.pdf.
European Commission (2002). *More Research for Europe, Towards 3 % of GDP*, http://europa.eu.int/comm/research/era/pdf/com³percent_en.pdf.
European Commission (2002). *Investing efficiently in education and training: an imperative for Europe*, Com 779, http://europa.eu.int/eur-lex/en/com/cnc/2002/com²002_0779en01.pdf.
European Commission (2003). *Communication Investing in research: an action plan for Europe*, http://europa.eu.int/comm/research/era/3pct/pdf/action-plan.pdf.
European Commission (2002). *Communication: The European Research Area: Providing New Momentum. Strengthening – Reorienting – Opening up new perspectives*, Brussels: Commission of European Communities, 16 October 2002, http://europa.eu.int/comm/research/era/pdf/era-newmomentum_en.pdf.
European Commission (2003). Communication: *The role of the universities in the Europe of knowledge*, Brussels: Commission of European Communities, February 5, 2003, http://europa.eu.int/eur-lex/en/com/cnc/2003/com²003_0058en01.pdf.
European Union (2002). *Sixth Framework program 2002-2006*, http://europa.eu.int/comm/research/fp6/index_en.html.

European University Association (2001). http://www.unige.ch/eua/.
European University Association and European Commission (2003). *Trends in Learning Structure in European Higher Education III*, EUA, Brussels, http://eua.uni-graz.at/Trends3-Graz-draft.pdf.
European University Association, (2003). http://www.unige.ch/eua/php/include/service/6/public/main.php3?interface_id=10&catid=1&newsid=97&state=.
Graz Declaration 2003 (2003). EUA – European University Association, Brussels, http://www.unige.ch/eua/welcome.html?http&&&www.unige.ch/eua/En/home.html.
Grin, J.-F. Harayama, Y. and Weber, L. (2001). "Responsiveness, Responsibility and Accountability in Swiss University Governance", in A. Arimoto (ed), *University Reforms and Academic Governance*, RIHE International Publication Series No. 7, Hiroshima, pp. 55-101.
Haug, G., Kirstein, J. & Knudsen, I. (1999). *Trends in Learning Structures in Higher Education. Project report for the Bologna Conference on 18-19 June 1999.* The Danish Rectors Conference, Copenhagen, http://www.bologna-berlin2003.de/pdf/trend_I.pdf.
Haug, G. & Tauch, Ch. (2001). *Trends in Learning Structures in Higher Education (II). Follow-up report prepared for the Salamanca and Prague Conferences of March/May 2001*, Finish National Board of Education, European Commission, Association of European Universities (CRE), European Training Foundation.
Higher Education Founding Council for England (2003). *Strategic plan 2003-2008*, http://www.hefce.ac.uk/pubs/hefce/2003/03_12.asp.
Lisbon European Council (2000). *Presidency conclusions*, http://ue.eu.int/Newsroom/LoadDoc.asp?BID=76&DID=60917&from=&LANG=1
Lourtie, P. (2001). *Furthering the Bologna Process. Report to the Ministers of Education of the signatory countries.* Report commissioned by the Follow-up group of the Bologna Process. Prague, May 2001, http://www.bologna-berlin2003.de/pdf/Lourtie_report.pdf.
Middlehurst, R. (2003). *Quality Assurance Implications of New Forms of Higher Education. European Network for Quality Assurance in Higher Education (ENQA)*, Occasional Paper No. 3, Observatory Reports, Helsinki, http://www.obhe.ac.uk/products/reports/.
Prague Communiqué (2003). http://www.bologna-berlin2003.de/pdf/Prague_communiquTheta.pdf.
Reichert, S. & Tauch, Ch. (2003). *Trend 2003; Progress toward the European Higher Education Area; Bologna four years after: Steps toward sustainable reform of higher education in Europe*, EUA and European Commission, Bruxelles.
Socrates (2003). http://europa.eu.int/comm/education/socrates.html.
Spinelli, G. (2003). *Final Report. Seminar on "Integrated curricula—Implications and Prospects".* April 11-12, 2003, Mantova, http://www.bologna-berlin2003.de/pdf/Mantova_Results.pdf.
Tauch, Ch. & Rauhvargers, A. (2002). *Survey on Master Degrees and Joint Degrees in Europe.* EUA, Genève, September 2002, http://www.bologna-berlin2003.de/pdf/Survey_Master_Joint_degrees.pdf.

The Council of Europe: *800 million Europeans* (2003). Council of Europe, Strasbourg.

The Danish Evaluation Institute (2003). *Quality procedures in European Higher Education. An ENQA survey.* ENQA Occasional Papers 5. European Network for Quality Assurance in Higher Education, Helsinki.

Weber, L. (2001). "Critical University Decisions and their Appropriate Makers: Some Lessons from the Economic Theory of Federalism", in Hirsch & Weber (eds), *Governance in Higher Education, The University in a State of Flux,* Economica, Paris pp. 79-93.

Zgaga, P., (2003). *Bologna Process between Prague and Berlin. Report to the Ministers of Education of the signatory countries.* Report commissioned by the Follow-up Group of the Bologna Process, September, Berlin, http://www.bologna-berlin2003.de/pdf/Zgaga.pdf.

MOST FREQUENTLY USED ABBREVIATIONS

ECA: European Consortium for Accreditation
ECTS: European Credit Transfer System
EHEA: European Higher Education Area
ENQUA: European Network for Quality Assurance
ERA: European Research Area
ESIB: The National Union of Students in Europe
EU: The European Union
EUA: European University Association
GATS: General Agreement on Trade in Services (GATS).

CHAPTER 4

The Dream of Reason brings forth Monsters: Science and Social Progress in an Era of Risk

Sir Howard Newby

"The dream of reason produces monsters" is the title of an etching by Goya. It captures the general sense of disappointment during the early decades of 19th-century Europe at the failure of the liberal Enlightenment to produce a more just and open society. How was it that a cultural, political and social movement based upon the values of liberty and rational enquiry could bequeath the opposite: a return to authoritarian dogma and an atavistic attachment to those fundamentalist urges – "monsters" – which continued to thwart the dreams of reason?

This paradox remains just as resonant today. The novelist, Malcolm Bradbury, in perhaps his best-known work, *The History Man* (1975), demonstrated the fragility of liberal ideals to the onslaught of dedicated dogma, in this case the relentless ratiocination of 1970s Marxism. His final novel, *To The Hermitage* (Bradbury, 2001) ironically contrasted the liberalisation brought to the Russian court of Catherine the Great by the values of the French Enlightenment with the relentless political correctness of 21st-century Scandinavia, itself a potential constraint on the freedom of thought and action which would not be altogether unfamiliar to the inhabitants of Tsarist Russia.

In our recent history, we have come to recognize that these issues are more than a source of comic irony for contemporary novelists. The terrorist attacks of September 11th 2001 on New York and Washington have brought into sharp focus in a very pertinent way how the dream of reason can indeed bring forth monsters. Now more than ever it appears difficult to argue the case for the Enlightenment, namely that the growth of knowledge results in social progress. Instead, in recent years, anti-Enlightenment sentiments appear to have been on the increase. If anything we have succumbed to a lack of faith in the notion of social progress and a suspicion amounting to an assertion that the growth of knowledge does not guarantee human happiness – rather the reverse. An increasing proportion of the population seems to distrust rational enquiry to establish both the facts and the uncertainties; rather they prefer their instincts, or even to celebrate anti-intellectualism.

In this paper I want to offer some thoughts on how this state of affairs has arisen. But I also want to re-enforce another Enlightenment principle: the unity of knowledge. Indeed, I want to argue that the increasing fragmentation of knowledge is acting as a hindrance to not only the public understanding of science, but also the scientists' understanding of the public. And with this has come the decline in public trust of all kinds of expert knowledge. In doing so I am reminded of the character in the novel *Atomised* by that enfant terrible of modern French fiction, Michel Houellebecq (2001), who, in an unconscious echo of the United Kingdom's 2001 Research Assessment Exercise (HEFCE, 2001), commented: "I am no longer an active researcher... maybe that's why I am starting to think of metaphysical questions late in the day"

ENLIGHTENMENT AND BEYOND

It is important to recall that both natural science, in its modern form, and social science are products of the European Enlightenment and have, from the 18th century onwards, shared both a common purpose and a core set of values – a deep attachment to rational enquiry, a relentless search for law-like generalisations and a strong commitment to the perfectibility of society. Scratch the surface of any researcher, whether in the natural sciences, the social sciences or the arts and humanities, therefore, and you will find a deeply held belief in social progress through the acquisition of knowledge. But, from the middle of the 19th century onwards, the various disciplines have diverged, not only through a necessary division of labour as the sum total of knowledge has expanded, but through the adoption of differing methodologies, divergent forms of organisation and, perhaps most important of all, different kinds of intellectual discourse.

Traditional disciplinary boundaries are not the only cause of the problem, however. There are also underlying conceptual obstacles. For example, it is a commonly held view within the natural scientific community that basic science proceeds through a wholly innate process of scientific discovery. Such discoveries are then translated into various forms of technological change and it is these changes in technology which provide the motor for social and economic progress. This does, of course, contain a simple truth: science does indeed change the world, as the history of the 20th century only too clearly demonstrates. But science alone does not change society: the history of the 20th century equally demonstrates that society can have a considerable impact on the nature of scientific activity. However, as soon as the natural scientific community has convinced itself that scientific progress is an external force acting on society, then there is the danger that it will regard society itself, in the sense of a wider public, as a mischievous irrelevance, something which hinders the untrammelled pursuit of scientific progress.

This in turn becomes both a cause and a consequence of a particular kind of scientific thinking. For example, the official credo of natural science comprises a "linear-additive" model of knowledge – that is, a positivist world of rational enquiry in which knowledge accumulates in a linear fashion by the progressive discovery of invariant laws of Nature. The whole process is tightly disciplined by rules of evidence. In this process, mathematics and logic are epistemologically privileged – that is, they raise the quality of the knowledge produced by scientific method above that produced by other methods – for example, intuition, religion, magic, witchcraft or metaphysics. In an idealized Newtonian world it was, therefore, possible to conceive of science as eliminating ignorance in this fashion. Eventually, all the laws of Nature would be discovered and we would know all there is to know about the world around us. Even today this model offers an adequate account for most natural scientists about what they do most of the time. This is because, for most natural scientists, science is a matter of practical problem-solving. For this purpose, the linear-additive model is perfectly adequate. As one of Houellebecq's (2001) characters puts it: "Personally, I think that I needed that basic, pragmatic positivism that most researchers have. Facts exist and are linked together by laws; the notion of cause simply isn't scientific. The world is precisely the sum of information we have about it."

However, for scientists with a more theoretical inclination, the linear-additive model was demonstrated throughout the 20th century to be increasingly inadequate. How else, for example, can we explain the paradox that the more we know, the more extensive our ignorance appears to be? And for each problem science solves, many new ones are identified that require solutions. On the one hand our level of reliable knowledge about the world, our ability to make predictions, has never been greater. NASA can now land a probe on an asteroid. A geneticist can tell from the DNA in a strand of hair at birth whether that child will contract Huntington's Disease in middle age. More generally, it has been estimated that the sum total of scientific understanding in the past 50 years has been greater than that in all previous history. Yet for all that we seem to know, the world appears to be an increasingly uncertain place. As a very perceptive article by Thomas Barlow in the *Financial Times* (of all places) put it, "...the knowledge we acquire about the world increasingly allows us to change it, and that in changing it we seem adept at making it incomprehensible again" (Barlow, 2002). In other words, certainty appears to breed even more uncertainty.

TECHNOLOGICAL ANGST

It is not too difficult to discern why this is the case. The growth of scientific knowledge and the pace of technological change are now such that there is no earthly possibility that the culture of any society can adapt sufficiently quickly to keep pace with it. The potentialities of material change are far outpacing the realities of cultural change, and out of this all kinds of social and cultural dislocations are emerging. As Barlow again puts it: "...we find ourselves suffering from a kind of technological angst, an ambivalence to change, and an escalating feeling that advances in science have begun to outpace human ability for making judgements about their application." (Barlow, 2001)

In the same article in the *Financial Times,* Barlow went on to present a litany of issues which relate to this idea: "Is nuclear power safe? Is overpopulation about to cause a cataclysm of disease and famine? Would pesticides give us all cancer? What caused the hole in the ozone layer? Does biodiversity matter? Is the greenhouse effect real? Is cloning ethically acceptable? Dare we eat genetically-modified foods?" (Barlow, 2001) Unfortunately these kinds of questions are not obviously open to common-sense solutions. Part of the problem is that many of the hazards of the modern world are inaccessible to the senses altogether. In some cases, indeed, the problems we face may be so remote and complex that even the experts have trouble grasping them.

In this context it is not surprising that the world appears a riskier place, even though, on any quantifiable statistical basis there is little doubt that the world is a much less risky place for its inhabitants than it was 50 or even 100 years ago. The sheer pace of technological change has created a generally heightened sense of uncertainty. The past is no longer a guide to the future; just as explanation may not be equivalent to prediction. In a world which has become, according to many, increasingly globalized, the individual may feel less control over his or her daily life. And this world is also a more complex world, one in which, because of the extreme division of labour in modern industrial societies, we must rely on the expertise of others on matters over which we ourselves are relatively ignorant. Risk, uncertainty, vulnerability, trust – this seems like a lexicon of the human condition as we move into the 21st century. In this sense, the discussion of risk is no more than a metaphor for a change in a society struggling to come to terms with itself. Ever since the Enlightenment we have been prepared to believe that human progress can be achieved via the pursuit of knowledge. Now there are many who have their doubts. The debate over risk is in part a debate over the contemporary state of the human condition.

All of this seems a long way from the linear-additive approach to the accumulation of knowledge. But it also explains a kind of paradox. We all stand in awe of the practical success of modern science. However much one may argue about this or that quantum of scientific knowledge, science demonstrably works. It is for this entirely pragmatic reason, at least in the minds of the general public, that science is elevated above other systematic means of creating knowledge. To say that something has been demonstrated scientifically remains, even despite recent vicissitudes, an ultimate test of the authenticity of knowledge and, therefore, of the authority of the speaker. Conventionally, those emanating from the humanities and the social sciences could only claim such authority when they, too, claim to be arguing "scientifically".

Ironically, the latter half of the 20th century was characterized by scientists asserting the provisional and uncertain nature of their findings rather than the reverse. It was Karl Popper (1959) who, by emphasising the provisional character of scientific knowledge, the rule of theory and the importance of scientific falsification rather than verification, pointed to some intriguing contrasts between scientific rhetoric and scientific reality. It did not take long for those who investigated natural science as it is actually practised to claim that scientists were simply engaged in a systematic deceit upon themselves. They did not spend their days trying to falsify hypotheses, as Popper had taught them they should, but, quite often, interpreted the observable facts to suit their pre-conceived theories.

SCIENCE AS A SOCIAL CONSTRUCT

In this regard, it is difficult to overestimate the influence of the work of Thomas Kuhn (1962), whose notion of scientific paradigms has now passed into everyday scientific discourse, even though, ironically, it is been treated with great scepticism even by those who share Kuhn's view of science as a social construct. Following Kuhn, we now recognize that the natural scientific community has its own culture, which enforces its own norms of what is and is not acceptable evidence, and which, via the subtleties of measurement and instrumentation, overwhelmingly operates in a verificationist fashion, and whose claim to speak with absolute certainty has to be interpreted with the same degree of scepticism with which one would greet similar claims from other brokers of knowledge and ideas.

Kuhn's work unleashed a veritable deluge of studies which sought to demonstrate that scientific knowledge was itself socially constructed. In its more vulgar form this sought also to demonstrate that the knowledge produced by scientific enquiry should be no more privileged than its predecessors – magic, religion, etc. In seeking to explain how scientific knowledge is created, Kuhn provoked a dangerous non sequitur – that scientific knowledge could be explained away.

Now social science does have a duty to demystify rhetoric and seek the underlying causes of human behaviour which lie behind self-justification. In this respect, the natural science community could be considered as no different to any other whose claims to authority risk being undermined by social scientific investigation. However, natural scientists, not surprisingly, found this approach extremely irritating. To them social science was simply seen as attempting to subvert the authority of natural science and offer little in return. The understandable reaction was to retreat behind the scientific barricades. Who needed this kind of sniping when there were important practical tasks to accomplish? Natural science remained confident in its ability to change the world for the better. Better, too, to ignore these turbulent (and it has to be said, at times, arrogant) critics and get on with the job?

However understandable this reaction, its consequences have been unfortunate. The scientific community has retreated from an engagement with society, just as society at large has been excluded from the real world of scientific method. As the biologist Steve Jones recently pointed out, the scientific community is now completely mystified by the idea that morals should direct its research, while those who seek to make science more publicly accountable are equally baffled by the logic and methods of science. The public now feels it is reduced to the role of a hapless bystander or, at best, the recipient of scientific advance and technological innovation which the scientific community believes it ought to want. If the public decides it does not want it, it is regarded as either ignorant or irrational. The scientific community therefore ends up frustrated by the public's apparent disdain for the fruits of its labours and the public's lack of sympathy for an endeavour which, as far as the scientific community is concerned, is for the public good.

In this situation, as one of Houellebecq's (2001) characters perceptively comments: "It is easy to imagine a fable in which a small group of men – a couple of hundred in the whole world – work intensively on something difficult, abstract, completely incomprehensible to the uninitiated. These men remain completely unknown; they have no apparent power, no money, no honours; nobody can understand the pleasure they get from their work. In fact, they are the most powerful men in the world, for one simple reason: they hold the keys to rational certainty. Everything they declare to be true will be accepted sooner or later by the whole population. There is no power in the world – economic, political, religious or social – that can compete with rational certainty". We are becoming dangerously close to Goya's nightmare of reason creating monsters here. All too often now the natural scien-

tist appears intimidating and remote. And all too often scientific communities treat the public with, at best, condescension and, at worst, as a threat.
Once the public trusted scientists, and scientists could speak with authority.
Now, both that trust and that authority have been somewhat eroded. Contemporary knowledge is not only unprecedentedly voluminous, but also
astonishingly fragmented, and the more we know collectively, the less capable an individual seems to be of interpreting matters outside his or her expertise. As a consequence, while many of the difficult and controversial decisions we must make in modern society are focused around scientific
questions, we find ourselves on virtually every topic of importance dependent
on advice from small, elite sub-groups of experts. Often we find that the
expertise necessary for solving problems is precisely that which created them
in the first place.

THE PERCEPTION OF RISK

A good example of this is the study of risk itself. Quantitative risk assessment
is now a highly sophisticated and reliable aspect of modern economic and
scientific activity. Yet both politicians and scientists continue to be taken by
surprise by the public reaction to technological innovations which they
assumed were not contentious. Waste disposal, genetically-engineered orga-
nisms, food irradiation, food additives – the litany could be extended at
length. Many people seem very happy, as has often been pointed out, to take
the most enormous risks in their private lives, but react violently against statistically tiny risks in the public domain. One only has to compare the public
debate which has recently surrounded accidents on the railways with the
daily death toll on our roads in the United Kingdom. It hardly needs to be
added that this in turn influences the political and policy framework governing the pace and direction of technological change and, ultimately, therefore, the legally defined conditions surrounding the pursuit of scientific
enquiry.

This is not because quantitative risk assessment is somehow inexact.
Rather, it misses the point. I am reminded of the famous quotation from the
American social psychologist, W. I. Thomas: "If men define situations as real,
they are real in their consequences" (Thomas & Thomas, 1928). Thomas
was pointing to something which today we would regard almost as a truism,
namely that people behave on the basis of their perceptions of reality –
including risk – rather than that reality itself. Therefore it is the perception
of risk which influences behaviour rather than the statistically objective,
quantifiable assessment of that risk. In this sense risk perception cannot be
reduced to a single subjective correlate of a particular mathematical model of
risk, such as the product of probability and consequences, because this

imposes unduly restrictive assumptions about what is an essentially human and social phenomenon. This is because risk is a social construct (although not only a social construct). And this applies as much to fruits of scientific understanding as anything else. For centuries we have been taught and conditioned to assume that science is certainty. If not today, then tomorrow, scientists would make the discoveries that would remove our worries about disease, hunger and even our social affairs. Yet now we can recognize just how incomplete this view is. The study of risk is just one area where we now find scientists delivering only soft, uncertain facts to decision-makers facing hard decisions. Politicians demand to know what is safe, whilst scientists can only ever state that nothing is risk-free. Typically we find that the facts are uncertain, values in dispute, stakes high and decisions urgent; and the framing of the problem involves politics and values as well as science.

Very many natural scientists find this role uncomfortable, since it disrupts the established taken-for-granted relationship between science and politics. It also presents a problem for politicians in search of scientific legitimacy for their decisions: an appeal to scientific "facts" is a handy device to shut down the much more messy debate necessary to manage uncertainty as well as to reconcile conflicting interests. The scientific study of risk cannot, therefore, be limited solely to "getting the science right". It is simply not the case that once you get the science right, so better decisions are sure to follow. The foot-and mouth-outbreak in England in 2001 surely demonstrated this. Scientists, I know, will feel uneasy about this. Equally, however, natural scientists will need to recognize that the perceptions of risk are shaped by complex social and psychological processes and that scientists' perceptions of the public are equally important as public perceptions of the science. Understanding and managing the distinction between risk assessment and risk perception is difficult, complex, and the outcomes are uncertain. It itself constitutes a risk. But in reality there is no alternative. The things which are perceived as real will be real in their consequences.

This leads me back to where I began. Rather than ignorance being bliss, probably what we all fear most is that which we do not understand. There is a sharp distinction to be made between the practice of science and the logic of scientific enquiry. Being critical of how science is organized and directed is not to be conflated with the criticism of rational enquiry itself. As the President of the British Academy, Viscount Garry Runciman, recently put it: "Both the natural and the human sciences are both objective and subjective, as both are at the same time value-neutral in so far as their results are directly and publicly testable and value-laden in so far as the underlying presuppositions and purposes are not. Both share the same two inescapable requirements: first, reasoned argument as opposed to dogmatic assertion; and second … docility to the evidence" (Runciman, 2002). Any serious practitioner of either the human or the natural sciences has no need to be told that there are no canonical narratives or definitive series of everything. Or, as Nietzsche put it a century ago: "...without a recognition of logical fictions, without a comparison of reality with the purely imagined world of the absolute and immutable, without a constant counterfeiting of the world by numbers, man could not live..." (Nietzsche, 1923)

RESTORING PUBLIC TRUST

In a less deferential age it will not be easy to restore the public trust in science to levels which pertained in a previously unquestioned authority of other professions and institutions in modern society. The scientific community is beginning to engage more with society at large, albeit hesitantly and tentatively, as it comes to recognize the potential consequences of failing to do so. Equally, the public understanding of what science can – but, more importantly, cannot – deliver has a long way to go. The public stands in awe of the products of recent scientific progress. But science is not magic, and the scientific community does not possess a collective magic wand. Modern science has not removed human moral fallibility.

There is no doubt then that Goya's dream of reason has produced monsters, but part of the Enlightenment tradition is to continue to strive to eliminate such fiends. In the wake of September 11th 2001 we have come to question our faith in social progress and in open human enquiry. But now is the time when we need to re-assert Enlightenment values and to ensure that the growth of knowledge is not impeded by a relapse into the celebration of ignorance.

REFERENCES

Barlow, T. (2001). Article in the London *Financial Times*, 12 May 2001, Financial Times Ltd, London.
Barlow, T (2002). Article in the London *Financial Times*, 5 January 2002, Financial times Ltd, London.
Bradbury, Malcolm (1975). *The History Man*, Secker and Warburg, London.
Bradbury, Malcolm (2001). *To the Hermitage*, Picador, London.
HEFCE (2001). *2001 Research Assessment Exercise: The outcome*, HEFCE, Bristol.
Houellbecq, Michel (2001). *Atomised*, Vintage, London.
Kuhn, Thomas. (1962). *The Structure of Scientific Revolutions*, University of Chicago Press, Chicago.
Nietzsche, F. (1923). *Beyond Good and Evil, The Complete Works of Friedrich Nietzsche*, edited by Dr Oscar Levy, volume 12, George Allen and Unwin Ltd, London.
Popper, Karl (1959). *The logic of scientific discovery*, Hutchinson, London.

Runciman, G. (2002) "Two bodies, One Culture", speech by Viscount Garry
    Runciman, President of the British Academy, to the Academy's Centenary Din-
    ner, 4 July 2002, British Academy, London.
Thomas, W. I & Thomas, D.S (1928). *The Child in America: Behavior Problems and
    Programs*, Alfred A. Knopf, New York.

PART II

•••••••••••••

Teaching and Research

CHAPTER 5

Innovation in undergraduate Teaching: Student-centred and Research-led learning

Roger G. H. Downer[1]

INTRODUCTION

I t is a remarkable testimony to the prescience of our academic forbears that most of the thousands of universities created globally during the last 900 years bear a close resemblance to the progenitor of Western Universities, founded at Bologna in the 11th century. There have of course, been some changes during almost a millennium of institutional evolution. New disciplines have developed and been introduced into the academic milieu and, particularly during the last 100 years, universities have embraced the philosophy of such visionary educators as Wilhelm von Humboldt and recognized the discovery, assimilation and application of new knowledge as an integral part of the university mission. By contrast with this growing emphasis on research and knowledge creation, the practice of teaching and the relationship of the teacher with the student have undergone relatively little change through the centuries.

CHANGING ROLE OF UNDERGRADUATE EDUCATION

More that 150 years after the publication of his seminal work, *The idea of a University*, there are few discussions about the role of undergraduate educa-

---

1 I appreciate the valued input of Dr Sarah Moore, Dean of Teaching & Learning, University of Limerick, to the preparation of this paper.

tion which fail to invoke the views of Cardinal John Henry Newman. New-man was unequivocal in his assertion that the university should provide an environment in which young men – the days of equal opportunity were still distant – could develop personally and intellectually, acquire a breadth of inter-disciplinary understanding and graduate with a capacity "to fill any post with credit and to master any subject with facility" (Downer, in press). Newman's ideals remain eminently worthy, and an important role for undergraduate education continues to be the development of an informed citizenry capable of rational, independent contributions to public debate and decision-making. However, in addition, the modern university has a societal responsibility to provide a highly skilled workforce who will contribute to economic competitiveness, professionals who can avail of the latest technological advances in the discharge of their professional responsibilities and, increasingly, universities are serving as essential partners of both the public and private sectors in providing career development and lifelong learning opportunities.

This diversity of roles is coupled with an increasingly diverse student population in which there is considerable variation in age, academic back-ground, intellectual ability, interests and aspirations. Such diversity suggests that no single form of pedagogy is universally suitable to satisfy the several roles identified for undergraduate education and the heterogeneity of the student population. Thus, there is a need to reassess the nature of the under-graduate experience in the modern university and the manner in which undergraduate education is provided.

STUDENT-CENTRED TEACHING

In most universities, the teacher continues to be considered as the fount of knowledge with a role to "profess" this understanding to eager, absorbent stu-dents. This attitude becomes particularly evident upon reading mission state-ments from a variety of universities in different jurisdictions. Most place high priority on the attainment of excellence in teaching, but, commendable as such statements may be, they fail to acknowledge that the ultimate goal of education is not excellent teaching, but, rather, excellence in student learning. The teacher-centred bias in much university education is unfortu-nate and, in its worst and all-too-common manifestation, places the teacher in an authoritarian role delivering factual content and opinion and reward-ing students for their ability to reproduce this dogma. Such didacticism leads to superficial learning and it is now recognized that the ideal learning envi-ronment encourages and enables students to assume ownership for their learning and allows them to question, interact, test, debate and explore both the process and the content of their learning. Goodwin et al (1991) cite the

1986 report of the Carnegie Foundation on higher education, which states: "The undergraduate experience, at its best, involves active learning and disciplined enquiry that leads to the intellectual empowerment of students."

The challenges of effecting the transition from teacher-centred to student-centred teaching should not be underestimated. Many academics are notoriously resistant to change and will not accept readily a top-down directive which might require considerable effort and the abandonment of a well-tried and trusted modus operandi. The intransigence of faculty is often exacerbated by the hegemony of academic departments which are likely to defend and protect their right to do what they perceive to be best for their particular discipline. Institutional structures may also obstruct the implementation of pedagogic change with inflexibilities in such factors as disciplinary compartmentalisation, scheduling and course prerequisites, contributing to a litany of "bureaupathologies" which hinder innovation and change. In spite of these inherent difficulties, there is little justification for the retention of a less than effective status quo and, therefore, universities must examine the appropriateness and effectiveness of current pedagogic practices.

Indeed, in that universities have a responsibility to ensure that available resources are deployed optimally to achieve the institutional mission, it is appropriate for them to consider if the commonly deployed, current pedagogy of lectures, note-taking and content-based examinations makes the most effective use of the contact time between the teacher and the student, and if it achieves an optimal learning environment. The traditional, content-based lecture can be justified in an era or situation in which books are scarce or expensive, but this is not the case in most universities today. Ready access to information is a feature of the modern educational environment with electronic databases, web-based learning programmes and CD-ROMs complementing traditional library resources. Consequently, most of the relevant content is available to students outside the lecture room and in a form that is often more comprehensive and understandable than in a formal lecture. If students are made responsible for at least some of the content before they enter the classroom, the interaction between the student and the teacher will be more productive, with the student transformed from the role of receiver to that of developer of knowledge. There are mutual benefits to this type of student/teacher relationship because, as most scholar/teachers will readily admit, students provide valuable challenges to entrenched hypotheses, offer fresh insights and contribute to enhanced understanding by both partners.

Such reforms would, of course, change the role of the university professor who, traditionally, has served principally as the provider of information. In student-centred teaching, the professor assumes a much more complex role located on the boundary between information and understanding. Good teachers have always fulfilled this function, but, in order to take full advantage of the opportunities presented by the information age, all teachers should assume the role of guides, mentors and facilitators who enable students to make the transition from factual content and information to true understanding and wisdom.

RESEARCH-LED TEACHING/PROBLEM-BASED LEARNING

Coupled with the need to move towards a more student-centred learning environment is the emerging concept of research-led teaching and learning. The Report of the Boyer Commission on educating undergraduates in the research university, *Reinventing undergraduate education*, recommends that research-based learning should be the standard form of undergraduate education in research universities.

Research-led teaching can embrace several pedagogic strategies, which are closely related to each other and are not mutually exclusive. In an extreme form, ongoing research activities are placed at the core of the undergraduate curriculum. Professors describe the research questions that are being addressed and introduce students to the underlying concepts required to understand the scope, nature and direction of the research. In upper-level courses, the material may be based entirely on the professor's personal research programme, whereas, in introductory courses, a broader range of research topics is usually required to ensure holistic exposure to the discipline.

Frank Rhodes has reported a variation of this approach in describing the teaching of an outstanding professor of engineering who presents students with practical problems and then proceeds to help them discover and understand the solutions (Rhodes, 2001). There is now an established field of pedagogical endeavour and innovation which can be encapsulated in the term "Problem-Based Learning" and which incorporates the values and orientations associated with research-led teaching. Indeed, in that not all universities have strong research programmes, the problem-based approach is more appropriate in many situations.

The utility of the approach and the manner in which it is applied varies greatly between disciplines, but the benefits, which occur, are generally acknowledged to include:

- the approach can be applied to any discipline and tends to transcend disciplinary boundaries by identifying problems and then applying knowledge from different disciplines to achieve a solution;
- in research intensive environments students are exposed to the excitement of cutting-edge research and are exposed to dynamic, committed researchers;

- students are encouraged to question, understand and become involved in the resolution of real-life issues;
- active participation in the resolution of problems is more likely to imbue learners with passion and enthusiasm for the subject;
- students develop skills associated with creative problem-solving.

In addition to its impact on curricular content, research-led teaching can influence also the way in which students are helped to appreciate the research method with emphasis placed on research methodology and the ways in which knowledge is accumulated in a particular discipline. This leads, ideally, to the type of student-centred, enquiry-based learning described in the previous section. Indeed, as envisaged in the report of the Boyer Commission, undergraduate students should, wherever possible and appropriate, be involved in the research process progressing from a role as junior members of a research team in first year to one which is equivalent to that of a first-year, post-graduate student by the final year. Irrespective of whether they proceed to graduate school or not, the research-based or problem-based learning experience will provide them with analytical and problem-solving skills which will be valuable in professional life and as thoughtful, informed citizens. Furthermore, in that the approach often involves group projects, students acquire team-working and communication skills which are increasingly deemed by employers to be of great importance.

UNDERGRADUATE TEACHING IN RESEARCH UNIVERSITIES

In the light of the foregoing discussion, it might be expected that some of the best examples of research-led teaching would be found in the TIER 1 Research universities of the United States. These are defined as universities which "offer a full range of baccalaureate programmes, are committed to graduate education through the doctorate with 50 or more doctorates graduated annually and give high priority to research with annual research income of $40 million or more." (Boyer Commission, 1999)

Unfortunately, analysis of the performance of undergraduate students in research-intensive universities suggests that the potential identified above is often not realised, and the learning productivity in some cases compares unfavourably with that in other types of third-level institutions (Kuh & Hu, 2001). Clearly in some instances, the universities surveyed had not adopted a research-led approach to teaching, whereas in others, it is likely that research "stars" had negotiated contracts with no or minimal undergraduate teaching responsibilities and delegated their teaching to post-graduate students or post-doctoral fellows whose primary goal is to do research and publish. This all-too-common occurrence reflects the erroneous perception that teaching and research are independent activities which compete for faculty time and resources. Rather, as Elton (2001) points out in his consideration of von Humboldt's 1810 monograph, university teaching "involves a joint endeavour between the teacher and the learner in a common search for knowledge". Indeed, based on his reading of von Humboldt, Elton (2001) suggests that this is what distinguishes a university from a school with the latter teaching only closed and settled bodies of knowledge, whereas university teaching, learning and research have, as their common outcome, the discovery of new knowledge and understanding. In the modern university, teaching, learning and research are part of a continuum of enlightenment and, should not be considered as separate, unrelated activities.

The finding that there is not necessarily a direct link between a strong research university and a good undergraduate-learning environment (Kuh & Hu, 2001) belies commonly accepted academic dogma. Elton (2001) has explored the basis for the mythology, and concludes that many of the studies which purport to demonstrate a positive correlation between research and teaching/learning were simplistic and lacked objectivity. For example, assessments of the quality of teaching are often conducted by highly respected researchers who consider good research performance to be evidence of good teaching (Elton, 2001).

Clearly it is naïve to expect that every good researcher will be a talented, inspiring teacher or, indeed, that only good researchers can be inspiring teachers. However, most successful researchers have a great enthusiasm and passion for their subject and the splendid examples established by such notables as Richard Feynman at Caltech and Carl Sagan at Cornell suggest that, whenever possible and appropriate, students should be provided with opportunity to learn from the best researchers on campus. Under such circumstances research-led teaching can greatly enhance the undergraduate learning experience.

RELATIONSHIP BETWEEN STUDENT-CENTRED AND RESEARCH-LED TEACHING

Although the foregoing account argues for adoption of a student-centred, problem-based approach to third-level teaching, it is recognised that teachers and students differ in their ability to deliver and respond to different forms of pedagogy. Therefore, as indicated previously, no single teaching strategy is optimal for every situation and every personality. Such variables as class size, sophistication of the student body, strengths and weaknesses of the teacher and the nature of the discipline will all determine the effectiveness of the teaching approach and the learning experience.

Even within a single course, a variety of pedagogic strategies may be used, but the overriding philosophies of student-centred, research-led teaching and learning should be central to the process. Figure 1 presents a matrix which illustrates the consequences of over- or under-emphasis of either strategy.

Figure 1. Consequences of over- or under-emphasis of student-centred and research-led teaching

		STUDENT CENTREDNESS	
		LOW	HIGH
RESEARCH FOCUS	HIGH	Incomplete coverage Faculty Inaccessible Learning has low priority	Content at cutting edge Inspirational teachers Students fully engaged STUDENT CENTREDNESS
	LOW	Impoverished content Uninspiring teachers Students and teachers disengaged	Content often bland and second-hand May lack rigour Lacks evidence

- *High Research Focus and Low Student Centeredness:* This scenario represents the extreme situation that is often criticised in research universities. High institutional priority is attached to research productivity and internal reward systems fail to recognise adequately the importance of individual contributions to the learning process. Consequently, professors invest little time in their teaching responsibilities, often "talk over the heads" of their students or delegate assistants to deliver lectures. An additional constraint arises when the curriculum is heavily biased towards the particular research interests of the professor and, as a result, some important curricular elements receive inadequate coverage. The overall result is a poor learning environment which frustrates students and denies professors the benefits of student insight into research questions.
- *Low Research Focus and High Student Centeredness:* The heavy emphasis placed on the learner is generally appreciated by students and, as a result, this approach often generates excellent student evaluations of teaching. Furthermore, in some situations, the strategy can be used effectively to enable students to acquire understanding of basic, underlying concepts and to stimulate interest and a desire to learn more about the subject. However, the material delivered is, at best, second-hand, often out of date, and the student is not exposed to the frontiers of disciplinary knowledge. The overall consequence is often a lack of rigour and intellectual challenge for the student.

- *Low Research Focus and Low Student Centeredness*: university teaching which fails to embrace either of the two concepts is, invariably, impoverished in content and uninspiring in delivery. The material presented is usually outdated, little opportunity is provided for discussion and student creativity is stifled. Such courses fail to stimulate student interest and, indeed, generate much of the criticism that is directed against the quality of undergraduate education in universities.
- *High Research Focus and High Student Centeredness*: This clearly provides the optimal learning environment with engaged students involved in the excitement of cutting-edge research or resolution of real-life problems and professors benefiting from the insights and fresh perspectives of students.

PROMOTION AND IMPLEMENTATION OF AN OPTIMAL LEARNING ENVIRONMENT

The learning environment envisaged above differs from that found in many modern universities and, therefore, change is needed in order to achieve this ideal. Unfortunately, the implementation of change is difficult in any workplace and, within a traditional academic environment, is likely to be particularly problematic. Any proposal to switch, even partially, from a familiar, trusted form of teaching to one that is less certain and more demanding of faculty time and institutional resources will inevitably raise concerns and generate resistance. Therefore, a careful implementation strategy is required.

A key factor in the successful implementation of change within organisations is strong leadership, and the introduction of pedagogic change in a university requires absolute commitment to the process on the part of each member of the senior executive team. However, experienced university leaders recognize that the best way to effect new initiatives is to be "pushed by faculty in the direction that you want to go". Accordingly, an essential element in the implementation strategy will be to identify faculty champions, with a passion for teaching and research, who will welcome the opportunity to participate in efforts directed towards the development of a culture of student-centred, problem-based learning. Ideally, these champions will represent a variety of academic disciplines and will infect colleagues with their enthusiasm for the new approaches. The efforts of the faculty champions must be strongly supported by the academic and administrative leadership of the university in a variety of tangible and highly visible ways. These include:

- *Resources*: One of the factors that contribute to the continuing practice of professors lecturing to large classes is that it offers an inexpensive, cost-effective method of "educating" undergraduate students. Student-centred teaching is more costly, requiring greater investment of faculty time and infrastructural support. Institutions wishing to undergo transition from traditional to student-centred, research-led teaching must be willing to commit additional funding to the teaching/learning enterprise. Such investment delivers a clear message to the academic community about the institutional resolve to effect the change. Parenthetically, it is an interesting reflection of institutional priorities that substantial monies are often made available to facilitate new research initiatives, whereas few funds are set aside to encourage innovations in teaching and learning.

- *Rewards*: The reality of promotion and tenure decisions in most modern research universities is that faculty who excel in research and neglect their teaching responsibilities will tend to be favoured over excellent teachers with modest research accomplishment. In that change is most readily achieved when there are obvious benefits associated with its implementation, it is evident that institutions must ensure that there are clearly defined incentives available to those who embrace and contribute to the process of change. This does not mean that professors should be rewarded for neglecting research in favour of teaching because, as indicated previously, in a true university the two activities are closely related and, indeed, part of a continuum of discovery. However, commitment to excellent teaching must be considered a prerequisite for promotion of academic staff in the same way as research productivity.

- *Support for Teachers*: The challenge for faculty who are undertaking the transition from traditional methods of teaching to student-centred, research-led strategies of learning is considerable and requires that they be provided with appropriate support. They will need time to restructure courses and they require access to professional pedagogic counsel. Institutional commitment to the process of change can be demonstrated also by the establishment of a teaching-resource centre and by the organisation and promotion of an ongoing series of workshops and seminars on relevant topics. The overall impact of such a supportive professional development environment will raise the profile of teaching within the institution and encourage faculty participation.

- *Support for Learners*: Most students entering university directly from secondary school and mature students who were educated in a traditional academic environment will not be prepared for student-centred, problem-based pedagogy. They will require remedial, transition courses to enable them to benefit fully from the learning opportunities presented. Tutorials and modules, which explain clearly the learning process and what is required of the students should be offered with such essential skills as use of databases, time management, working in teams and report-writing also emphasised to complement the disciplinary learning process.

CONCLUSION

Universities serve essential societal roles in the education of an informed and responsible citizenry and as a source and repository of knowledge. Both roles are of pivotal importance for national competitiveness in the Knowledge Age and, therefore, it behoves universities to ensure that best practices are followed in the execution of these missions. The current paper argues that effective learning is best achieved if it is directed by the interests and curiosity of the student and if it is founded on current, frontier research issues.

REFERENCES

Boyer Commission on Educating Undergraduates in the Research University (1999). *Reinventing Undergraduate Education: A blueprint for America's Research Universities*.

Downer, R.G.H. (in press). "The Idea of a University – Newman Revisited," *The Journal of the Irish College of Physicians and Surgeons*.

Elton, L. (2001). "Research and Teaching: Conditions for a positive link," *Teaching in Higher Education* 6, pp. 42-56.

Goodwin, L., Miller, J.E. & Cheetham, R.D. (1991). "Teaching Freshmen to Think – does active learning work?" *Bioscience* 41, pp. 719-722.

Kuh, G.D. & Hu, S. (2001). "Learning Productivity at Research Universities", *Journal of Higher Education* 72, pp. 1-18.

Rhodes, F.H.T. (2001). *The Creation of the Future*, Cornell University Press, Ithaca and London.

CHAPTER

The Changing Nature of Research and the Future of the University

James J. Duderstadt

INTRODUCTION

The contemporary research university reaches into every aspect of modern society. It educates the graduates that sustain commerce, government, and professional practice; it performs the research and scholarship so essential to a knowledge-driven global economy; and it applies this knowledge to meet a diverse array of social needs including health care, economic development, and national security. Although the changing needs and nature of society were important factors in shaping the evolution of the university over the centuries, so too has been the changing nature of research and scholarship. Intellectual transformations ranging from scholasticism to the scientific revolution have played a major role in defining the nature of the university in the past and are continuing to do so today. This paper attempts to identify some of the changes occurring today in scholarship and research, and speculates about the impact on the future form of the research university.

First, however, it seems appropriate to establish a benchmark by summarizing how changes in the nature of research over the past 50 years have been important determinants in shaping the contemporary research university. Although much of this discussion will be focused on the American experience, many of these factors have influenced the evolution of research universities in other nations and are even more likely to do so in the decades ahead as the nature of learning, research and scholarship becomes increasingly international.

THE AMERICAN RESEARCH UNIVERSITY, CIRCA 2000

The character of today's American research university was shaped some 50 years ago by the seminal report, *Science, the Endless Frontier* produced by a World War II study group chaired by Vannevar Bush (Bush, 1945). The central theme of the document was that the nation's health, economy and military security required continual deployment of new scientific knowledge; hence the federal government was obligated in the national interest to ensure basic scientific progress and the production of trained personnel. It stressed a corollary principle: that the government had to preserve freedom of inquiry, to recognize that scientific progress results from the "free play of free intellects, working on subjects of their own choice, in the manner dictated by their curiosity for explanation of the unknown". Rather than attempting to build separate research institutes or academies, the federal government decided instead to rely on a partnership with the leading American universities by supporting research on the campuses through a system of competitive, peer-reviewed grants and a framework for contractual relationships between universities and government sponsors. Faculty investigators were encouraged to work on research of their own choosing, with the anticipation that eventually this unconstrained research would lead to significant social benefits.

The resulting partnership between the federal government and the nation's universities has had an extraordinary impact. Federally supported academic research programmes on the campuses have greatly strengthened the scientific prestige and quality of American research universities, many of which now rank among the world's best. The academic research enterprise has not only provided leadership in the pursuit of knowledge in the fundamental academic disciplines, but through the conduct of more applied-mission-focused research, it has addressed national priorities such as health care, environmental sustainability, economic competitiveness, and national defence. It has laid the technological foundations for entirely new industries such as microelectronics, biotechnology, and information technology. Furthermore, by combining research with advanced training, it has produced the well-trained scientists, engineers, and other professionals capable of applying this new knowledge.

Yet it is also clear that while the research university model evolving during the latter half of the 20th century has been remarkably successful, many of its most distinguishing characteristics have been mixed blessings. The single-investigator model of sponsored research, in which individual faculty members are expected to secure whatever resources are necessary for research and graduate training in their narrow area of scholarship, has driven the dominance of disciplinary specialization and reductionism. Faculty have learned that the best way to attract funding in a competitive, peer-reviewed research culture is to become as specialized as possible, since this narrows the group of those likely to review their proposals (perhaps even to their colleagues), thereby driving even more the disciplinary fragmentation of the academy. As a result, academic disciplines dominate the modern research university, developing curriculum, marshalling resources, administering programmes, and doling out rewards.

Since competition for grants and contracts play such an important role in supporting research and graduate education, it is not surprising that research universities tend to set their sails to track the ever-shifting winds of federal research priorities. For example, as the space race of the 1960s was succeeded by the social programmes of Lyndon Johnson's Great Society and concern about the environment of the 1970s, research universities throttled back academic programmes in the physical sciences and engineering in favour of the applied social and health sciences (e.g. education, social work, medicine, dentistry and public health). Today the health concerns of an ageing baby-boom population have stimulated a doubling of the budget of the National Institutes of Health, triggering a massive shift from the physical and social sciences into the life sciences on many campuses, as universities have sensed the shift of federal priorities from "guns to pills". More specifically, during the past decade the budget of the National Institutes of Health increased by more than 150 %, to $27 billion for FY2003, while the research budgets of those agencies such as the Department of Energy, Department of Defense, and the National Aeronautics and Space Administration remained relatively stagnant or declined. Even the National Science Foundation experienced only modest growth, to roughly $5 billion in FY2003. Today, roughly 62 % of every federal research dollar flowing to the campuses is in biomedical research (Committee on Science, Engineering and Public Policy, 2003).

The faculty members of research universities are well aware that their careers – their compensation, promotion, and tenure – are determined more by their research productivity, as measured by publications, grantsmanship and peer respect, than by other university activities such as undergraduate teaching and public service. This reward climate helps to tip the scales away from teaching and public service, especially when quantitative measures of research productivity or grantsmanship replace more balanced judgements of the quality of research and professional work. So too, the fragmentation of disciplines driven in part by increasing specialization of scholarship has undermined the coherence of the undergraduate curriculum. There appears to be a growing gap between what faculty members like to teach and what undergraduate students need to learn (Shapiro, 1991).

Just as the research interests of the faculty drove the fragmentation of undergraduate education, so too, graduate education has been reshaped largely to benefit faculty research. In a sense this was natural since Ph.D. programmes have traditionally seen their role as training the next generation of academicians, that is, self-replication. All too often, however, the current research-driven paradigm tends to view graduate education as either a by-product activity, driven by the level of research funding, or as a source of cheap labour for research projects. Such exploitation of students for the benefit of faculty research extends to the postdoctoral level as well. Postdoctoral students have the sophistication to be highly productive research assistants. They are highly motivated and work extremely hard. And they are cheap. Hence, it is not surprising that in many fields the postdoctoral student has become the backbone of the research enterprise. In fact, one might even cynically regard postdocs as the migrant workers of the research industry, since they are sometimes forced to shift from project to project, postdoc to postdoc appointment, even institution to institution, before they find a permanent position.

The growing pressures on faculty, not only to achieve excellence in teaching and research, but also to generate the resources necessary to support their activities, are immense (Clark, 1998). At a university like Michigan, with roughly 2,700 faculty members generating over $700 million of research funding per year, this can amount to an expectation that each faculty member will generate hundreds of thousands of research dollars per year, a heavy burden for those who also carry significant instructional, administrative, and service responsibilities. Pressures on individual faculty for success and recognition have led to major changes in the culture and governance of universities. The peer-reviewed grant system has fostered fierce competitiveness, imposed intractable work schedules, and contributed to a loss of collegiality and community. It has shifted faculty loyalties from the campus to their disciplinary communities. Faculty careers have become nomadic, driven by the marketplace, hopping from institution to institution in search of higher salaries, more generous research support and better colleagues.

As one junior faculty member exclaimed in a burst of frustration: "The contemporary university has become only a holding company for research entrepreneurs!"

THE CHANGING NATURE OF RESEARCH AND SCHOLARSHIP

What changes in the nature of research and scholarship might we identify as significant factors in determining the nature of the university in the century ahead?

Disciplines or Dinosaurs

It is important to acknowledge the dynamic nature of the disciplinary character of scholarship. What we regard as entrenched disciplines today have changed considerably in the past and continue to do so. New ideas and concepts continue to explode forth at ever-increasing pace. We have ceased to accept that there is any coherent or unique form of wisdom that serves as the basis for new knowledge. We have simply seen too many instances in which a new concept has blown apart our traditional views of the field. Just as, a century ago, Einstein's theory of relativity and the introduction of quantum mechanics totally revolutionized the way that we thought of the physical world, today's speculation about dark matter and quantum entanglement suggest that yet another revolution may be under way. The molecular foundations of life have done the same to the biomedical sciences.

In part the knowledge explosion is driven by the increasingly sophisticated nature of the experimental apparatus used to gather data and the digital technology used to store, curate and communicate knowledge. But it is also due simply to the fact that an ever-increasing population ever more dependent upon knowledge for economic prosperity has driven a major expansion in the numbers of scientists, engineers, and other scholars. There are also qualitative changes in the nature of research itself. Twenty-first-century science is marked by increasing complexity that frequently overwhelms the reductionist approach of the disciplines.

Basic vs. Applied Research

There is a definite hierarchy of academic prestige – or, perhaps better stated, an intellectual pecking order – within the university. In a sense, the more abstract and detached a discipline is from "the real world", the higher its prestige. In this ranking, perhaps mathematics or philosophy would be at the pinnacle, with the natural sciences and humanities next, followed by the social sciences and the arts. The professional schools fall much lower down the hierarchy, with law, medicine, and engineering followed by the health professions, social work, and education at the bottom. Clearly, within this culture of academic snobbery, the distinction of basic ("curiosity-driven" or Baconian) versus applied ("mission-oriented" or Newtonian) research becomes significant, perhaps tracing back to the Humboldtian ideal of pure *Wissenschaft*.

In reality, however, the progression of basic knowledge from the library or the laboratory to societal application is far from linear, and the distinction between basic and applied research is largely in the eye of the beholder (Sonnert & Holton, 2002). Furthermore, there is yet another mode of research that represents a conscious combination of basic and applied research:

so-called Jeffersonian science (using as an analogy the Lewis and Clark expedition, which was justified to Congress as discovering paths to further westward expansion, and portrayed to the Spanish as a purely scientific expedition, sampling unknown fauna and flora). Such research aims at providing the fundamental knowledge essential to address a key social priority (also known as Pasteur's quadrant [Stokes, 1997], referring to Pasteur's discovery of micro-organisms when trying to find a better way to brew beer) is not only important in its own right, but it creates the opportunity to make public support of all types of research more palatable to policy makers and taxpayers. Contemporary examples would include the neuroscience and cognitive science necessary to create better schools, the atomic and quantum physics necessary for nanotechnology, and, of course, the molecular biology necessary for progress in health care (providing an excellent case study through the growth in the NIH budget of the effectiveness of Jeffersonian research in building the case for strong public support).

The Conduct of Research

The process of creating new knowledge is evolving rapidly away from the solitary scholar to teams of scholars, often spread over a number of disciplines. This is driven by many factors. The enormous expense of major experimental facilities such as high-energy physics accelerators, astronomical observatories, and biochemical laboratories compel scientists to work in teams consisting not only of primary investigators but specialists such as systems engineers and software developers that may number in the hundreds. Similarly the complexity of contemporary research topics such as protein function or global change span many disciplines that require multidisciplinary teams.

While this may be a marked departure from the Humboldtian notion of the isolated scholars attempting to attain objective truth, it is actually more consistent with the nature of human social interactions. In the past, these scholarly communities generally occurred within disciplines, at the department level within universities, or scholarly communities scattered across the globe in highly specialized areas. Today these communities are increasingly multidisciplinary teams aimed at the investigation of complex research topics.

The International Nature of Scholarship

Any discussion about the future of the research university must account for the impact of the pervasively international character of research. To be sure, international cooperation in research is demanded by large and expensive facilities such as high-energy accelerators or astronomical observatories; for projects requiring coordinated research programmes such as global climate change; and for cross-national comparisons of health, education and economic development. However international cooperation is much more than joint financial support of major facilities with other nations. Scholarship is a global enterprise in which nations must participate both for their own benefit and that of the world.

Information and communications technologies have provided a powerful new tool to facilitate and extend international scholarship. By forging new national and international alliances and by carefully exploiting the new communications technologies on the horizon – putting the entire world in nearly instantaneous low-cost contact through the Internet (and its successors) – we can link to our scientific and scholarly colleagues throughout the world. Driven by information technology, the network has become more than a web which links together learning resources. It has become the architecture of advanced learning organizations (Dolence & Norris, 1995). Information, knowledge, and learning opportunities are now distributed across robust computer networks to hundreds of millions of people around the globe. The knowledge, the learning, the cultural resources that used to be the prerogative of a privileged few are rapidly becoming available anyplace, anytime, to anyone.

The Tools of Research

The tools of research continue to evolve, increasing dramatically in power, scope and, of course, cost. Research university leaders and funding agencies have long pointed to the staggering size and cost of the experimental facilities characterizing the physical sciences, e.g. the high-energy physics accelerators such as the Large Hadron Collider or astronomical observatories such as the Keck telescopes or the Hubble Space Telescope. But today many research universities are making even larger investments in the biomedical sciences, building new "life sciences institutes" to achieve the critical mass of facilities and scientists to tap the massive funding flowing into molecular genetics, proteomics, and biotechnology. Over the longer term, one might well question whether these research facilities will soon follow the path of high-energy physics and astronomy, becoming too large and expensive for single institutions – and perhaps even nations – and instead requiring international consortia of institutions, sponsors, and scientists.

The rapid evolution of digital technology also poses both new opportunities and challenges. A new age has dawned in S & E research, pushed by continuing progress in computing, information and communication technology, and pulled by the expanding complexity, scope and scale of today's challenges. The capacity of this technology has crossed thresholds that now make possible a comprehensive cyber-infrastructure on which to build new types of knowledge environments and organizations and to pursue research in new ways and with increased efficiency. The emerging vision is to use cyber-infrastructure (Atkins, 2003) to build more ubiquitous, comprehensive digital environments that become interactive and functionally complete for research communities in terms of people, data, information, tools and instruments and that operate at unprecedented levels of computational, storage and data-transfer capacity.

The Relationship Among Research, Education, and Learning

For decades, the conventional wisdom in the United States has been that research and teaching were mutually reinforcing and should be conducted together, at the same institutions by the same people (Pelikan, 1992). Higher education has long attempted to weave together research and education, particularly in making the case for public support of the research mission of the university. Yet the relationship of research to teaching quality is far from obvious. For example, in most research universities there is an ever-widening gap between the research activities of the faculty and the undergraduate curriculum.

There is a certain irony here. The research university provides one of the most remarkable learning environments in our society – an extraordinary array of diverse people with diverse ideas supported by an exceptionally rich array of intellectual and cultural resources. Yet we tend to focus our educational efforts on traditional academic programmes, on the classroom and the curriculum. In the process, we may have overlooked the most important learning experiences in the university.

Increasingly, we realize that learning occurs not simply through study and contemplation, but through the active discovery and application of knowledge. From John Dewey to Jean Piaget to Seymour Papert, we have ample evidence that most students learn best through inquiry-based of "constructionist" learning. As the ancient Chinese proverb suggests "I hear and I forget; I see and I remember; I do and I understand."

Perhaps it is time to integrate the educational mission of the university with the research and service activities of the faculty by ripping instruction out of the classroom – or at least the lecture hall – and placing it instead in the discovery environment of the laboratory or studio or the experiential environment of professional practice.

From Partnership to Procurement

We noted earlier the profound shift in federal research priorities that has occurred over the past several decades, shifting from the support of the physical sciences and engineering (e.g. in areas such as microelectronics and aerospace engineering) to support the Cold War and the space race, to the bio-medical sciences, reflecting the demands for better health care from an ageing population. There is growing recognition that our nation needs to address possible imbalances among the fields of science and engineering – at a time when many fields are increasingly interdependent for achieving opti-mal results in the productivity of the economy and the pursuit of knowledge.

Perhaps even more disturbing are signs suggesting that the basic principles of the extraordinarily productive research partnership that has existed for the past half-century between the federal government and the research univer-sity have begun to unravel. The government is increasingly shifting from being a partner with the university – a patron of basic research – to becoming a procurer of research, just as it procures other goods and services. This view has unleashed on the research university an army of government staff, accountants, and lawyers all claiming to want to make certain that the uni-versity meets every detail of its agreements with the government. This situa-tion is compounded by an array of new legislation and policies seeking both to demand and measure the performance associated with programmes sup-ported by federal tax dollars such as the Government Performance Results Act (GPRA) of 1992 and the more recent Performance Assessment Rating Tool imposed by the current administration.

The Commercialization of the Academy

The efforts of universities and faculty members to capture and exploit the soaring commercial value of the intellectual property created by research and instructional activities create many opportunities and challenges for higher education. To be sure, universities recognize and exploit the increasing commercial value of the intellectual property developed on the campuses as an important part of their mission. But there are also substantial financial benefits to those institutions and faculty members who strike it rich with tech transfer. This has infected the research university with the profit objec-tives of a business, as both institutions and individual faculty members attempt to profit from the commercial value of the products of their research and instructional activities. Universities have adopted aggressive commer-cialization policies and invested heavily in technology transfer offices to encourage the development and ownership of intellectual property rather than its traditional open sharing with the broader scholarly community. They have hired teams of lawyers to defend their ownership of the intellec-tual property derived from their research and instruction. On occasions some institutions and faculty members have set aside the most fundamental values of the university, such as openness, academic freedom, and a willingness to challenge the status quo, in order to accommodate this growing commercial role of the research university (Press & Washburn, 2000).

SOME IMPLICATIONS FOR THE 21ST CENTURY RESEARCH UNIVERSITY

Intellectual Architecture

The changes in the nature of scholarship, from disciplinary to multi/inter-trans/cross-disciplinary, from specialization and reductionism to complexity and consilience, from Baconian or Newtonian to Jeffersonian, from analysis to creativity, will likely reshape the intellectual architecture of the university, as well as its organizational structure. Clearly top-down organizations, imposed by administrators with little experience or understanding of life in the intellectual trenches, will fail to tap the energy and creativity of faculty and students. Managing intellectual change in the university is not about putting centralized command-and-control systems in place. On the other hand, leaving the future of the university to faculty entrenched in traditional disciplines would similarly doom it to ossification. The organization of the university will become increasingly driven by innovative scholarship, teaching, and learning at the grassroots level. To preserve vitality will require flexible, decentralized structures, competing with one another for survival.

The increasingly rapid and non-linear nature of the transfer of knowledge from the library and laboratory into practical application suggests that more basic research activities may shift from the academic disciplines into professional schools. For example, the clinical applications (and revenue) associated with molecular genetics and proteomics have already drawn much of the most exciting basic research in the life sciences into clinical departments such as immunology and internal medicine. So too, engineering is becoming increasingly dependent upon and involved in basic research topics such as quantum computing and nanoscience. Some of the most exciting basic work in the social sciences is now found in professional schools such as business, public policy and law.

The development of information and communications technologies, the increased mobility of people and the migration of populations driven by economic, social and political factors will provoke even greater cultural contact and the internationalization of public life, education and scholarship, and academic institutions. If universities are to be able to capitalize on discoveries made elsewhere and facilities located elsewhere, they must have world-class researchers who maintain constant communication and work frequently in collaboration with the best scholars throughout the world. International science and technology cooperation is also necessary in order to make progress on many common problems that require a global perspective, i.e. stopping new infectious diseases, understanding volcanic hazards, cataloguing biological diversity and reversing soil degradation.

NEW PARADIGMS FOR THE RESEARCH UNIVERSITY

So what might we anticipate as possible future forms of the university? The monastic character of the ivory tower is certainly lost forever. Although there are many important features of the campus environment that suggest that the most universities will continue to exist as a place, at least for the near term, as digital technology makes it increasingly possible to emulate human interaction in all the senses with arbitrarily high fidelity, perhaps we should not bind teaching and scholarship too tightly to buildings and grounds. Certainly, both learning and scholarship will continue to depend heavily upon the existence of communities since they are, after all, highly social enterprises. Yet as these communities are increasingly global in extent, detached from the constraints of space and time, we should not assume that the scholarly communities of our times, constrained to a physical campus, would necessarily dictate the future of our universities.

As illustrations, let me suggest several possible visions of the future, that progress ever more toward an unpredictable and unknowable future (and, as some might contend, toward the lunatic fringe...)

The Core-in-Cloud University

Many research universities are already evolving into so-called "core-in-cloud" organizations (Gibbons, 1994) in which academic departments or schools conducting elite education and basic research, are surrounded by a constellation of quasi-university organizations – research institutes, think tanks, corporate R & D centres – that draw intellectual strength from the core university and provide important financial, human, and physical resources in return. Such a structure reflects the blurring of basic and applied research, education and training, the university and broader society.

More specifically, while the academic units at the core retain the traditional university culture of faculty appointments (e.g. tenure) and intellectual traditions (e.g. disciplinary focus), those quasi-academic organizations evolving in the cloud can be far more flexible and adaptive. They can be multidisciplinary and project-focused. They can be driven by entrepreneurial cultures and values. Unlike academic programmes, they can come and go as the need and opportunity arise. And, although it is common to think of the cloud being situated quite close to the university core, in today's world of emerging electronic and virtual communities, there is no reason why the cloud might not be widely distributed, involving organizations located far from the campus. In fact, as virtual universities become more common, there is no reason that the core itself has to have a geographical focus.

To some degree, the core-in-cloud model could revitalize core academic programmes by stimulating new ideas and interactions. It could provide a bridge that allows the university to better serve society without compromising its core academic values. But, like the entrepreneurial university, the cloud could also become a fog, scattering and diffusing the activities of the university and creating a shopping mall character with little coherence.

New Civic Life Forms

Today, as knowledge becomes an ever more significant factor in determining both personal and societal wellbeing, and as rapidly emerging information technology provides the capacity to build new types of communities, we might well see the appearance of new social structures (Benton Foundation, 1996). A century ago, stimulated by the philanthropy of Andrew Carnegie, the public library became the focal point for community learning. Today, however, technology allows us to link together public and private resources such as schools, libraries, museums, hospitals, parks, media and cultural resources. Further, communities can easily be linked with the knowledge resources of the world through the Internet. Perhaps a new "civic life form" will evolve to provide community education and knowledge networks that are open and available to all. These might evolve from existing institutions such as libraries or schools or universities. They might be a physically located hub or virtual in character. However, they also might appear as entirely new constructs, quite different than anything we have experienced to date. Perhaps it is time to consider a blank-sheet approach to learning, by setting aside existing educational systems, policies and practices, and instead first focusing on what knowledge, skills and abilities a person will need to lead a productive and satisfying life in the century ahead. Then, by considering the diversity of ways in which people learn, and the rich array of knowledge resources emerging in our society, one could design a new ecology of learning for the 21st Century.

The University à la Neuromancer (Gibson, 1984)

Ray Kurzweil's The Age of Spiritual Machines provides a provocative vision of possible futures for our society by projecting Moore's Law – the exponential evolution of digital technology – over the next several decades. He suggests that over the next decade intelligent courseware will emerge as a common means of learning, with schools and colleges relying increasingly on software approaches, leaving human teachers to attend primarily to issues of motivation, psychological wellbeing, and socialization (Kurzweil, 1999).

More specifically, Kurzweil speculates that by the end of this decade, although schools are still not on the cutting edge, the profound importance of the computer as a knowledge tool will be widely recognized. Many children will learn to read on their own using their personal computers before entering grade school. Within two decades, most learning will be accomplished using intelligent software-based simulated teachers. To the extent that human teachers do teaching, the human teachers are often not in the local vicinity of the student and will be viewed more as mentors and counsellors than as sources of learning and knowledge.

Within three decades (2030), Kurzweil suggests that human learning will be primarily accomplished using virtual teachers and enhanced by the widely available neural implants that improve memory and perception (although not yet able to download knowledge directly thereby bypassing formal education entirely). Although enhanced through virtual experiences, intelligent interactive instruction and neural implants, learning still requires time-consuming human experience and study. This activity comprises the primary focus of the human species, and education becomes the largest profession as human and non-human intelligences are primarily focused on the creation of knowledge in its myriad forms. Finally, a century hence, Kurweil speculates that learning will no longer be the struggle it once was. Rather the struggle will be discovering new knowledge to learn.

While many would argue (indeed, many have argued) with Kurzweil's view of the future, it does illustrate just how profoundly different the future may be both for our society and our universities.

CONCLUDING REMARKS

As one of civilization's most enduring institutions, the university has been extraordinary in its capacity to change and adapt to serve a changing society. Far from being immutable, the university has changed considerably over time and continues to do so today. The remarkable diversity of institutions of higher education, ranging from small liberal arts colleges to gigantic university systems, from storefront proprietary colleges to global "cyberspace" universities, demonstrates the evolution of the species.

Today we have entered yet another period of rapid change, as an array of powerful economic, social and technological forces are transforming social institutions such as the university. This impending revolution in the structure and function of higher education stems from the worldwide shift to a knowledge-based society. Educated people and the knowledge they produce will increasingly become the source of wealth for nations. The knowledge produced on our campuses is expanding exponentially with no slowing in sight.

As we look to the profound changes ahead of us, as we explore possible visions for the future, it is important to keep in mind that throughout their history, universities have evolved as integral parts of their societies to meet the challenges of their surrounding environments. This disposition to change

is a basic characteristic and strength of university life, the result of our constant generation of new knowledge through scholarship that, in turn, changes
the education we provide and influences the societies that surround us. In a
very real sense, the university is both driving and being driven by technological, social and economic forces at work throughout the world.

This propensity of universities to change is nicely balanced by vital conti-
nuities, especially those arising from our fundamental scholarly commitments
and values and from our roots in democratic societies. While the emphasis,
structure, or organization of university activity may change over time to
respond to new challenges, it is these scholarly principles, values, and traditions that animate the academic enterprise and give it continuity and meaning. An integral part of the life of the university has always been to evaluate
the world around us in order to adjust our teaching, research and service
missions to serve the changing needs of our constituents while preserving
basic values and commitments. We must always bear in mind those deeper
purposes of the university that remain unchanged and undiminished in
importance. Our institutions must remain places of learning where human
potential is transformed and shaped, the wisdom of our culture is passed from
one generation to the next, and the new knowledge that creates our future is
produced.

REFERENCES

Atkins, D. (chair), (2003). *Revolutionizing Science and Engineering Through Cyberinfrastructure, Report of the National Science Foundation Blue-Ribbon Advisory Panel on
Cyberinfrastructure*, National Science Foundation, Washington, D.C.

Benton Foundation. (1996). *Buildings, Books, and Bytes: Libraries and Communities in
the Digital Age, A Report on the Public's Opinion of Library Leaders Visions for the
Future*, Washington, DC. Funded by the W. R. Kellogg Foundation.

Bush, V., (1990). *Science, the Endless Frontier, A report to the President on a Program for
Postwar Scientific Research* (Office of Scientific Research and Development, July
1945), National Science Foundation, Washington, D.C., p. 192.

Clark, B., (1998). *Creating Entrepreneurial Universities: Organizational Pathways of
Transformation*, Oxford, New York.

Committee on Science, *Engineering, and Public Policy*, (2003). *Observations on the
President's Fiscal year 2003 Federal Science and Technology Budget*, National Academy Press, Washington, D.C.

David, P. (October, 1997). "The Knowledge Factory: A Survey of Universities." *The
Economist*. 345, pp. 1-22.

Dolence, M. & Donald M. Norris, (1995). *Transforming Higher Education: A Vision for
Learning in the 21st Century*, Society for College and University Planning, Ann
Arbor.

Gibbons, M., (1994). *The New Production of Knowledge: The Dynamics of Science and
Research in Contemporary Societies*, Sage, London.

Gibson, W., (1984). *Neuromancer*, Ace, New York.

Kurzweil, R. (1999). *The Age of Spiritual Machines: When Computers Exceed Human Intelligence*, Viking, New York.

Pelikan, J. (1992). *The Idea of the University: A Reexamination*. Yale University Press, New Haven, p. 238

Press, E. & Washburn, J., (2000) "The Kept University", *The Atlantic Monthly*, 285(3), pp. 39-54.

Shapiro, H., (1991). *The Functions and Resources of the American University of the Twenty-First Century*. University of Chicago Symposium, Chicago.

Sonnert, G. & Holton, G., (2002). *Ivory Bridges: Connecting Science and Society*. MIT Press, Cambridge.

Stokes, D., (1997). *Pasteur's Quadrant: Basic Science and Technological Innovation*. Brookings Institute, Washington, D.C.

CHAPTER 7

Closing the European Knowledge Gap? Challenges for the European Universities of the 21st Century

Frans A. van Vught

INTRODUCTION

This paper discusses the present condition of European universities in the context of the European ambition to be a world-class knowledge economy. It explores both this political ambition and the realities of the European knowledge economy. In addition, it compares these European realities with the performance of the United States knowledge economy and analyses the background to the "knowledge gap" between Europe and the U.S.

In the second part of this paper the traditional European academic culture and some key European university characteristics are discussed. The argument presented is that both this culture and these sometimes "distorted" characteristics need to be fundamentally changed in order to allow Europe to realize its ambitions to become a world-class knowledge economy. At the end of the paper some suggestions are formulated to enhance the role of the European universities in the knowledge economy as well as with respect to a number of crucial policy initiatives in the European higher education and research system.

GLOBALIZATION AND THE KNOWLEDGE ECONOMY

Since the 1970s the world has been going through a rapid process of increasing globalization. Partly as a result of this globalization the world's economic production has increased six-fold over the past 50 years, while the world's population has increased only by a factor of two-and-a-half. The result has been increasing prosperity for a large number (but unfortunately not the whole) of the world's population. The ongoing economic integration that has characterized the world since the Second World War appears to be an important source of increasing prosperity. Globalization is a process that is characterized in economic terms by a sharp increase in trade in goods and services, as well as, more recently, an expansion of international flows of capital. The crucial driver behind these developments is the rapid development of technology over recent decades that has led to significant cost reductions in production, communication and transport, and a major increase in our capacity to process information. Clearly international policy agreements concerning free trade and the limitation on tariff barriers have played their role, but technological advances appear to be the most important cause of the continuing integration of markets.

In the meantime, the significance of these developments and their effects grows even more powerful. The competitive strength of companies increasingly rests on their ability to respond to the wishes of customers at the right moment. Adequate information processing and flexibility and efficiency in production are important advantages in this respect. Regions, countries and even entire continents benefit from the increased competitiveness of their business and industry sectors and concentrate increasingly on attracting investment for economic activities. The result is a growing competition between geographical entities.

In this context knowledge is a crucial factor. Globalization has given rise to a situation in which economic and social development is increasingly based on knowledge. Today we live in a knowledge society and our economy is strongly dependent on the creation and distribution of knowledge. Our markets, production processes and institutions are knowledge-based. Our working and living conditions are determined by knowledge.

THE EUROPEAN KNOWLEDGE ECONOMY

Europe stands on the threshold of a number of major socio-economic changes. The coming years will see fundamental changes not only in the sphere of politics and governance, but also in the areas of social life and economic structures – some of these changes have already been set in motion. Europe will have to meet the challenge of ever increasing globalization (Van Vught a.o., 2002).

Europe realizes that it has arrived in the era of knowledge and that European and national policies must be grafted on to this new reality. This was most clearly seen when the political leaders of the European Union governments met in Lisbon in March 2000 to agree on strategic goals. They agreed that in 2010 (less than 10 years from now) the European Union must be the world's most dynamic and competitive knowledge economy. To achieve this more knowledge must be created faster, and more knowledge workers must be educated.

But Europe is changing in terms of the composition of its population. Demographic indicators show that the proportion of Europeans in the world's population is declining to an unprecedented level: from 35 % in the 1950s to 13 % today, and a predicted 8 % in 2050. Alongside this trend is the phenomenon of ageing. Europe is already the continent with the largest proportion of the population 65 years or older. and this percentage is increasing: it is expected to double from around 14 % today to almost 28 % in 2050. The "greying of the population" in Europe is the fastest in the world (European Commission, 2003a, p. 5). A European demographic policy is clearly called for and needs to be a counterpart to the strategic approach to the knowledge economy.

A declining labour force requires a major immigration of new knowledge workers. In Germany it has been calculated that until 2020 an annual immigration of a million immigrants is needed to maintain its labour force at current levels. The focus here needs to be on young, highly educated researchers of which there are already significantly fewer in Europe than in the United States (European Commission, 2003a, p. 253).

Even if Europe succeeds in achieving an effective immigration of young talent and limits the decline in the labour force, there still remains a need to achieve a significant increase in labour productivity. If we want to maintain our current levels of welfare, then we need to improve our international competitiveness, our economic growth and our productivity. This is why the emphasis on knowledge is critically important. Only through technological progress and a highly educated labour force will we be in a position to achieve heightened levels of productivity. In a knowledge economy, investment in education and research is the most important factor in guaranteeing long-term welfare and prosperity.

As indicated earlier, Europe realizes that it has arrived in the era of the knowledge economy. Since the 1970s the European economic structures have undergone a number of changes whereby the economy has developed from an industrialized to a knowledge intensive economy. The emphasis on labour, raw materials and available capital has shifted to the creation, distribution and application of knowledge. Most notable is the structural intensification of research activity. In the knowledge economy, economic growth depends more on investment in knowledge than on traditional factors of production. In a production function where knowledge has become the most important factor, the quality of human capital is decisive. It is, after all, the professional skills of researchers and those who apply knowledge that make the development and application of knowledge possible.

The development of the knowledge society appears to bring with it a number of social effects that warrant our attention. Now that the production and distribution of knowledge have reached a pace unknown before in our history, it appears that there is a range of attendant social consequences. Institutional and organizational changes seem necessary, existing patterns of rules and agreements are no longer adequate, while new professions and ways of organising work appear to be developing. Knowledge seems to change not only economic production processes, but also penetrates our social, institutional and organizational structures and processes. We live not only in a knowledge economy, but also in a knowledge society.

In this knowledge society, technological progress is not an exogenous fact. Technological progress does not reach us from outside, but is the result precisely of these structures and processes within the knowledge society. The way in which we organize our knowledge society determines to a large measure the nature and extent of technological progress. This progress does not happen automatically – the production and application of knowledge must be organized and stimulated. In other words, political and executive responsibility has to be taken for active policy in this field. The cornerstone of such policy should be an investment strategy to increase the possibilities of the generation, distribution and application of knowledge – in short, an investment policy for education and research.

AMBITIONS AND REALITIES IN THE EUROPEAN KNOWLEDGE ECONOMY

At a European level such a policy is currently in development. The ambitions of Europe's top political leadership, for example, have been translated into a new form of steering referred to as "the open coordination method". This steering instrument (which implies a leading role for the European Commission) aims to compare the policy achievements of E.U. member states in relation to the Lisbon objectives using indicators and benchmarks. Through this process a form of peer pressure is brought to bear on less well achieving member states who feel almost forced to match the policy results of the better performing countries. In addition, the Lisbon ambition has been given further effect by the agreement reached during the top political meeting in Barcelona (15 and 16 March, 2002) that each member state should strive to spend 3 % of GNP on research.

Let us be absolutely clear that we in Europe still have a long way to go. The ambitious goals set in Lisbon – to be the world's most competitive and dynamic knowledge economy by 2010 – are still a long way away from being realized, and it is a legitimate question to ask whether the goals are still achievable. The reports published to date by the European Commission on the progress made in terms of the Lisbon strategy make it clear that much work remains to be done. The European Union continues to lag behind the U.S.A. and Japan both in terms of levels of investment in the knowledge economy (for example, expenditure on R & D and education) and the growth in these investments. This disappointing picture is also seen in the indicators used to measure the performance of the European knowledge economy (such as the number of patents). Europe as a whole does not perform as well as the U.S.A. In addition, the rates of growth in the performance of European countries appear too limited to close the existing gap between Europe and the U.S.A. by 2010 (European Commission, 2003a; 2003b).

This brings us to the question of the nature of the difference in knowledge economy achievements between Europe and the U.S.A. What actually explains this clear "knowledge gap" between America and Europe? Much has been spoken about the "European paradox" since the 1980s. On the one hand, Europe has become the world's largest producer of scientific publications, but, on the other hand, Europe is clearly behind the U.S.A. when it comes to turning scientific knowledge into economic growth (Soete, 2002). Recent statistics demonstrate that the E.U. member states' combined share of the world's scientific publication output since 1997 exceeds that of the NAFTA countries (U.S.A., Canada and Mexico). Europe is thus unquestionably the world's leading producer of scientific output (European Commission, 2003a, p. 279).

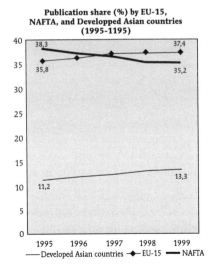

Publication share (%) by EU-15, NAFTA, and Developped Asian countries (1995-1195)

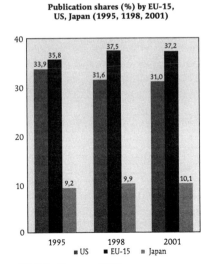

Publication shares (%) by EU-15, US, Japan (1995, 1198, 2001)

Source: DG Research, Third European Report on S&T Indicators, 2003
Data: ISI, CWTS (treatments)

However, if we look at actual investment in higher education and in R & D see a completely different picture. The average expenditure on higher education within the European Union amounts to 1.1 % of GNP. In the U.S.A. this figure is more than double at 2.3 %. The difference can be traced mainly to the near absent private contribution in European higher education (0.2 % compared to 1.2 % in the U.S.A.). (European Commission, 2002b; 2003c, p. 12)

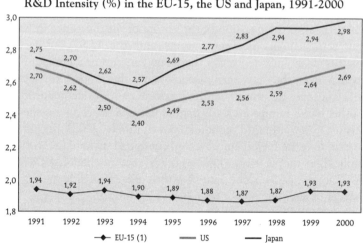

R&D Intensity (%) in the EU-15, the US and Japan, 1991-2000

Source: DG Research, Third European Report on S&T Indicators, 2003
Data: OECD – MSTI database (STI, EAS Division) with DG Research provisional estimates
Note: (1) L data are not included in EU-1 5 average

European expenditure on R & D as a percentage of GNP has hovered around the level of 1.9 % since 1990. It is anticipated that without changes in policy this will fall somewhere between 1.8 and 2.2 % in 2010 – considerably lower than the 3 % target agreed at the political summit in Barcelona.

In the United States, expenditure on R & D is increasing – from a low of 2.4 % in 1994 to almost 2.7 % in 2000. In 2000 Japan had already reached almost 3.0 %. For the United States, 3 % is seen as a realistic future expenditure level.

Europe thus lags behind both the U.S.A. and Japan in terms of R & D intensity (expenditure as a proportion of GDP). And the gap is growing – in 1994 it was 0.5 %, by 2000 it had reached 0.8 %.

THE EUROPEAN 'KNOWLEDGE GAP'

Let us look more closely at how this gap can be interpreted. Government R & D expenditure in the E.U. and U.S.A. is at a comparable level (in 1999 0.8 % of GDP in the U.S.A. and 0.7 % in the E.U.). However, in Europe (as in the U.S.A.) there is concern that government expenditure may decline – an alarming situation when seen against the Barcelona target.

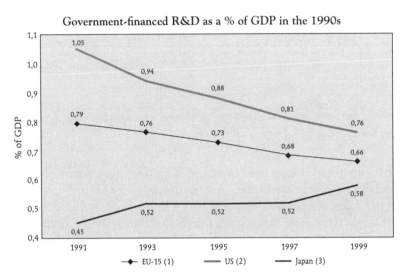

Government-financed R&D as a % of GDP in the 1990s

Source: DG Research, Third European Report on S&T Indicators, 2003
Data: OECD; DG Research
Notes: (1) L data are not included in EU-15 average. (2) US: excludes most or all capital expenditure. (3) JP: 1996 instead of 1995.

R & D expenditure by business and industry companies in the U.S.A. appears to be considerably higher than in Europe, and is growing more rapidly. The following figure Soete (2002) shows the extent of this largest part of the "knowledge gap" between the U.S.A. and the E.U. – a gap that appears to be increasing.

It could well be that these differences in both private investment and the expenditure by business and industry between the U.S.A. and Europe provide an explanation for the European paradox. In Europe, investment in higher education and research is still seen primarily as a task for government, while in the U.S.A. individuals also invest in their higher education, and business and industry invest more broadly in R & D. In the U.S.A. the focus on the relevance of the application of knowledge is evidently stronger than in Europe, which could also be the reason why in the U.S.A. more economic growth is generated from knowledge than in Europe.

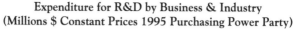

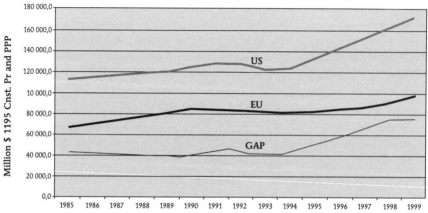

Source: Soete, 2002.

This hypothesis is supported by statistics on the proportion of researchers in the labour force. In the U.S.A. in 1999 this was 8.7 FTE (full-time equivalent) per 1,000 employees, compared to 5.4 in the E.U. In the U.S.A. there are thus relatively more "knowledge workers" active in the economy than in Europe. Furthermore, these knowledge workers are predominantly employed by companies in the U.S.A. (almost 83 %), whereas in Europe 50 % are in positions in government or universities (European Commission, 2003a, p. 183). This is another indication that companies in the U.S.A. appear to be more orientated to knowledge than their counterparts in Europe.

The "knowledge gap" between America and Europe can be traced back to differences in investment in higher education as well as in R & D. In the U.S.A. higher education is not only publicly financed, but there are also significant private contributions. Investments in R & D in the U.S.A. are made not only by government, but also to an important extent by business and industry. In Europe higher education and scientific research are seen as activities to be financed from public sources. In Europe higher education and scientific research have traditionally been seen as the primary domain of the universities – which in Europe are almost exclusively (semi-) public institutions.

In Europe the generation of knowledge predominantly takes place in largely publicly funded universities, and these European "knowledge institutions" are exceptionally good at this. In the European universities knowledge generation is a goal in its own right. Knowledge as a resource directed towards economic productivity, however, is a concept still relatively novel in Europe. In the U.S.A. there is a more pragmatic approach to the social function of knowledge. Although much of the fundamental, cutting-edge, leading research in the world takes place at American research universities, focused attention is nevertheless paid to an intensive relationship between science and economic productivity. In particular, the number of patents and spin-off companies has grown rapidly since the American universities were given the opportunity to commercialize their own scientific output in 1980 (by the Bayh-Dole Act). An important outcome has been a substantial increase in job opportunities in the high-tech sector.

Now that we in Europe realize that the era of the knowledge economy has arrived, we need to ask whether adjustments are needed to the ways we organize our processes of knowledge generation and application. The knowledge economy creates challenges that cannot be bypassed. This applies not only to political leadership at a European level, but to European universities as well. Developments concerning the knowledge society, and European ambitions and achievements to date, must challenge universities to reassess their own outlook and their own functioning.

THE HUMBOLDTIAN IDEOLOGY

Knowledge plays a role in the knowledge society and knowledge economy in four ways. First and foremost is the creation of knowledge, primarily through scientific research. Secondly, the transmission of knowledge through higher education. Thirdly, the distribution of knowledge through knowledge transfer (and naturally through publications). Finally, the application of knowledge primarily through technological and other innovations. These four functions become increasingly interwoven in the knowledge society. Whereas in the past each could be performed by distinct processes and organizations, they now appear to be integrated in networks and cooperative linkages. Universities occupy a unique place in such cooperative linkages. Although they no longer have a monopoly on knowledge production and transfer, they nevertheless play a crucial role in modern knowledge-intensive processes.

European universities are responsible for 80 % of Europe's fundamental research and employ 34 % of its knowledge workers. Universities (and other higher-education institutions) train almost all of Europe's highly educated citizens. Universities are clearly important institutions in the knowledge society. However, the European ambition to become the leading knowledge economy confronts the European university with new challenges that reach to the very heart of the classical European academic culture.

The roots of the European university lie in classical antiquity. Plato founded the Athenian Academy in 387 BC with the goal to remove the "veils of ignorance" from students and to bring them into contact with "eternal knowledge". Plato's Academy served as the model for the diverse variants of the European University. If we consider the continental monastery universities of the Middle Ages (such as those in Bologna and Salamanca) or the British academic guild communities (Oxford and Cambridge), the driving force was the disinterested search for true knowledge.

On the European continent the proposals of Wilhelm von Humboldt for the establishment of the University of Berlin (written around 1810) have had a far-reaching influence on the structure and functioning of the European universities over the past 200 years. Von Humboldt's lucid but succinct proposals grew over time into an academic ideology that has guided many European universities and the academics that work in them to this day. Since the publication of his proposals, an almost endless stream of essays about and references to his work have been published, and Von Humboldt crops up frequently in the current literature on universities.

Von Humboldt's – at the time radical – proposals were aimed particularly at constructing an institutional framework for modern science that would prevent the search for new knowledge being corrupted or even destroyed by others – themselves legitimate social forces such as politics, the economy or religion. The solution proposed by Von Humboldt was state-guaranteed autonomy for the universities and academic freedom for those within them whose business was the search for true knowledge. In his famous words, this search should be undertaken in "solitude and freedom" (*Einseimkeit und Freiheit*) and universities and academics should enjoy the greatest possible autonomy (Nybom, 2003). When Von Humboldt's proposals for almost unlimited autonomy were embraced, the result was that German (and many other European) academics surrendered their political and other social ambitions so that they could dedicate themselves to science without disturbance. In the end this arrangement had exceptionally positive academic consequences, but it strengthened the conviction amongst academics that beyond their academic work they had no further social obligations (Lepenies, 1992).

The Humboldtian ideology brought much academic success and great prestige to the European universities. At the end of the 19th century, European universities enjoyed high social respect. The late 19th-century German universities served as a model for the European university supremacy at that time, and it was these universities that were the source of inspiration for the establishment of the American research university. The Humboldtian ideology, however, has also served as a facade behind which universities and academics have found it easy to hide. The ideology has become a more or less taken-for-granted, intrinsic dimension of European academic life. Many academics use this ideology to distance themselves from societal issues and the contribution that science might possibly make to social development.

THE DISTORTION OF UNIVERSITY CHARACTERISTICS

The position adopted by European universities to pay only scant attention to societal issues contributed in the second half of the 20th century to what can be described as "the distortion of university characteristics". These university characteristics are directly linked to the most essential feature of the university – that it is in the business of knowledge. In universities knowledge is created, stored, transferred and (even if sometimes reluctantly in Europe) applied. As a result of this essential feature, universities all over the world are characterized by a strong emphasis on the professional autonomy of academic experts, by extensive organizational fragmentation (where the constituent elements of the university are only "loosely coupled" to each other) (Weick, 1976) and by a wide distribution of decision making authority (Clark, 1983).

On the face of it, there is nothing wrong with these characteristics of the university. The professional character of the university organization, organizational fragmentation and wide distribution of authority are seen as an important explanation for the miraculous historical stability of the university (Van Vught, 1995). The fact that the form of the university as an institution has changed little since its medieval form may well be related to these fundamental organizational and governance features. These ensure a high level of redundancy that allows universities to adapt themselves to a wide variety of environmental conditions, including those that cause the failure of a constituent part(s) (Landau, 1969).

Nevertheless, the European university also faces the danger of its fundamental characteristics being distorted. The risk of such distortion occurs when these organizational and governance principles permeate the university in extreme form. What are these principles, and what dangers do they entail?

First and foremost is the increasing specialization of professional academic experts. Both the natural sciences and the human and social sciences have witnessed acceleration in the division of fields of knowledge, particularly since the second half of the 19th century. Universities have developed a large number of new scientific fields of study, with the result that what was originally a clear scientific territory has now come to resemble an academic labyrinth. In all fields new disciplines and sub-disciplines are created, and the university becomes a conglomerate of narrower and narrower sub-disciplines. The university of today is a university of specialists. This increasing specialization implies that even within a speciality new sub-specialities develop and these are so narrowly separated from each other that for many scientists high-level, mutual discussion of their work is now impossible. Scientific hyper-specialization, however, is also the key to scientific success. Through hyper-specialization the modern scientist reaches the international publication fora which bring not only recognition and prestige, but also tenure and an enhanced salary.

But these hyper-specializations also have disadvantages. As indicated, scientific communication is seriously inhibited – even within the specialist group scientific discussion takes place less and less. Researchers are compelled by necessity to retreat inside the bastions of their specialist areas of knowledge, communicating only by e-mail with handfuls of colleagues elsewhere in the world. In the university this extensive permeation of hyper-specialization seems to lead to a form of academic atomism. The division of scientific fields has resulted in the almost inevitable scientific isolation of individual specialists, and in an inability to communicate with others at a scientific level. Researchers find themselves more and more restricted to their own specialities to which are linked their desires for recognition and status. The interests of the university recede further into the background. The university threatens to become a coincidental location for a barely coherent and ostentatious collection of specialities. Collegiality as a binding force is slowly being siphoned out of our universities.

The second characteristic of the university, organizational fragmentation, can also take an extreme form. This fragmentation threatens to lead to a Balkanization with extremely negative consequences when seen from an academic perspective. Many European universities and academics view the current American research universities as the paragon of the modern university. The world's best education and its leading research take place there, and more importantly, these are held in a mutually strengthening equilibrium. The American research universities are a product of the end of the 19th century and were a modification of the Humboldtian ideals of the German universities applied to the practical realities of earlier American colleges. The establishment of Johns Hopkins University in 1836 marked the birth of the modern research university (Geiger, 1986), and it was soon followed by sister institutions such as Stanford and Chicago. The original American colleges (with their traditional, English educational model) adjusted either rapidly (such as Harvard and Columbia) or followed dragging their feet (such as Yale and Princeton) (Kennedy, 1995). The research universities consolidated their position in the first decades of the 20th century and soon developed into an attractive model for many universities across the world.

The model of the research university in combination with the Humboldtian ideology led the late 20th-century European university to embrace the principle of the organizational separation of scientific fields into distinct faculties, institutes, centres and schools. Every self-respecting group of specialist researchers drew from the research university model a right to be an independent organizational entity, with in consequence as little interaction as possible with the other units within the university. In the extreme case this leads to the various university entities behaving as small sovereign states with little interest in their outside world.

The former President of Harvard, Derek Bok, suggests that successful specialist groups have the tendency to slide into self-sufficiency and introversion, and to distance themselves from academic debate about the university as a whole (Bok, 1990, p. 111). Independent academic entities limit themselves to scientific communication with like-minded specialists outside their own institution and have no interest in discussion inside or outside the university. In addition, in our contemporary universities a non-interventionist mentality appears to be on the rise. Given the irreversible trend towards further specialization and the dominance of the ideology of the Humboldtian principles of autonomy and academic freedom, researchers are reluctant to engage in serious assessment of each other's work. The danger of extreme organizational fragmentation within the university is that it becomes a random and ineffective federation of sovereign mini-states that are concerned only with their own interests – they are not interested in the welfare of their federal allies, nor of the institution as a whole, nor of the society of which they form part.

The third characteristic of universities is the wide distribution of decision-making authority. This characteristic also contains the risk that it will become a threat to the European university. In particular, in combination with the extreme organizational fragmentation and the development of a non-interventionist mentality discussed earlier, the wide distribution of authority can become an effective block to any change in the university. Universities have the reputation of being places that are difficult to change. The higher-education literature is full of witnesses to the conservative character of academic institutions (Kerr, 1982; Van Vught, 1992). Behind extreme conservatism lurks a real and not to be underestimated danger: that of a widening gulf between university and society. Since the Second World War, European universities have grown rapidly to become mass institutions, but in the process they have lost prestige. Their proverbial conservatism and their somewhat haughty emphasis on their autonomy have led to a widening gulf between university and society. In many European countries social and political support for universities has declined since the 1980s, and in some cases there is even a certain aversion to these previously very prestigious institutions.

MAJOR NEW CHALLENGES

The advent of the knowledge society has seen a resurgence in the political and social interest in universities in Europe in recent times. Various governments, and certainly the European Commission, realize that universities have an important role to play in the knowledge society. European universities, however, need to recognize that they are now in a different position compared to where they stood in the times of Von Humboldt. The knowledge society and knowledge economy demand more than an ideological affirmation that the generation of knowledge is a primary goal. They also demand a greater social involvement than has often been evidenced in the academic isolation and conservatism of the European universities over previous decades. The knowledge society does not benefit from universities that elevate themselves above their societies as ivory towers. It requires knowledge institutions able to give effect to the integration of knowledge functions (creation, transmission, distribution and application) in a broad social context. Knowledge in the knowledge society is not just a goal in its own right, but also a resource directed at productivity and economic growth.

Here lies the greatest challenge for European universities. They must have the courage to cast off the old Humboldtian ideology, or at least to complement it with a pragmatic, utilitarian vision of knowledge. They must ensure that the characteristics of the university are not transformed into distorted characteristics. In this regard the European universities have much to learn from their American cousins. In the same way that the American research universities were based on the model of the 19th-century German university, so can the European universities of today learn valuable lessons from their American peers.

European universities are no longer the best in the world. They have had to surrender their supremacy of the 19th and early 20th centuries to their American colleagues. This can be seen most clearly in the award of Nobel prizes: before the Second World War only 11 % of the prizes were awarded outside Europe, since then 75 % have gone to American universities (Davis Graham & Diamond, 1997, p. 10; Lindqvist, 2003).

European universities also appear to be less popular with foreign students than American universities. In 2000, European universities attracted some 450,000 foreign students, while American institutions enrolled 540,000 (primarily from Asia). American universities are also more successful in recruiting students to the natural sciences and technological disciplines that are critical for the further development of the knowledge economy. Perhaps even more importantly, American universities are able to retain more of their foreign graduates and Ph.D.s. Even in the case of European graduates of American universities, half stay in the U.S.A. for a number of years or even permanently (European Commission, 2003c, p. 7).

The American research universities clearly offer a more attractive working environment for top researchers as well as for foreign students. They obviously have considerably greater financial capacity than European universities – they have between two to five times the financial resources per student at their disposal that European universities have. Ultimately this is a result of the higher private contributions for higher education in America. In particular, American research universities are able to generate considerable income from private sources and donations (including from alumni organizations) alongside their public income (from their States and Federal research programmes). This private income mirrors the social formation of these American universities. From the beginning of the 1980s American universities "embraced the notion of economic relevance, specially furthering economic development through technology transfer and closer involvement with the productive economy" (Geiger, 1999, p. 65). Apart from the generation of knowledge, many American research universities have incorporated the goal of distributing and applying knowledge. Knowledge transfer is an essential part of their mission, as is evident in, for example, the research parks associated with Stanford, the Harvard-MIT axis and the North Carolina Research Triangle. "In the knowledge-based economy of the future, the American research universities are proven engines for knowledge creation-'"(Davis Graham & Diamond, 1997, p. 221).

European universities must intensify their relations with business and industry if they are to play a meaningful role in the knowledge society. Universities in Europe must orientate themselves more than in the past to the distribution and application of knowledge. They must concentrate on operating in networks and, in cooperation with companies and other organizations, on the registration of patents and the starting of new businesses. They must expand links with commerce and industry, strengthen their regional role and make their services and facilities available to third parties. In short, European universities must meet the challenge of transforming their traditional – Humboldtian – academic culture to a culture of external orientation and cooperation directed at economic productivity.

In addition, European governments as well as the European Commission face some major challenges. In order to be able to reach the high ambition of the European political summit of Lisbon 2000, the following policy-initiatives need to be taken.

First, the "European higher education area" and "the European research area" will have to be further developed. Compared to the U.S. system of higher education, the European system still hardly exists. The European higher-education system is a multi-national system with little in the way of common organizational forms or professional standards. Compared to the U.S. higher-education system, there is no higher-education market and student and staff mobility is very limited. In order to create a European higher-education area, the so-called "Bologna process" (which aims to bring about a European higher-education space without borders) will have to be intensified.

The creation of a European research area should be developed further in order to bring an end to the tendencies of national protectionism in European research. The scale of a pan-European research market will be necessary to address the problems of the lack of sufficient funding for R & D in Europe. Moreover, critical mass, mobility of researchers, integrated research networks and especially one or more European research councils will all be needed to face global competition in knowledge creation (Weber, this book).

A special problem Europe needs to solve with respect to its research capacity is the lack of young researchers. The European Commission has calculated that if Europe wishes to have as many researchers at its disposal as the U.S.A. by 2010 there will need to be 850,000 extra researchers in that year, or approximately 80,000 per year – this implies a 6 % annual growth rate compared to 2.6 % at present (European Commission, 2003a, p. 189). The lion's share of new researchers needs to be in the natural and technological sciences. To be able to increase the number of young researchers, European universities will have to attract far more foreign graduate students than they are doing so far. European immigration incentives for young academic talent are an obvious instrument in this context.

Secondly, the higher-education and research systems of Europe will have to be functionally diversified. Compared to the U.S. university system, the European system lacks a base for the classification of institutions. The implicit assumption in European higher-education appears to be that all universities are alike. A "pseudo uniformity" of institutional functions appears to exist, based on the Humboldtian ideology that all institutions and all academics should have the opportunity to be equally involved in academic activities. However, only about 100 of the 3,000 higher education institutions in the U.S.A. are judged to be real research universities. Why should this be different for the 3,300 higher-education institutions of the European Union, or the nearly 4,000 of greater Europe? We need the courage in Europe to identify our best research universities and to develop and implement research stimulation policies that strive for top quality.

Finally, in order to face the challenges of Europe's ambition with respect to the knowledge economy, both the private sector (especially business and industry) and universities should be stimulated to increase their mutual cooperation. The private sector should be stimulated to increase its financial support for R & D, especially by co-funding university research programmes. Universities should be stimulated to address their research efforts to the needs of the knowledge economy and the knowledge society. If Europe wants to close the knowledge gap, it needs strong bridges between society and its universities.

REFERENCES

Bok, D. (1990). *Universities and the Future of America*, Duke University Press, Durham.

Clark, B. R. (1983). *The Higher Education System*, University of California Press, Berkeley and Los Angeles.

Davis Graham, H. & Diamond, N. (1997). *The Rise of the American Research Universities*, The Johns Hopkins University Press, Baltimore and London.

European Commission (2002a). *European Benchmarks in Education and Training: follow-up to the Lisbon European Council*, COM 2002 final, Brussels.

European Commission (2002b). *Key Data on Education in Europe*, Office for Official Publications of the European Communities, Brussels and Luxembourg.

European Commission (2003a). *Third European Report on Science & Technology Indicators*, Office for Official Publications of the European Communities, Brussels and Luxembourg.

European Commission (2003b). *Choosing to Grow: knowledge innovation and jobs in a cohesive society*, COM 2003, final, Brussels.

European Commission (2003c). *The Role of Universities in the Europe of Knowledge*, COM 2003 58 final, Brussels.

Geiger, R. L. (1986). *To Advance Knowledge, the growth of American research universities 1900-1940*, Oxford University Press, Oxford.

Geiger, R. L. (1999). "The Ten Generations of American Higher Education", in Altbach, Philip G., Berdahl, Robert and Gumport, Patricia J. (eds.), *American Higher Education in the Twenty-first Century*, The Johns Hopkins University Press, Baltimore and London, pp. 38-70.

Kennedy, D. (1995). "Another Century's End, Another Revolution for Higher Education", *Change*, May/June, pp. 8-15.

Kerr, C. (1982). *The Uses of the University*, Harvard University Press, Cambridge.

Landau, M. (1969) "Redundancy, Rationality and the Problem of Duplication and Overlap", *Public Administration Review*, 29 (4), pp. 346-358.

Lepenies, W. (1992) *Aufstieg und Fall der Intellektuellen in Europa*, Campus Verlag, Frankfurt am Main.

Lindqvist, S. (2003) Contribution to the seminar "The European Research University, a Historical Parenthesis", Stockholm 16 & 17 May, 2003.

Nybom, Th. (2003). "The Humboldt Legacy: Reflections on the Past, Present and Future of the European University", *Higher Education Policy* 16 (2), pp. 141-160.

Soete, L. (2002). *Background Note for the Innovation Lecture 2002*, The Hague, 9 December 2002.

Van Vught, F. A. (ed.), (1992). *Governmental Strategies and Innovation in Higher Education*, Jessica Kingsley, London.

Van Vught, F. A. (1995). "The New Context for Academic Quality", in (pp. 194-211): Dill, D. D. & Sporn, B. (eds.), *Emerging Patterns of Social Demand and University Reform: Through a Glass Darkly*, Elsevier, Oxford, New York and Tokyo.

Van Vught, F. A., van der Wende, M. & Westerheijden, D. (2002). "Globalisation and Internationalisation: Policy Agendas Compared", in Enders, J. and Fulton,

O. (eds.): *Higher Education in a Globalising World*, Kluwer Academic Publishers, Dordrecht, Boston and London, pp. 103-121.

Weber, L. E. (this book). "Financing the research university: a European perspective," in Weber, L. E. and Duderstadt, J. J., *Reinventing the Research University*, Economica, London.

Weick, K. F. (1976). "Educational Organisations as Loosely Coupled Systems", *Administrative Science Quarterly*, 21 (1), pp. 1-19.

PART III

....

The Research University
and the wider Community

CHAPTER

On Classifying Universities: Policy, Function and Market

Robert Zemsky

One of the tensions characterizing higher education around the globe derives from the classifiers' passion for pigeonholing each and every university and from the equally passionate conviction on the part of those universities that they are truly unique and hence should not be classified, stapled, or otherwise mutilated. The classifier believes that there is an underlying logic governing the nature and functioning of institutions – that form and function along with governance and financing are matters of policy rather than institutional choice. Institutions, for their part, mostly accept the designations the classifier bestows, as long as the definition limits neither opportunity nor funding.

Thirty years ago, it was the classifier who held sway. In the Soviet Union as well as those institutions whose systems of higher education followed the Soviet model, the classification of institutions reflected a remarkably narrow set of industrial and employment classifications. What a university did and the kind of graduates it produced was clearly as well as specifically defined in its title. In parts of Europe, for example in Belgium, university forms and titles reflected important ethnic and political settlements in which language and religion more than academic specialty provided the defining elements. In the U.K. there was a hard and defining line separating universities and polytechnics. In Germany there was a parallel separation between universities and *Fachhochschulen*. The former were the generators of knowledge; the latter focused on profession and vocation, on the one hand, and applied as opposed to generative science, on the other. In France there was a different, but no less definitive line separating that country's universities and its *grandes écoles*. In the U.S., the Carnegie Classification was predominant, defining four separate kinds of universities based on the amount of sponsored research and the number of graduate degrees awarded and the disciplines in which those degrees were granted. In Japan, the classification of universities and other institutions of higher education reflected in part the role of the government and in part the growing importance of a limited number of private universities. Still, at the top of that hierarchy, were the national universities – those whose students had the highest test scores, whose graduates were the most sought-after, and whose faculty and staff were civil servants attached to the Ministry of Education.

A SHIFTING LANDSCAPE

Today, however, it is the classifier who is losing ground. The line separating universities and polytechnics in the U.K. has been erased – they are all universities, at least in name. In Russia and across eastern Europe and China, the Soviet higher education model of vocational- and industrial-based universities supplemented by research academies has been recast. In Japan, the government is in the process of divesting itself of its national universities, removing faculty and staff's civil service status and generally preparing the way the privatizing of universities across Asia. Many observers believe Germany will soon follow suit – making major adjustments to its two-tier system while similarly divesting universities of their standing as governmental agencies. Even in France, higher education could lose its distinctive labels, as the system begins to resemble the dominant European model. And, in the U.S., any and all attempts at distinctive labelling or classification have simply been abandoned, as "university" becomes the label of choice for most institutions – including the for-profit University of Phoenix.

There are basically two root causes underlying these changes. The first is that most governments have lost interest in preserving the purity of their classification systems. With growing numbers of people demanding access to higher education and intensifying competition for governmental support among and between institutions and other public agencies, there is little appeal for preserving what it "really means to be a university."

Governments also have contributed to the second underlying cause of this shift away from using distinctiveness as a criterion for classifying institutions of higher education. Unable to meet the cost of educating an increasing proportion of their young adults, most governments have begun either experimenting with or actually implementing tuition and fee policies that have universities charging real prices in order to raise substantial revenue. As that barrier is breached, universities become increasingly subject to market forces as they seek to recruit faculty, garner research support, and enrol students who see in the new market realities an opportunity to increase their own socioeconomic mobility. To the extent that Europe becomes an integrated higher education market, it is likely that the homogenizing effect of market forces will further reduce the distinctiveness of the labels historically applied to European universities.

It is, of course, in the U.S. where the impact of market forces has been the greatest and where the outlines of a "declassified" system of higher education are most strongly etched. To understand what is happening in the U.S. today, it is helpful to look back at the landscape of the early 1970s. At that time, most taxonomies of U.S. higher education followed the general outlines of the Carnegie Classification. (See Figure 1.) There was a basic symmetry to the system: first, a split along the lines of governance and finance (public or private); then, a split along the length of the standard undergraduate curriculum (four years or two years); then, a parsing of institutions according to the traditional college/university division; and, finally, definitions that separated the research universities (principally those belonging to the Association of American Universities, or AAU) from what Carnegie came to consider "lesser" doctoral and comprehensive universities. Among the two-year institutions, all community colleges were public and most junior colleges were private. Among the nation's colleges there were essentially two flavours: private liberal arts colleges and public state colleges, many of which had started out as normal or teachers' colleges.

Figure 1: The U.S. Higher Education Landscape in 1970

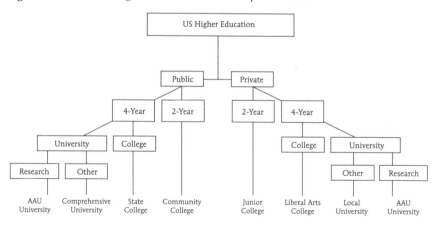

Thirty years later, this landscape has been substantially reshaped. (See Figure 2.) To the traditional public/private split has necessarily been added a third category: for-profit institutions. While this category remains small in terms of its total number of students, its principal occupant, the University of Phoenix, looms large: more than 90,000 students enrol in what is essentially a store-front operation that has now aggressively branched out into online distance education.

Other changes are evident. In Figure 2, the private sector has been com-
pressed and shifted toward the right. Gone are the private, two-year junior
colleges. The entire college category is being diminished (hence the shading
of the box in Figure 2). Where once-premier liberal arts colleges the likes of
Amherst, Williams, and Swarthmore competed head-to-head with Harvard,
Yale, and Princeton for both students and faculty, that competition is now
decidedly more one-sided. Almost always the comparable university wins,
simply because it offers both more options and more support. Liberal arts
colleges with lesser reputations are finding that the best way to compete and
survive is to mimic the university – often coming to call themselves universities, while adding a variety of post-baccalaureate vocational master's programmes (a shift indicated by the arrow in Figure 2). (Zemsky et. al., 2001)

Figure 2: The U.S. Higher Education Landscape in 2000

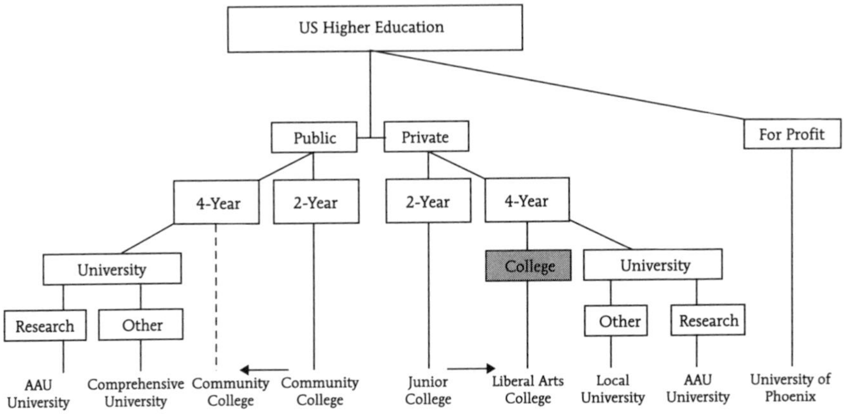

The public sector has undergone a parallel transformation. Most state colleges are now called universities, with many seeking the research and graduate education portfolios that once exclusively belonged to their state's flagship campuses. The nation's public community colleges are being similarly
recast. Estimates of the number of students currently enrolled in a community college who already possess a baccalaureate degree range upwards from
20 % – suggesting the shifting role of the community college as a general
supplier of work-related skills, including those skills essential for white-collar
careers. At the same time, a number of community colleges are actively
exploring, and a few have actually instituted, four-year programmes leading
to the baccalaureate degree or its equivalent.

THE PUSH OF MARKET FORCES

Most of these changes reflect the push of market forces, as institutions of nearly every stripe have sought to ensure sufficient revenue either to stay in business or to fulfill their ambitions. With these market forces has come a second, closely related set of innovations and changes in the form of the "dreaded rankings". The first, and still most powerful, are those published annually by U.S. News & World Report, classifying not just the quality of universities in terms of their baccalaureate programmes, but increasingly in terms of their graduate programmes as well. Everybody pays attention to the rankings, regardless of what they may say when their institution fares less well than expected. And, increasingly, institutions have altered their practices simply to improve their place in the rankings. The admissions practices of U.S. law schools offer perhaps the clearest example of how the process works. When it became clear to the top 25 or so law schools in the U.S. News rankings that the editors were placing a heavy weight on how the applicant scored on the Law School Admission Test (LSAT), most law schools began adjusting their admissions formula to give more weight to the LSAT.

The irony is that there is little reason to believe the rankings measure quality, and a great deal of evidence to suggest that the rankings are in fact just a surrogate for market position. Five years ago, the Institute for Research on Higher Education (IRHE) at Penn first published its market taxonomy for higher education. The taxonomy was derived from a regression model using just a handful of variables to predict the prices both public and private universities charged. One of the questions we asked was whether the same regressions might also predict U.S. News rankings – and the answer was a resounding "yes." To group universities into the tiers reflected in the U.S. News rankings, all one needs to know is the percentage of each university's entering class that earns a baccalaureate degree within six years of matriculating. It is a remarkably consistent relationship: the higher the graduation rate, the higher the price the university charges, and the higher the rankings tier to which the university belongs (NCPI, 2002).

In many ways the market structure revealed both in the U.S. News rankings and the IRHE taxonomy has replaced the more traditional ways of classifying U.S. institutions of higher education. In all, IRHE classified just under 1,500 baccalaureate institutions into five market segments (See Figure 3). Substantially fewer than 10 % were classified as medallion institutions – literally, the top of the heap. In this segment are all the Ivy League institutions plus Stanford, Duke, and the University of Chicago, along with a dozen major public universities led by the Universities of Michigan, California (five separate campuses), Wisconsin, Illinois, and Virginia. In the next segment are approximately 200 name-brand institutions, all of whom are well-known to the public and most of whom spend considerable time, energy, and resources trying to become medallions. The core of the market, dominated by public comprehensive universities and local private universities, accounts for just over half of all U.S. institutions. The market segments on the right side of the divide contain colleges and universities that are in many ways the most market dependent – smaller, often struggling private and public institutions who often compete on basis of price, hence the label "good buy." Finally, there are the institutions that cater, sometimes almost exclusively, to part-time and intermittently enrolled students: younger adults, for the most part, who are pursuing a baccalaureate degree one course at a time and often from a variety of institutions.

Figure 3: Distribution of U.S. Baccalaureate Institutions

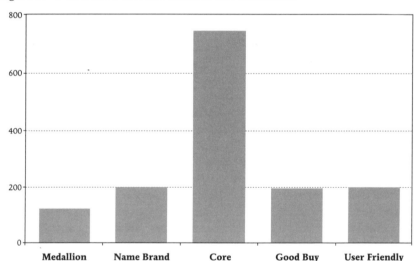

One way to interpret this new classification of U.S. universities and colleges is to understand how much it reflects the different confidences and aspirations of higher education's student customers. On the left are those institutions whose students are the most certain they will complete their baccalaureate education, who know from the outset that four years at a university will not be enough, and – because they perceive the importance of a medallion undergraduate degree for winning admission to a prestigious graduate or professional school – are willing to pay extraordinarily high prices. Arrayed on the right, in sharp contrast, are institutions whose students are quintessential shoppers, choosing their courses and institutions on the basis of convenience as well as price. Students in the middle are just that

– persuaded they need a college degree, but not yet sure they are ready to earn one. For these students, enrolling in a university is a matter of trying it to see if you like it.

CHANGING CLASSIFICATIONS

It is interesting to note how the AAU and the Carnegie Foundation for the Advancement of Teaching (CFAT), arbiters of the higher education classification system, have reacted to the changing circumstances that markets have introduced into American higher education. CFAT has decided that a single classification scheme will no longer suffice, in substantial part because both the public and the institutions being classified had come to see the Carnegie categories as rankings: "We are currently engaged in a fundamental reconsideration of the Carnegie Classification. We plan to develop a more flexible system that will permit institutions to be grouped in several ways, in recognition of the fact that a single classification scheme can conceal the many ways that institutions resemble or differ from one another. This work will result in a series of distinct classification schemes, as well as an interactive facility that will enable users to generate their own, customized classifications" (CFAT, 2003).

Individuals will be encouraged to design their own classification systems, while institutions will be rewarded for presenting themselves in different ways to different constituents or clients or markets. Institutions like Harvard will be festooned with designations, merit badges really – one for being a research-intensive university, another for its large-scale graduate and professional programmes, another for being an urban university, yet another for its commitment to undergraduate education, and so on. One can only wonder what will be left of that once elegantly simple system in which there were research universities, liberal arts colleges, specialty colleges, and community colleges.

The AAU faces a similar problem of definition as it has sought to determine which additional universities to admit as members. Its answer, however, has been to refine and make more detailed the characteristics of a research-intensive institution. On its website, under the general heading of AAU membership, is posted a statement of the organization's "Membership Policy" that specifies five Principles of Membership and nine Membership Indicators, which collectively draw on more than 27 designations of faculty achievement and nearly that many sources of research support and accomplishment. What the AAU increasingly faces is the market-oriented challenge: "Tell me what my institution has to do to win AAU membership and we will do it." While the final judgment remains a vote of the membership, the scorekeeping in fact becomes an implicit index of market accomplishment. (AAU, 2003)

The emergence of a structured, highly competitive market for higher education is creating a second problem for AAU – the growing disparity between its members with the best and least market positions. Of the 26 private American universities belonging to the AAU, all but four are medallions. Among the more than 30 public universities belonging to the AAU, only 12 are medallions and five are actually part of the core market segment – a category that has no private AAU members. (See Figure 4.)

Figure 4: Market Distribution of AAU Universities

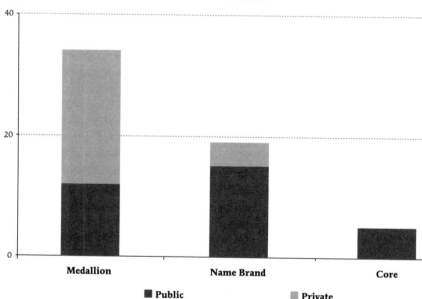

What is at stake here is not just status, but, more importantly, money. The private medallion research universities with their large endowments, top-dollar tuitions, and robust applicant pools are putting more and more distance between themselves and the rest of the pack. Of the large, public research universities, the University of Michigan is probably unique in its ability to keep pace with the big privates in terms of its capacity to grow its revenue base year in and year out. One of the concerns of those who watch the AAU from the outside is that it may be in the process of becoming a two-tier organization, with the market playing the lead role in determining which institutions belong to which tier.

The relevance of these developments for universities outside the United States remains an open question. What is clear, however, is that the more

European and major Asian universities rely on market income to finance both their operations and their ambitions, the more subject they will become to the homogenizing influences of the market. What will be put at risk is the ability of both governments and institutions to maintain those finely-wrought distinctions that historically have been used to classify higher education institutions. The term university will become generic. In pursuit of different markets – for students, for research, for faculty and staff – institutions will take on different hues, often simultaneously. There will be less concern with consistency, less willingness to turn to public policy or governmental authority to separate the wheat from the chaff. Instead, and perhaps with audible resignation, that task will be left to the market – letting institutions become, regardless of what they call themselves, what the market wants and is willing to pay for.

REFERENCES

Association of American Universities – AAU (2003). Website (as of November 5, 2003) at http://aau.edu/aau/Policy.pdf.

Carnegie Foundation for the Advancement of Teaching – CFAT (2003). Website (as of November 5, 2003) at http://www.carnegiefoundation.org/Classification/future.htm.

National Center for Postsecondary Improvement – NCPI (2002). "The Landscape", *Change*, March-April, pp. 47-50.

Zemsky, R., Shaman S. & Shapiro D. (2001). *Higher Education as Competitive Enterprise: When Markets Matter*, Josey-Bass Publishers, San Francisco CA.

CHAPTER 9

The Modern University and its Main Activities

André Oosterlinck

AUTONOMY AND RESPONSIBILITY

In the industrialized world, universities are concerned first of all with basic research and with research-based education. Research and education are closely and indissolubly intertwined. In most of Europe, education is considered as a fundamental human right, which must, therefore, be guaranteed by government. In some countries, this is expressed by including this right to education in the constitution. Consequently, governments must commit themselves to the suitable financing of universities, to enable universities to materialize this fundamental right. These subsidies must be sustainable and sufficiently reliable for the foreseeable future. The fact that universities depend on public financing, however, does not mean that they lose their essential autonomy. Universities are, and must be, autonomous institutions. This autonomy is nothing new. As a matter of fact, "corporate independence" has been a main characteristic of universities ever since their inception in the Middle Ages. In some instances, this independence even included judicial autonomy, sometimes even allowing the rector of the university to put troublesome professors or students in the university prison. Where are the good old times? Some of my colleagues may regret that this is no longer the case...

A university's autonomy needs to be deserved and justified because of its reliance on public money. Accepting subsidies implies accepting responsibility to spend them wisely, efficiently and transparently. One of the consequences is that universities must commit themselves to careful financial management, and that this management is under public control. Although universities are quite different from corporations and from companies, they should at all times apply the principles of top-quality corporate governance. They must also make sure that they are accountable for their independent decisions. The bottom line is that universities must live up to a complicated set of expectations, namely the expectations of their wide range of stakeholders.

ACADEMIC FREEDOM

What is true on the "corporate" level is also true on the individual level. The age-old concept of academic freedom must continue to exist, but it should be understood in the proper way. Academic freedom can never be an excuse for poor performance or for refusing internal or external quality control. Academic freedom includes the inalienable right to decide upon one's own research content, and to express one's opinion in the classroom, the only limitations being the standards of scientific method in general and of the particular discipline in which one is active. Simply put: academic freedom includes the right to pursue the truth, no matter what the truth is. As Rector Pieter De Somer, my predecessor in Leuven[1], once expressed it during his speech at the occasion of Pope John Paul II's visit to our university, academic freedom includes the right to err, the right to make a mistake. Academic freedom, however, does not include the right to perform poorly.

Academic freedom does not exist for itself. It exists to serve the greater purpose of the university, which is the creation, accumulation and dissemination of knowledge. Academic freedom, therefore, is not absolute. It is a freedom with a particular purpose. Consequently, academic freedom automatically includes academic responsibility, both for the university as a whole and for the individual professor or researcher.

Academic freedom is what our stakeholders grant us, on the condition that we deserve it, i.e. that we live up to the expectations of our stakeholders. These are quite varied. Obviously, the students, as well as our staff, are our stakeholders. But society at large also has a set of expectations. Many subdi-

---

1 Founded in 1425, the K.U.Leuven belongs to the group of the 30 oldest universities in the world. It is Belgium's largest university, with some 28,000 students. About 30 % of its 3,000 doctoral students are of international origin. Its total budget amounts to 450 million Euro. Less than half of this budget consists of government subsidies, which is spent for education purposes. More than half of its budget finances research. From this segment, 28 % consists of contract research with industry, in the broad sense of the word. K.U.Leuven has been the source of more than 50 spin-offs. K.U.Leuven Research & Development is the university's special interface office, which is responsible for negotiating contract research, scouting for research valorization, intellectual property and patent filing, and for interfacing with industry. It is also very closely involved with finding and investing seed money, which the university organizes in its own seed money fund (Gemma Frisius Fund).

visions can be made, for instance: cultural life, public health and so on. Paying attention to all these stakeholders' expectations is the essential responsibility of all universities.

CORE ACTIVITIES

This statement is far too general, of course. How does a university actually do that? How do we live up to what our stakeholders expect us to do? I think it is wise to take a look at the traditional threefold mission which we find back in most universities' basic documents. These three core activities are not equally old, however.

The oldest function of a university, dating back to the Middle Ages, is knowledge distribution. This is what universities have done for many centuries, without bothering too much about knowledge creation. Only towards the end of the 18th and the beginning of the 19th centuries, did universities feel the need to contribute to knowledge progress, and to actively create new knowledge. Von Humboldt and the German intellectual elite of his time spread this idea worldwide. At the same time, this was the birth of our individual academic freedom. Before this period, academic freedom mainly meant institutional freedom. The third essential activity, apart from knowledge distribution and knowledge creation, is still younger. We have to wait till the second half of the 20th century to witness the birth of what is called knowledge transfer to society at large. This meant that universities started to realize that they are not located in an isolated ivory tower, but that they have responsibilities to fulfil which go beyond knowledge creation and knowledge distribution, not only among our students, but in society at large, which should benefit from the very existence of universities.

Let us now focus on these three activities separately. I will briefly sketch a few characteristics of each one of them, and indicate the way they are interrelated. As I will point out, the unique and distinctive feature of a university is, in my opinion, to be found in this carefully balanced set of connections between the three core activities.

RESEARCH

Academic research is clearly the basis of modern universities. Research, as we see it now, has a personal and a societal purpose. We do research because we want personal development, out of personal curiosity and because we want to contribute to the progress of science and society. Modern academic research has a double aspect. There is fundamental research, on the one hand, without too much concern for external relevance or economic applicability, and there is applied research, which focuses on economic relevance. Fundamental and applied research are not, however, separated to a great degree. Both are clearly linked, and neither can exist without the other. Essential synergies exist and must be nurtured.

University research is undergoing important changes. One of them is rather worrying. Compared to what multinational companies can spend on research, university research budgets are very small, especially the part which is subsidized by government. It must be stressed that governments must maintain healthy levels of financing, especially to allow universities to continue their fundamental research. It is equally important that universities are given the necessary freedom to engage in applied research, because this gives them access to much-needed extra finances. Industry-based research may be equal to university research as far as quality is concerned, but it lacks the obligation to publish which is so characteristic of university research. Universities publish their ideas to the entire scientific community in order to get feedback from their peers, or even for society as a whole. This is not possible, or at least not to the same extent, for industry-based research, which by its nature must be concerned in the first place with the future of the company in which the research is performed. This is done by non-disclosure clauses and by various legal provisions for the protection of intellectual property. Sometimes, this difference can obstruct collaboration between universities and industry. In my opinion, there should be no problem, provided universities accept the idea of a certain delay in publication, long enough for the protection of intellectual property to be implemented. For instance, sufficient time should be allowed for a patent to be filed.

Another important change in academic research is the focus on interdisciplinary areas, and the urgent need to establish sufficient critical mass. The time of the lone researcher may not have completely vanished, but research has definitely become a team effort. This has quite noteworthy implications for the way universities are organized. Ever since the Middle Ages, the most characteristic organizational unit in a university has been the faculty. In many cases, faculties operate as smaller kingdoms within a greater framework. Very often, real walls exist between faculties, jeopardizing or often limiting research, certainly in the case of large-scale interdisciplinary research. Maybe the time has come to reconsider these walls, no matter how venerable they are.

Research is related to the other two basic activities of a university. The link with education is not universally accepted. Some plead for a separation between teaching universities and research universities. In my opinion, this is not very wise. Professors must be researchers in order to be able to transfer the research attitude to their students, especially at the graduate level. Obviously, not all students will become researchers, and the presence of research in the classroom will definitely be less at the undergraduate level.

However, even professors who lecture only to bachelor students, must have research experience. From the very first day, students need to be exposed to the spirit of innovation and to a critical attitude, both resulting from research experience.

Input from research is also required in order to keep education up to date. This is especially true for postgraduate university courses, whose main purpose is not only to refresh the basics, but primarily to gain access to new developments and insights.

The role of research in the university's service to society is obvious. By its research, universities contribute to society's general progress.

EDUCATION

Let us now turn to education, the second core activity of any modern university. On the one hand, in tomorrow's Europe, which will be governed by the principles of the Bologna Agreement, and which will be far more internationalized than it is today, research, and definitely basic research, will be the most important element to determine the quality of universities, and will certainly be used in the ranking process. But, on the other hand, we should not forget that most, if not all, first-year students want a marketable diploma, rather than top-level research. Simply put: students are looking for education, not for Nobel Prizes. Modern university education is aiming at self-learning, flexibility and learning how to learn. Encyclopedic knowledge transfer is no longer appropriate.

Throughout Europe, the Bologna Agreement is having far-reaching ramifications for university programmes. The introduction of the so-called Bachelor-Master Structure necessitates a thorough overhaul of all programmes. Up to now, in most educational systems of continental Europe, university degrees had no significant value after the first level (the candidature). This will change dramatically, since the Bologna Agreement stipulates that the Bachelor's degree should have a value on the labour market. Obviously, this compels universities to reorganize their programmes from the very first year onward. In most European countries, this reorganization is now in full progress.

One of the basic considerations to start the Bologna process was to make European education more competitive on a global level. By 2010, Europe should become a single "higher-education area". Students should be able to move throughout Europe without too much difficulty, and programmes should be comparable from one end of Europe to the other. At the present time, this is clearly not the case. Even though diplomas may carry the same name, their value and their contents can be quite different. In a few years time, European education should be far more transparent than it is now.

Transparency does not mean similarity, however. Programmes will continue to differ from each other, but these differences will no longer be hidden under similar names. A system of evaluating and possibly classifying the programmes will enable students (and employers) to judge the relative value of any given curriculum credit or full programmes.

For a long time, university financing was directly related to the number of students they attracted. Fortunately, this is starting to change. This may lead to a decrease in the number of fashionable programmes, which were aimed not so much at quality, but at short-term attraction.

Education is related to research, of course. It is the cradle of future researchers. Good education is the best way for a university to guarantee its future research success.

Education is also related to a university's service to society. In our knowledge society, there is an increasing need for permanent education and life-long learning, which universities are very well suited to provide. Obviously, they can also improve cultural diversity, the ongoing social debates on a variety of topics, etc.

SERVICE TO SOCIETY

The third core activity of a modern university is the most recent one. Service to society is the area where universities interact with their stakeholders. In this contact, universities prove their wider relevance, not just to their own staff and students, but to society at large. They can show that their research leads to the creation of new jobs, that it can get rid of societal bottlenecks etc. This is also the area where universities can engage in new types of activities. Furthermore, this is the area where universities can prove their relevance by spreading their knowledge through intensive media contact.

Through the valorization of their research results, universities can engage in certain forms of economic activities, for instance by revitalizing existing companies, introducing new technologies, new approaches to the market, and the optimization of existing processing, so that they can better compete in the international world. Also important is the creation of spin-offs. Most of these start on campus, and can be used as an example and a model for young entrepreneurial students and entrepreneurs of the future. Interacting with society will also indicate new areas of research and new needs of education. Obviously, universities will have access to additional financial opportunities and new forms of recognition. On the other hand, economic applicability can never the main target of university research as a whole.

CORPORATE GOVERNANCE AS A BALANCING ACT

It goes without saying that the three essential activities of modern universities require continued attention and awareness, even more so because they need to be in constant balance. Therefore, it makes good sense to comprehensively describe them in a mission statement, which can serve as a guideline for important policy- and decision-making, and in a vision statement and a strategic plan, describing the goals and the ways to achieve the essential targets and the organizational structure they require.

These three activities will serve as the criteria with which a university's performance will be measured. Therefore, they will also be the main basis for the university's continued request for autonomy and, in short, for its future. Due diligence and consideration about research, education and service to society are, therefore, a prerequisite for our university's future possibilities.

The delicate balance between a university's three core activities requires constant attention. A disequilibrium can cause a university to become a research institute, a specialized vocational school or an economic actor. Although all of these have their own raison d'être, none of them can ever be a university. Without a balance of the three core activities, there can be no university. Obviously, this has far-reaching managerial consequences. From a rigid business point of view, fundamental research or even educating students could be considered a waste of effort and money. From the point of view of some researchers, engaging in economically relevant activities could be considered inadmissible. Even providing education might be considered by some as a waste of time which could be spent on research. Once again, however, the uniqueness of the university lies in the balance.

This balance requires university management to be of a special nature. It should reconcile contradictory interests. It should endeavour to bring highly individual personalities together to pursue the same goals. It should try to give equal importance to various groups of stakeholders, each one of them with their own genuine interest in what the university does.

So what kind of wizard or miracle workers should university management consist of? The problem is that there is no clear-cut answer to this question. Every university has its own managerial "climate", sometimes with considerable differences from one institution to another. For instance, in Leuven, "extreme democracy" is the ruling principle. Provided he or she manages to collect 30 supporting signatures, all professors can, in principle, become rector of the university. But at the moment, external managers cannot. In most universities in Holland, quite the opposite is true, and the top of university management is not elected, but appointed. There is probably something to be gained from both systems. Modern universities are facing such a tremendous set of expectations that we probably cannot hope to find the best person for every managerial function simply by trusting fully democratic elections. On the other hand, imposing outside managers on the academic community could have paralyzing effects. The best solution, therefore, would be to carefully design a profile of the "ideal university president", an optimal combination of a good researcher, a good professor and a good manager. This profile can only be the result of a wide and open discussion within the academic community, because it not only serves as a "checklist" used in finding suitable candidates for managerial positions, but also as a blueprint for the future which the university wants for itself.

CHAPTER 10

The Research-led University and the Wider Community

Nils Hasselmo

INTRODUCTION

Trying to design the University of the Future does, of course, present an academic like me with the temptation of creating the University of Utopia, devoted to the pursuit of pure knowledge, feasible because all the issues that would require the troublesome involvement with "the wider community" would have been solved. "UU" would have no need for involvement with society for financial reasons, being amply funded by, maybe, a substantial land grant from the Elysian fields. One could pursue the monastic tradition in universities to the full. I will not yield to that temptation.

But, nor will I succumb to describing what some of our more pessimistic colleagues fear will be the University of Dystopia, a university totally mired in the narrowly utilitarian and politically expedient, whose funding would be totally dependent on endless catering to commercialization and political whim. I will not pursue a university that is totally driven by the market.

The University of the Future that I will attempt to charter will be firmly rooted in the tradition of the free and open pursuit of knowledge and understanding by scholars and scientists – and students – who are driven by their curiosity, in a community of critical peers, to explore all aspects of our universe and our human existence. But this University of the Future will also, in a somewhat idealized form of the American land-grant tradition, be connected with, and serve, the society of which it is a part – and notably a society that is global, but not monolithic or mono-cultural.

127

Land-Grant Act: "AN ACT Donating Public Lands to the several States and Territories which may provide Colleges for the Benefit of Agriculture and Mechanic Arts." (First Morrill Act, 1862)

Summary: Morrill Act of 1862 established the Land Grant university system. On July 2, 1862, President Abraham Lincoln signed into law what is generally referred to as the Land Grant Act. The new piece of legislation introduced by U.S. Representative Justin Smith Morrill of Vermont granted to each state 30,000 acres of public land for each Senator and Representative under apportionment based on the 1860 census. Proceeds from the sale of these lands were to be invested in a perpetual endowment fund which would provide support for colleges of agriculture and mechanical arts in each of the states.

FIRST MORRILL ACT. July 2, 1862: AN ACT Donating Public Lands to the several States and Territories which may provide Colleges for the Benefit of Agriculture and Mechanic Arts.

SECOND MORRILL ACT. August 30, 1890. AN ACT To apply a portion of the proceeds of the public lands to the more complete endowment and support of the colleges for the benefit of agriculture and the mechanic arts established under the provisions of an act of Congress approved July 2, 1862.

The University of the Future must moderate between "the monastery and the market"![1]

The essence of the relationship with the wider community

First and foremost, the University of the Future will contribute to the wider community by being a free and open centre for discovery and learning. This is paramount, and underlies all that I say in this paper concerning specific interaction with the wider community.

The University of the Future will address a broad array of important concerns and needs of the wider community, drawing on the rich store of knowledge and understanding accumulated through its disciplinary and interdisciplinary pursuits, as well as on continuous interaction with society and its decision-makers and practitioners. The essence of the relationship between the University of the Future and the wider community will be this interplay between, on the one hand, fundamental knowledge and understanding and, on the other hand, practice and real-world problem-solving.

The University of the Future will contribute directly to the wider community in a variety of ways, ranging from data gathering and analysis to transfer of know-how and technology to the development of policy options, from economic development to cultural enrichment, from the local to the global.

---

1 Quote from Illinois, Champaign-Urbana, Chancellor Nancy Cantor in recent speech.

It is also important to note that the University of the Future will provide evaluation and critique of societal performance and actions. Properly combining these two types of roles – being a contributor to the development of society and at the same time being a critic of society – is a fundamental challenge.

Issues and prerequisites for pursuing them

In what follows, I will identify some issues that I believe the University of the Future will have to address in order to connect with, and serve, its wider community. I will also touch on some of the prerequisites to the effective pursuit of these issues in terms of the governance, organization, financial management, regulation, personnel policies, information services, and "culture" of the university.

The issues involved must be addressed by the University of the Future in collaboration with other universities of that future, as well as other institutions of the wider community of the future. The University of the Future will not be able to fulfil its noble mission without such collaboration.

The community of the future must also ensure proper governance for the universities, with guarantees of institutional independence and individual academic freedom, because the agenda that the University of the Future will pursue for, and with, the wider community will be fraught with conflict. I am tempted to say that the more important the university's role as arbiter of knowledge and critic of society becomes, the greater the potential for conflict.

Issues to be addressed by University of the Future in its interaction with wider community

Before outlining some of the issues I believe will be important in the research university's future direct interaction with the wider community, let me again emphasize that its role in undergraduate, graduate, and professional education and in research will, of course, continue to be its most fundamental responsibility. One of the important ways it will directly serve the community, perhaps especially its own alumni, will be through lifelong learning. Service to the "wider community" should increasingly include contracts for continuing learning by the university's "students for life".

As we consider the research university's direct interaction with the community, the following sets of issues seem to me to be paramount:

• Security, democratic values, and world peace
• Cultural diversity
• Economic development

- The environment
- Health
- Education
- The arts

Security, democratic values, and world peace

Security issues have been a high priority since 9/11. There is no reason to expect that they will not be important also in the future that we are probing.

It is an essential role for the University of the Future to help ensure that the perspective on security is broad and deep. The university is responsible for seeing to it that the perspective includes an understanding of the major forces that drive world events as well as of the values that are fundamental to democracy.

The university is responsible for ensuring that the government and important community agencies have access to experts who have the knowledge and understanding of events and their contexts to provide analysis and policy recommendations based on sound judgments.

The university must itself, through its research activities, provide independent analysis and critique of what is happening in regard to various cultural, religious/ideological, and political movements around the world, as well as in the nation where the university is located, including critique of the national responses to world events.

What about advocacy? Is it a proper role for the University of the Future? Certainly, in the United States the first amendment and the guarantee of academic freedom give to each scholar/scientist the right to advocacy. In the context of the university as an institution, it is important that academic freedom should be exercised with responsibility, including civility, but the sanctions against "irresponsible words and actions" should be those of critique in open debate rather than censure or other action, unless physical threat is involved.

What about advocacy by the university as an institution through its leaders, that is, primarily through its president and the board? Advocacy for basic democratic and academic values is, of course, appropriate for the university. I would include in those categories both issues of diversity, that is, of equitable participation, and issues of research ethics. The University of the Future should by no means be value-neutral in these regards. When it comes to even more directly politically charged issues, such as domestic and global economic policies or foreign policy, we need to give serious consideration to the extent to which university boards and presidents should take a stand. We ought not automatically, or superficially, to assume that taking an institutional stand on such issues is illegitimate, but extremely careful judgment has to be exercised in each case. The line is not easy to draw between legitimate, and necessary, institutional advocacy on fundamental values and inappropriately taking sides on "purely" political questions. The critical dividing line may be whether the university has a direct interest in the outcome of the issue or not; if the former is the case, there should be no hesitation in taking a stand.

Which leads me to a second set of important issues, those of cultural diversity.

Cultural diversity

The University of the Future is, of course, going to have to be heavily involved in issues of cultural diversity. Through its research activities, it will need to provide knowledge and understanding of different cultures as well as of cultural diversity, within its own nation and globally.

The university must conduct advanced education for experts in languages and cultures, and on multiculturalism, as well as undergraduate education in these fields. The university will have the responsibility to ensure that qualified teachers in these areas are educated for the primary and secondary schools. It will have the responsibility to provide opportunities for the general public, on a lifelong basis, to learn other languages and become informed about other cultures, and about the nature of multiculturalism.

One of the difficult questions that the university must help the wider community deal with through its research and teaching is that of what is and what is not acceptable in a culture. There are, of course, many examples of cultural practices and beliefs that are incompatible with democratic values, for example, various expressions of racism and religious intolerance, and certain so-called "honour codes" that require killing somebody for the sake of personal and family honour, and female circumcision.

Obviously, the more fraught with conflicting values an issue is, the more important it becomes that a university, as an independent agency where data-gathering, analysis, critical give-and-take and evaluation can take place, will address the issue.

Economic development

The dual role of the University of the Future as, on the one hand, an important agent in furthering certain kinds of development in society and, on the other hand, a critic of those same developments, is probably found in all my examples, and it certainly shows up with force in the area of economic development.

The importance of the university, especially the research university, to economic development has become abundantly clear during the past decades. Witness the scramble among politicians in the United States to ensure that their region has one or more such universities – and for earmarks to nourish their research!

The fact that more and more of the funding of universities is coming through collaboration with business and industry has become a problem as well as being a potential boon. The perception, and potential reality, that what I called "narrowly utilitarian" concerns have dangerously encroached upon academe will have to be addressed also by the University of the Future.

Not only has collaboration with business and industry increased because of initiatives by these sectors and the universities, the government has begun to set priorities for funding that are tied more and more to specific economic development goals. In the United States, we find both federal cross-agency investment priorities and state investment initiatives for research based on economic considerations.

Overarching priorities at the federal level

Among the priorities that have emerged in recent years at the federal level are:

- Nanotechnology (FY2003: $774 million)
- Networking and Information Technology (FY2003: $2 billion)
- Climate Change Science Program (FY2003: $1.7 billion)
- Education R & D – "research-based programs and practices called for in No Child Left Behind" (FY2004: $50 million)
- Recently added: Science and Technology to Combat Terrorism (FY2004: $900 million).

State Research Initiatives: Michigan (1)[2]

"In the State-of-the State address, (newly elected) Governor Granholm announced the Technology Tri-Corridor initiative to research, develop, and commercialize advancements in the life sciences, automotive technology, and the emerging homeland security sector. The tricorridor will focus new technology, business recruitment and development in these three critical areas."

The Governor is quoted as stating: "In the knowledge economy, business and education are linked; you cannot succeed at the former if you do not excel at the latter."

State Research Initiatives: Michigan (2)

Life Sciences Corridor: For example, the University of Michigan has established a Life Sciences Institute to serve as a hub for cross-disciplinary

---

2 From summary provided by University of Michigan.

research and teaching in the life sciences. Between 20 and 30 faculty members, housed in a $100-million facility under construction. The proposed research agenda:

- Developing more effective gene therapies for cancer
- Learning how a key blood coagulation protein changes with age
- Creation of a new biosensor to detect bacteria and viruses
- Studying the effects of "good" cholesterol protein on heart disease
- Finding the gene for macular degeneration – leading cause of blindness
- Developing new high-resolution mammography technology
- Clinical trials of a bioartificial kidney
- Developing new drugs to treat heart attacks and cardiovascular disease
- Testing a substance that kills bacterial. Viral and fungal contaminants in blood

University of Michigan, Michigan State University, Wayne State University, and the Van Andel Institute have joined to form the Core Technology Alliance for innovation.

State Research Initiatives: Michigan (3)

Automotive Corridor: Includes University of Michigan's Transportation Research Institute. The research agendas include:

- Powertrain systems (thermal and energy systems)
- Fuel cells
- Hybrid electric vehicles
- Vehicle structural design, including crashworthiness
- Materials and processes, including metals, polymers, adhesives, and manufacturing processes
- Environmental concerns, including emission controls
- Intelligent transportation systems, including crash avoidance and smart sensors
- Enterprise systems, including supply chain management, modular vehicle design, supplier involvement in product development.

State Research Initiatives: Michigan (4)

Homeland Security Corridor: The research agendas include:

- Environmental monitoring for contaminants in air and biological media

- Rapid-detection methods of various kinds
- Infrastructure monitoring
- Infrastructure design and vulnerability
- Robotics, including automated guided vehicles on land and under water
- Development of vaccines
- Treatment of contaminated soils and water
- Security systems in urban areas
- University of Michigan in 2002 established a Bioterrorism Preparedness Initiative as a means to address such issues.

The important R & D function of universities must continue in the future, but it must continue under conditions that do not undermine the fundamental role of universities as independent arbiters of knowledge and critics of economic policies and actions, nationally and internationally.

The environment

The University of the Future will, of course, continue to enhance our understanding of the environment, and our ability to manipulate it, including through genetic engineering. It will be important that the role of the university in making it possible for us to manipulate, and actually preserve or destroy the environment remain strongly coupled with its role as arbiter of objective knowledge about the effects of manipulation, and as critic of policies and practices that affect the environment.

Health

Similarly, the University of the Future will continue to be a major contributor to the knowledge and understanding of our physical and mental well-being, and of disease, as well as to our ability to deal with these issues through public health measures and clinical practice.

The university has already encountered conflict between different values in the case of genetic manipulation, including stem cell research, cloning and other forms of genetic selection. The freedom to pursue certain research, potentially providing cures for serious diseases, is running up against concerns about undue manipulation of human life, partly based on religious beliefs. The difficult issues society faces in determining what is ethically acceptable of what is technically possible will require the active involvement of the University of the Future in the form of both analysis and education and thoughtful advocacy.

Statement on cloning by the Association of American Universities, Winter 2002

"The Association of American Universities has a long history of supporting academic and scientific freedom. It also recognizes the importance of conducting research consistent with ethical, legal, and safety requirements.

AAU strongly opposes human reproductive cloning, and supports legislation to ban this practice. The National Academy of Sciences (NAS) has concluded that cloning procedures are currently not safe for humans and that no responsible scientists or physicians are likely to undertake to clone a human. We generally do not support legislation to limit fields of research, but since some organizations have announced an intention to clone humans, we concur with the NAS that a legal ban is more likely to deter any attempt to clone a human than would any voluntary system or moratorium. The ban should be reconsidered at five-year intervals, based on current scientific knowledge.

In contrast to human reproductive cloning, AAU continues to support human stem cell research. Once necessary research in animal models is conducted and important donor and patient safety issues are satisfactorily resolved, AAU can also support nuclear transplantation to produce stem cells, which is also known as somatic cell nuclear transfer, as nonreproductive cloning, and as therapeutic cloning. We concur with the NAS that nuclear transplantation to produce stem cells has considerable potential for advancing our fundamental knowledge and developing new medical therapies to treat life-threatening diseases, and that this research should proceed in parallel with other types of stem cell research, including human embryonic and adult stem cell research."

As in the case of the other issues that I have identified, the university must be a forum for free and open debate of the pros and cons of different stands on these issues.

It will also be responsible for the effective implementation of policies and practices that will ensure compliance with adopted regulations, under the pressures of constantly evolving technical possibilities and commercial opportunities.

It will be responsible for leading the development of ethical practices as well as for educating decision-makers and the public about the choices and their implications.

Again, we encounter the need for the university, through its research and teaching, to play the role of critic, be it of practices such as smoking, or of dietary fads, or of the effects of general lifestyle on health, sometimes in conflict with both tradition and commercial interests.

Finally, through its research and teaching, as well as, in some cases, as an actual health-care deliverer, the university will have a role to play in regard to the effectiveness of the health systems that are adopted, or being considered; this is another set of issues fraught with politics and commercial interests.

Education

To say that the University of the Future must address education may seem to be too obvious to even mention. There are, however, several reasons why I think it is important to include this topic among my examples of university responsibilities vis-à-vis the wider community, even as many others are left out.

First, the effectiveness of the education universities themselves provide, not least the research universities, needs continuing attention, both at the graduate and undergraduate level. I believe that it is essential for the University of the Future to adhere to the Humboldtian idea that a certain kind of learning can best take place in the setting of scientific and scholarly inquiry. The university needs to deal with what Burton Clark (1995, p. 189ff) has called "research drift", the tendency to isolate research from teaching, and "teaching drift", the tendency to isolate teaching from research.

But this is not the place to argue that matter. As far as the role of the university vis-à-vis the wider community is concerned, it is, however, important to stress the role of the university in educating teachers for primary and secondary schools, and in conducting pedagogical research that can lead to educational reforms based on sound experimentation rather than fads. We face massive challenges as we try, across terrifying cultural, social, and economic – and, even today, racial – barriers, to ensure that the next generation will be able to participate in a society where a certain amount of "book" knowledge and access to, and ability to use, information are becoming more essential than ever.

The needs of the wider community as well as the potential of information technology hold out the possibility that the University of the Future will be able to provide educational opportunities anywhere, at any time, on a life-long basis. The University of the Future has the potential of becoming the ubiquitous university.

The arts

Many research universities provide not only humanistic scholarship and scientific research but also artistic activity. Like scholarship and research, the arts have much to contribute to the wider community. It is hard to overvalue the impact of universities on the arts in their communities, or for that matter nationally, be it in the form of music, theatre, dance, painting, sculpture, architecture, or other arts.

Especially in a society of mass culture, franchise culture, the University of the Future must play a major role in fostering, and supporting, individual and local artistic activity. The university will provide its own facilities and pro-grammes for the arts, but can also play an important role in the establishment and maintenance of arts institutions such as orchestras/concert halls and museums.

The University of the Future must provide opportunities for artistic activity by its faculty and students, but it must also interact with the wider community by offering access to performances and exhibits, and by having faculty and students participate in community arts activities, including important internship opportunities for students.

Having briefly outlined some of the many issues that I think the University of the Future must address in its interaction with the wider community, let me now turn to some of the implications of, and prerequisites for, pursuing such an agenda.

"Opera on the Farm"[3]

An example of the arts contributing to the wider community in the spirit of the land-grant university is the University of Minnesota's "Opera on the Farm" programme. This programme was conducted by the university's School of Music and its director at the time, Professor Vern Sutton, in the mid-1990s. Aaron Copland's "The Tenderland" and Gaetano Donizetti's "The Elexir of Love", operas that are both set on farms – although the former in America and the latter in Italy – were performed by faculty and students on farms in western Minnesota and the Dakotas, with local church choirs serving as choruses, and a local "Beth" in "The Tenderland" at each locality. Thousands of people attended the performances, most of whom had never before seen an opera.

SOME IMPLICATIONS OF PURSUING RESEARCH UNIVERSITY'S AGENDA WITH WIDER COMMUNITY

I will consider:

- Governance
- Organization
- Financing
- Regulation
- Personnel policies and practices
- IT
- The "culture" of the university
- "Hubs and spokes"

---

3 Information provided by the University of Minnesota.

Governance

The main feature of the governance of the University of the Future must be to ensure independence. And I will add: with accountability! Independence is necessary to ensure that the most creative minds – of which we expect to have a fair share in the university, although certainly no monopoly – will be able to set and pursue the basic agendas in the search for knowledge and understanding. In the tradition established, almost miraculously, at Paris and Bologna eight centuries ago, when the university as we know it was born, the governance system must protect the practitioners of the search for knowledge.

A system must be found, however, that can deal with the problem of protection coupled with continued productivity and renewal.

Tenure must, I believe, continue to be a bulwark protecting free and open inquiry. It has been the key to the prospering of universities over the centuries, sometimes in the face of frontal attacks by political and other vested interests, often in the face of external interests of one kind or another that would rather not see certain findings made public, or certain issues pursued at all.

Effective performance reviews, including post-tenure reviews to ensure continued productivity, must also be part of the future university. The review system must strike the sometimes difficult balance between evaluation by immediate peers (and potential competitors) and by representatives of the university who can help ensure that new, and sometimes controversial, research gets its due. The choice of alternative responsibilities (focused alternatively, for example, on research, teaching and service) at different stages of a scholar's or scientist's career may offer opportunities for continued productivity and renewal.

The governance system must also help connect the University of the Future with the wider community by participating in the identification and evaluation of the kind of agenda that I have outlined. Priorities will have to be set! It will also be important for the board – even under the conditions of independence that I have stressed – to provide for appropriate accountability procedures. These procedures should be both internal, assuring that the university is serving its mission and achieving its objectives, and external, assuring the community that important societal objectives are effectively served by the university. The board members should be selected for their mature judgment, their knowledge and their personal independence from narrow political and other considerations.

The governance system should connect and protect!

Organization

The main feature of the organization of the University of the Future must be its flexibility. While the traditional disciplinary structures have served us very well over the centuries, we must find ways of ensuring that interdisciplinary activities can be undertaken and prosper.

The flexibility must include both a process that allows new interdisciplinary ideas and activities to be tested – with some kind of sunset provisions – and a process that will provide more permanent structures for successfully tested ideas and activities.

It is especially important that flexible structures are made available for interaction with the wider community. The departmental structures are rarely suitable for the kind of agenda that I have outlined. We will need to build, and expand, structures on the model of the land-grant university's extension service and more recent knowledge and technology transfer enterprises. The new structures – and much experimentation is going on – ought to accommodate participation both by scholars and scientists across the university's disciplines and interdisciplinary programmes and by practitioners from the wider community. Consortia of various kinds have been used to address, for example, the needs of children, youth and families, economic development for sectors of business and industry and for communities and regions, and local and regional planning, and such arrangements must, subject to periodic evaluation, be part of the University of the Future.

Financing

Some mechanism must be found to allocate resources to activities, units and individuals for the pursuit of the agenda. Again, flexibility will be important. Budgets cannot be allowed to be frozen into atrophying units, or into what a friend of mine calls "extinguished volcanoes". There must be funds available for constant experimentation as well as for successfully tested new activities. A matrix budgeting system is appropriate, where the traditional departments, or other established units, are the columns, receiving funding in the traditional mode, and new interdisciplinary activities, often spanning several traditional units, are the rows, receiving funding that is then portioned out for the specified purpose to participating units.

It will undoubtedly be necessary to pursue many sources of funding. The financing system must allow, and assist, the leaders of new activities in such pursuits, and ensure that proper incentives are created and maintained for the acquisition of external funding.

The Consortium on Children, Youth, and Families (CYFC), University of Minnesota[4]

The Consortium on Children, Youth, and Families was established in 1991 under the leadership of University faculty, working in collaboration with community professionals.

1. Background

The basic motivation for the project was described by the leadership as derived from "a social/economic/political zeitgeist that has raised our collective consciousness, irrespective of our individual disciplines." (From "Guiding Principles")

The University's Institute for Child Development provided a strong foundation for the effort.

The leadership saw an unusual opportunity in that society's attention – often fleeting when it comes to even the most pressing issues – was clearly focused on issues having to do with children, youth, and families.

The major weaknesses were identified as the scattered nature of the university's programmes and the lack of connection with community agencies, policy-makers, and practitioners.

The "two cultures" phenomenon was seen as a threat: a deliberative university culture where knowledge is generated and disseminated, often in very traditional ways, and an action-oriented community culture of service-providers. The tension led to perceptions that the university was arrogant, and that its research was irrelevant to solving the real problems, and its education and training inadequate in preparing graduates for their actual work.

2. The Restructuring Process

The project was identified as one that central administration would encourage and support under its "Strategic Investment Pool" programme.

A planning retreat was held in 1990 with participation of 39 faculty members and 11 community representatives (selected by the Steering Committee). A set of guiding principles was adopted, and a strong call for further action was issued.

- What hindered? A general scepticism in the community had to be overcome. The university "talked a lot", but would it "actually deliver?" The fact that the university's own activities were scattered in a dozen or more units throughout the university, from the College of Education to Human Ecology, the Medical School, and the Extension Service, made bringing faculty together for more than inspirational meetings an important task. The "culture" of disciplinary isolation was a major obstacle.

- What helped? It was generally recognized, in the university and nationally, that the Institute of Child Development was one of the best in the country. There was great respect for the leadership of the consortium project because it was first drawn from this unit. Clearly the time was ripe both inside and outside the university. The enthusiasm of the originators caught on with a broad range of potential participants. Minimal as the funding from central administration was, it did help that the consortium had central sanction and support.

---

4 Information provided by the University of Minnesota

Regulation

The University of the Future will still have need for policies governing the conduct of its work. As in so many other areas, independence is important in regard to regulation, although general policies will, of course, have to be set by government. This will continue to place great responsibility on the board, the administrators, and the individual researchers for integrity, watchfulness and ability to spot troubles, if self-regulation is going to work and be allowed by society.

Conflict of interest will be especially important in interaction with the wider community, because university and community personnel, funds, facilities, etc. are likely to be intermingled as common agendas are pursued. The idyllic days when a well-funded extension service could just give everything away to the users are gone. The financing schemes that have arisen in support of joint university-community efforts do need careful oversight, if the University of the Future is going to be able both to provide effective knowledge and technology transfer and serve as independent arbiter of knowledge and as critic of society.

Conflict of Interest: From Recommendations by Task Force of the Association of American Universities (AAU, 2001)

The Task Force concluded that the problem is rarely a particular conflict itself (individual or institutional conflict of interest) – rather it is the question about what is done with the conflict....

The Task Force concluded that a university's institutional financial conflict of interest processes – for both financial holding-related conflicts and those involving senior officers – should follow a threefold approach:

1) disclose always;

2) manage the conflict in most cases;

3) prohibit the activity when necessary to protect the public interest or the interest of the university.

A key goal is to segregate the decision-making about the financial activities and the research activities, so that they are separately and independently managed...

The partnership between research universities and their principal research sponsors – including the federal government – must be based on the conviction that universities are accountable for the research they perform. If research universities do not demonstrate their ability to maintain accountability for individual and institutional conflict of interest, more prescriptive approaches may well be pursued by either the executive or legislative branches of government, or both.

Personnel policies and practices

I have already stressed the need for protection of the university's scholars and scientists, if they are going to be able to pursue the taxing agenda that I have suggested, and do it with the kind of independence that is necessary to truly serve society. The University of the Future is going to have to deal thoughtfully with the challenge of developing procedures that combine protection with assurance of continued productivity.

In order for the university to pursue an appropriate agenda in its interaction with society, the scholars and scientists must be able to represent all major sectors of society, in cultural, social, racial, and economic terms. "Being able to represent" should include actual representation, not only for, but from a variety of groups in society.

What will happen to the traditional faculty role? Will what has in many ways been a single, if multifaceted, concept of the "faculty member" be preserved? I will only touch on what I see as the requirements of the kind of interaction with society that I am addressing in this paper, and not deal with the larger question of whether the triple-threat faculty member, performing teaching, research, and service, will be viable in the University of the Future.

It seems that the effective pursuit of the kind of agenda that I have outlined will require a division of labour.

The scholar/scientist will discover and, in interaction with the community, analyse and criticize. Taking research findings to a state where they can be translated or converted into use by and for the community requires a different set of skills. It is important that the latter role should be defined to emphasize interaction operating both ways, translating/converting discovery/analysis/criticism to community use and bringing issues and problems from the community to the researchers.

The university may be well served by giving a more definite expression to the latter role in its personnel system. (I am, of course, here ignoring great differences among types of interaction, ranging from technology transfer to policy interpretation, from clinical activities of various kinds to economic development). It is also possible that one and the same person at different stages of a career might be interested, and serve well, first in the discovery role and later in the role of providing actual interface with society.

Promotion and salary-setting procedures must be tied effectively to the definition of positions, and be based on regular evaluations of performance.

Information technology

Interaction and sharing of the kind I have discussed in this paper will undoubtedly be significantly affected by IT, and IT may well find new uses within the agenda I have outlined. For one thing, IT gives us the opportunity to network more effectively, and in new ways, both inside universities and among universities, and between universities and the wider community. New methods and opportunities for data gathering, discovery, analysis and dissemination of findings are developing. Ease of access to information is being greatly enhanced. Since much of the interaction between the university and the wider community that we are talking about involves sharing and dissemination of information, it is safe to predict continued escalation of IT-based networking as "Moore's law" continues to apply with its regular doubling of capacity relative to cost.

Will there be a qualitative change as well in the interaction and sharing? Will the human interaction of the university representative to the community with representatives of that community be replaced by a more impersonal, albeit perhaps expanded, virtual interaction by computer? Here I can only raise the question, and leave it to the reader to do further conjecturing. In general, it is not safe to assume that IT will simply facilitate existing modes of interaction. The nature of interaction is very likely to change.

IT Network to Provide Access for the Community[5]

Details on the Master Gardener programme: The Master Gardener programme in Minnesota is an educational programme designed to train volunteers to help other people in their communities with horticulture. The programme was created in 1977 and is administered by the University of Minnesota Extension Service. Most of the 87 counties in Minnesota have active Master Gardeners. Volunteers receive professional training in home horticulture by university specialists in exchange for volunteer time. This training sets Master Gardeners apart from other home gardeners and allows them to be effective resources in their local communities. Working with local county Extension offices, Master Gardener activities benefit schools, community education programmes, garden centers, farmer's markets, historical sites, and many other programmes...

Classes are held in the Twin Cities of Minneapolis and St. Paul, various other locations in Minnesota, and on the Internet.

Food Safety Food Service Certification: Every restaurant in the state has to have certified food safety manager on staff. Currently the University of Minnesota offers this training in traditional classrooms. However, the university is in the final stages of testing the online version of this programme. We anticipate the response to online training will be strong. It is flexible and food service workers don't work standard shifts. Food service also has extremely high turnover and the online training can be completed quickly if the facility loses their employee with certification. An employee can complete it within days instead of having to wait for the face-to-face course to come to their area.

---

5 Information provided by the University of Minnesota.

The "culture" of the university

All the features of the University of the Future that I have identified come together in what we might regard as the "culture" of the university. For the university to serve the wider community effectively, this totality is important. Unless the board, the president, the administration, and a sizeable portion of the faculty and staff are imbued with a spirit of willingness to serve the wider community, the enterprise will not be fully successful. One of the many challenges of the University of the Future will thus also be to create such a spirit through its planning, priority-setting, reward system, budgeting, regulations, IT and personnel policies and practices.

"Hubs and spokes"

Finally, a few words about the physical structures of the University of the Future. I believe that we will continue to be well served by physical locations where scholars and scientists can work and interact with each other in real time in a collegial atmosphere, and where many disciplines are represented. The research university may survive as such an intellectual "hub" for discovery. I expect that the typical hub will also provide learning opportunities for students who would be apprenticed to the resident scholars and scientists, especially to learn what scholarship and science are about, and how research is done.

Needless to say, these hubs should have the characteristics of our finest campuses, with exciting and functional architecture and much green space!

In order to interact with the wider community, "spokes" will need to connect the university hubs with that community. These spokes may be physical locations, where university representatives interact with community representatives, but they will also increasingly be virtual networks through which the knowledge and understanding produced at the hubs will be translated and transferred.

I suggest this "hubs and spokes" model with some trepidation, because I am concerned that my University of the Future might be misinterpreted as a system burdened with heavy bureaucracy and rules and regulations. The hubs and spokes of the University of the Future must be organized to ensure both independence, room for, and ease of, innovation and entrepreneurship, and productive, and continually renewed, coordination and collaboration.

CONCLUSION

The exercise of trying to charter a University of the Future is exhilarating in many ways.

I do note that I have not been able to break away from much that is traditional, and that already exists. What I have actually done is, of course, first to re-emphasize the basic values of the university as it has emerged over the last few centuries, with much trial and tribulation, the values that are embodied in words such as "free and open inquiry," and secondly to idealize and expand the land-grant tradition of service to the wider community beyond its traditional rural and agricultural boundaries. These values, and the basic institutional structures and policies that sustain them, will need to be preserved.

What is new?

What is new is mostly, perhaps entirely, expansion and systematization of structures, policies, procedures and activities that are already found in many universities. It is all based on my conviction that the University of the Future must, and will, be at once at the centre of society, of the emerging knowledge society, providing it with indispensable knowledge, understanding, and know-how, and independent enough from society to be able to be a true arbiter of knowledge and a critic. In order to serve in that demanding role, the University of the Future needs both an expanded and enriched agenda that does not shy away from the difficult and controversial issues facing society, and flexible structures and procedures that can accommodate continuing innovation and renewal.

How will we know when we have gotten there?

The Kellogg Commission on the Future of the Land-Grant University (2001) identified "a seven-part test" for what they termed "the engaged university". This is a brief summary of the "guiding characteristics" that were identified:

- Responsiveness: a matter of asking the right questions and listening to the communities to be served.
- Respect for partners: a matter of working with the community to identify problems, seek solutions, and evaluate success.
- Academic neutrality: which I would rather call "academic objectivity – a matter of ensuring that the university's resources are used appropriately in dealing with controversial matters.
- Accessibility: a matter of ensuring that our structures and practices are as transparent and as user-friendly as possible.
- Integration: a matter of combining the university's missions in inquiry and learning with its mission in service.
- Coordination: a matter of making sure that the different parts of the university know what the other parts are doing.

"From The notion of engagement" (Kellogg Commission, 2001)

"From Executive summary"

"We issue this final letter with some sense of urgency and concern. Our message is not private pleading from a special interest group, but rather the public expression of our conviction that if this nation is to succeed in a new century, the covenant between our institutions and the public they serve must be renewed and again made binding."

...

"A New Kind of Public Institution"

"This Commission's prior letters have provided reasonable responses to that broad question. If the recommendations in our prior reports are heeded, the shape of today's university will still be visible in a new century, but it will have been transformed in many ways, major and minor. It will truly be a new kind of public institution, one that is as much a first-rate student university as it is a first-rate research university, one that provides access to success to a much more diverse student population as easily as it reaches out to "engage" the larger community. Perhaps most significantly, this new university will be the engine of lifelong learning in the United States, because it will have reinvented its organizational structures and re-examined its cultural norms in pursuit of a learning society."

"A new covenant"

"Thus for our part of the covenant, we commit to support:
• Educational opportunity that is genuinely equal because it provides access to success without regard to race, ethnicity, age, occupation, or economic background;
• Excellence in undergraduate, graduate, and professional curricula;
• Learning environments that meet the civic ends of public higher education by preparing students to lead and participate in a democratic society;
• Complex and broad-based agendas for discovery and graduate education that are informed by the latest scholarship and responsive to pressing public needs;
• Conscious efforts to bring the resources and expertise at our institutions to bear on community, state, national, and international problems in a coherent way;
• Systems and data that will allow us periodically to make an open accounting of our progress toward achieving our commitment to the public good; and
• Intensive, on-going monitoring of the progress of the Kellogg Commission's recommendations."

• Resource partnerships: a matter of properly combining funding for service activities from university, government, and private-sector sources.

Taken together, these characteristics help shape the culture that is necessary, if the research university is to serve the wider community.

What will wither away? Will the research university itself as we know it survive?

I think that what we have come to call "the research university" – or in the phrase used by the sponsors of this symposium, "the research-led university" – will survive for quite some time in a form that we will continue to recognize. To be sure, this institution has undergone, and will continue to undergo, much change. The question of the viability of the particular institutional configuration that we associate with the term in the United States (including such clearly extraneous activities as intercollegiate athletics) is being raised repeatedly, not least in connection with considerations of the impact of information technology. I have assumed for the purposes of this discussion that the University of the Future will retain the essential features of the current major American research university. But, I do want to stress that the impact of IT – with its potential for new networking and for unpacking responsibilities and activities – undoubtedly will be significant (and may well surprise us), and that many of the activities, policies and practices described are likely to be affected by it. Some activities will remain "real" in place and time, many others will be "virtual". While many aspects of the research university will remain, the University of the Future will break some of the shackles of place and time!

REFERENCES

First Morrill Act (1862), granting federal land to states for the purpose of establishing universities to serve the people of the state. (Internet, Morrill Land-Grant Acts).

Clark, Burton R. (1995). *Places of Inquiry: Research and Advanced Education in Modern Universities*, University of California Press, Berkeley, California.

AAU Task Force on Research Accountability (2001). *Report on Individual and Institutional Conflict of Interest, Association of American Universities*, Washington, D.C.

The Kellogg Commission on the Future of the Land-Grant University (2001). Final report. The commission was convened by the National Association of State Universities and Land-Grant Colleges and published a series of reports between 1995 and 2001.

CHAPTER 11

Social Diversity in Research Universities

Marcel Crochet

INTRODUCTION

U niversities were created in Europe more than 900 years ago. With determination, they have pursued their fundamental missions: research, scholarship and education. They have greatly contributed to the development of humanism, to the discovery of science and techno-logy, to medical research. A not unimportant role has been to educate an elite, i.e. those who are willing to assume responsibilities in their social, cul-tural or economic environment. It would be difficult today to imagine a world without universities!

At an early stage, universities were organized along very similar patterns, with the same faculties and the same degrees. It was an exceptional time for universities: in the 15th century, students would travel along the major roads of science, from Hastings to Venice, all the way through Louvain, Köln, Hei-delberg, Strasbourg and Basel... Quite unfortunately though, wars, revolu-tions and moving borders gradually led to diverging systems of higher educa-tion, up to the point where every single country would establish its own nomenclature and educational approach, to the dissatisfaction of those who promote a new and consensual Europe through the mobility of students as well as graduates offering their services.

Quite suddenly, as a follow-up to the events which shook the continent in the early 90s, the political world realized that universities needed to be reuni-fied if the future of Europe was to be based on the younger generations. How would it be possible to unite a continent and to promote mobility with a variety of educational systems as rich as its cultural diversity? The impetus to concretize the new vision has been exceptionally strong and efficient: those active in the educational world will remember the Sorbonne (1998), Bologna (1999), Salamanca and Prague (2001), Graz and Berlin (2003) as major milestones in the setting up of a new European organization of higher education which should be fully effective by 2010. With the Bologna declaration as a starting point, the whole process will have taken a little more than ten years which, by comparison with timescales proper to university life, is indeed very rapid.

On 19 September 2003, Ministers responsible for higher education from 33 European countries met in Berlin in order to review the progress achieved and to set priorities and new objectives for the coming years, with a view to speeding up the realization of the European Education Area (2003). Participants at the meeting expressed their general satisfaction, considering the astonishing progress accomplished over the four previous years; most countries have adopted new legal frameworks to integrate the Bologna Process in their educational structures. Although such a process meets wishes expressed in earlier conclusions of European Councils (2000 and 2002) aimed at making Europe a very competitive and dynamic economy, it is interesting to quote the very first paragraph of the "considerations, principles and priorities" set forth by the Ministers:

"Ministers reaffirm the importance of the social dimension of the Bologna Process. The need to increase competitiveness must be balanced with the objective of improving the social characteristics of the European Higher Education Area, aiming at strengthening social cohesion and reducing social and gender inequalities both at national and at European level. In that context, Ministers reaffirm their position that higher education is a public good and a public responsibility."

Such a declaration is well inspired and highly laudable, at a time when some countries might view education as a commercial good; it is also an appropriate response to the fears of those who consider the Bologna Process as a purely economic instrument. It raises, however, significant questions. While it is relatively easy to establish an inventory of European degrees, what do we know about present social inequalities in student populations? While road sheets are available to meet the 2010 objective of curriculum and degree harmonization, what should we do to reduce such social inequalities? Additionally, the Bologna Process will undoubtedly encourage the emergence of a limited number of prestigious research universities. How diversified will be the origin of their students?

The premise of the declaration is that, in a democratic country, the student population should reflect the socioeconomic diversity of the population. More precisely, in a region where a given percentage of the families live on a low income, the student population should be made up of the same percentage of children from such families. In most European countries, very low tuition fees, compulsory school and study grants are obvious indicators of their will to promote equality of opportunity for every young student, whatever his or her history. What is the success of such policies and, in case of failure, what are the reasons?

In the present chapter, we wish to analyse statistics collected within a specific region and from a specific university[1]; they seem, however, to reflect a situation prevalent in Europe as they emphasize the need to reinvent some educational paths.

THE SAMPLE

Belgium is a trilingual country, where people speak Dutch, French and German; it is divided into three "communities", each of which organizes education on the basis of its language. The French Community of Belgium (FCB, for brevity) represents some 4.15 million people. Education is compulsory until the age of 18; primary and secondary schools both offer six-year programmes. Higher education is based on a binary system. The *Hautes Ecoles* (literally High Schools, not to be confused with the American terminology) offer professional education with mostly three-year programmes; they don't practise research. Universities offer a variety of programmes and they all base their teaching on research. In 2002, students at the *Hautes Ecoles* and the universities numbered 75,000 and 61,000 respectively.

A recent study devoted to the student population in the FCB contains a diagram which illustrates the movement of students between their entrance in primary school and the end of their educational trajectory; it is shown in Table 1 (Droesbeke, Hecquet & Wattelar, 2001). Every year, some 50,000 children in FCB enter primary school. Out of 1000 children, 759 students undertake secondary school while 630 of them obtain their six-year certificate. Beyond that level, 89 interrupt their education, 223 register at the university and 318 at the *Hautes Ecoles* (the latter also receive 78 students who leave the university system). Eventually, 96 students complete their university curriculum while 238 obtain a degree from the *Hautes Ecoles*. It is interesting to note that, at the freshman level, universities in FCB fit the UNESCO definition of "mass universities", since they register more than 15 % of a student generation; the situation is different at the other end, where only 9.6 % obtain a degree. We note however that 334 students out of 1000, or 33.4 %, obtain a degree from higher-education institutions

The question raised is the possible correlation between the curriculum of these students and their families' socioeconomic situation. Or else, is there a

---

1 The present chapter is based on a report prepared in 2001-2002 by a joint commission of the Université catholique de Louvain and the MOC (Mouvement Ouvrier Chrétien).

Table 1. Path followed by 1000 students entering primary school in the French-speaking community of Belgium. A number of students leaving primary or secondary school choose professional training.

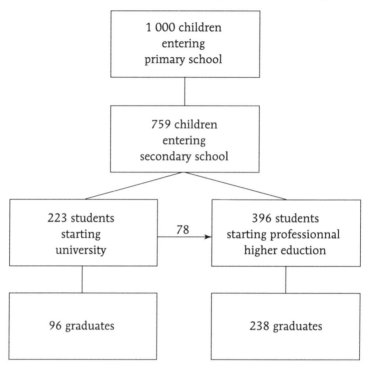

relationship between their parents education level and their own progress on the educational scale? Answers to such questions are essential when one analyses the evolution of the university population over the last 35 years: in 1967, 33,000 students were registered at university in FCB, while today they amount to 61,000. One may wonder whether, despite political efforts towards democracy, access to university education has followed the desired trend. It is not easy to answer, because of the lack of systematic surveys using the same questions over long periods of time, which would allow us to make a precise diagnosis and measure social progress in education. A partial response is provided below on the basis of surveys by A. Beguin (1976) and L. De Meulemeester (2001) devoted to the student population of the French-speaking Université catholique de Louvain (UCL, located in Louvain-la-Neuve).

UCL has some 20,000 students, i.e. one third of the student population in FCB, and offers programmes in all disciplines. Systematic studies have been undertaken since 1968 with first-year students; crosschecks with more general but less systematic surveys allow us to claim that our observations globally apply to the student population of FCB, although local differences are evident. The central location of FCB in Europe and its average economic situation suggest that these observations make sense within a European perspective.

SOCIOECONOMIC ORIGIN OF THE FATHER

It is customary to classify professions into three categories: modest, average and high. Typically, small farmers, labourers and railroad workers belong to the first category, qualified employees and teachers to the second, holders of a liberal profession to the third. The same categories have been used for many years in inquiries conducted at UCL.

Table 2 shows how the distribution of the students' fathers along these categories has evolved between 1967 and 1999. One observes significant changes between 1967 and 1986: the proportion of students originating from a high socioeconomic category rose from 31.6 % to 40 %, while those from modest and average categories were decreasing somewhat. No significant change was observed beyond 1986. Such a table provides little information if the evolution is not compared to that of the general population. This is difficult to measure because national statistics do not refer to same categories, as they are relevant for the whole Belgian population. However, surveys of the workforce published by the National Institute of Statistics allow one to compare the percentage of students from modest socioeconomic origins with the percentage of men aged 39 to 59 years within the Belgian population.

Table 2. Percentage of students' fathers belonging to so-called modest, average and high socioeconomic categories from 1967 to 1999.

Year	1967	1986	1996	1999
Modest	21.8	20.4	17.0	17.6
Average	42.2	36.2	37.2	34.2
High	31.6	39.8	40.9	41.2

Table 3 shows that in 1967 the percentage of men belonging to the modest class was about 50 % while only 22 % of university students were born from a father belonging to the same group. The ratio between these two percentages has improved somewhat between 1967 and 1986, but it has stagnated ever since: students from the modest socioeconomic class are underrepresented at the university.

Table 3. Percentage of the male population belonging to the modest socioeconomic category from 1967 to 1999 compared with the distribution of students' fathers.

Year	1967	1986	1996	1999
In Belgium	51.0 (in 1970)	37.4 to 40.8	37.0 to 39.9	36.1 to 38.5
Students' fathers	21.8	20.4	17.0	17.6

EDUCATIONAL LEVEL OF THE PARENTS

We call first-generation students those who register for the first time in higher education. Quite fortunately, extensive data are available on the level of education of the parents of such students; UCL has collected them for many years at registration time. Additionally, global statistics on the educational level of the Belgian population are also available. We limit ourselves to the analysis of data collected in 1999; they are representative of an essentially static situation.

The first line of Table 4 shows the distribution of the educational level of men aged 39 to 59 in 1999 within the Belgian population. The second line shows the same distribution among the fathers of students who registered for the first time at UCL in 1999. Quite clearly, these lines highlight major differences.

Table 4. Distribution in % of the educational level in 1999 of the male Belgian population and of the fathers of new students; *I: primary school, II: inferior secondary school, III: superior secondary school, IV: professional higher education, V: university.*

Level of education	Unknown	I	II	III	IV	V
Belgium		19.9	25.9	29.3	14.4	10.5
Students' fathers	4.6	3.2	8.4	14.7	26.7	42.4

While some 20 % of the male population have not gone past primary school, only 3 % of the students' fathers belong to that group. At the other extreme, while 10 % of the male population hold a university degree, 42 % of the first generation students are sons and daughters of a university graduate. Such a situation is not new: in 1986, the Belgian male population counted 6 % of university graduates, while 37 % of the students had a father with a university degree.

Table 5. Rate of success in % of the first year at university as a function of the educational level of the father and of the mother; the indicated levels are the same as in Table 4.

Level of education	I	II	III	IV	V
Students' fathers	26.1	33.9	36.3	40.8	55.4
Students' mothers	18.8	35.5	32.3	48.0	60.5

It is thus obvious that, today, the chances of a child entering university are intimately related to the educational level of his or her parents; further statistics at UCL show that the same can be said about its chances of passing first year at the university. The first line of Table 5 indeed shows the rate of success of the first year as a function of the educational level of the father. The second line is even more revealing: it shows the influence of the education of the mother on the success of first generation students. While the rate of success varies between 26 % and 55 % with the father's diploma, it ranges between 19 % and 60 % when one considers the educational level of the mother.

To summarize, what were the chances for a child born in 1981 in FCB of entering university in 1999 and passing first year? The answer is given in Table 6. Statistical data show that 50,500 children were born in 1981 in FCB; on the basis of the first line of Table 4, we know how to distribute the educational level of their fathers. Eighteen years later, 9,500 students entered the university in FCB; on the basis of the second line of Table 4, we can again show their distribution as a function of the father's education. We calculate that the chances of getting to university were respectively 3.2 % and 79.6 % for children born from fathers who had completed primary school or the university. What were their accumulated chances of entering university and passing first year? We use the first line of Table 5 and obtain the last two lines of Table 6. The respective chances were 0.8 % and 44.1 %! Taking into account their mother's education would enhance the discrepancy.

Table 6. Chances of entering university in 1999 and of passing their first year for children born in 1981 as a function of the educational level of their father; the indicated levels are the same as in Table 4.

Level of education	I	II	III	IV	V
50500 children	10050	13080	14797	7272	5303
9500 students	319	836	1464	2659	4222
ratio (in %)	3.2	6.4	9.9	36.6	79.6
successful first year	83	284	531	1085	2339
ratio (in %)	0.8	2.2	3.6	14.9	44.1

DISCUSSION AND CONCLUSIONS

The final data of Table 6 are astonishing: they show that an educational system based on the best intentions may lead to unexpected results; in FCB, as
in most European countries, primary and secondary schools are essentially
free and compulsory, higher education is heavily subsidized and generally
open to everyone. Such modes should favour equality of opportunity. It is,
however, obvious that students from a modest socioeconomic origin are less
present in higher education. Who are those who miss the university? First,
those who can't register because they have not completed secondary school;
they represent 37 % of a generation. Secondly, those 9 % who complete secondary school, but decide not to pursue their education. Finally, those who drop
out of higher education.

Further research is needed on the reasons that govern these trajectories.
One may wonder why so many students don't complete secondary school.
One might argue about a deficit of social and cultural conditions in favour of
intellectual work, lack of information, of experience or advice, or else the
absence of horizons other than their initial social condition. The "non-
choice" of higher education, more frequent in the modest class, may also
originate from many factors such as school trajectories in options which do
not favour the pursuit of higher education or the cost of expenses related to
education. Erroneous representations of student life, of the chances of success, of perspectives for the future or, in some cases, the mirage of material
success without education should also be mentioned.

The relationship between the rate of success in first year and the educational level of the parents is also of major concern. The objective assets of a
student with ideal working conditions, with the necessary equipment and
without financial worries are considerable. Additionally, the moral support of
parents who have gone though the "system" and their awareness about how it
works can be very helpful. Finally, it is clear that the type of school attended
at an early age has a major influence on the educational path.

In a way, nobody is directly "responsible" for the inequalities described
above. We observe an inexorable segregation that develops all along the educational trajectory, with its apex at the university. The phenomenon is not
recent. It is another manifestation of the reproduction of elites described by
Bourdieu and Passeron (1985).

The Bologna process in Europe might however enhance the inequality. It
is clear that, in the future, a number of students will want to obtain their
bachelor's degree in their home country and pursue their education in
another. Such paths are likely to become more accessible to those who benefit from more favourable socioeconomic conditions.

What should be the role of research universities? Should they simply accept a situation for which they do not consider themselves responsible and pursue their secular task, or should they react? It seems obvious that, in order to fulfil its humanist mission, the research university should undertake pro-grammes towards a better integration of society into their student body. Among a number of possible paths, they should:

- Collect data about their own students and evaluate the progress of social integration and equality.
- Offer their scholarly competence to the political world in order to detect the anomalies of the educational system and elaborate solu-tions.
- Cooperate with secondary schools and help them to open horizons for those who have not yet discovered them.
- Create paths of "second chance" for those who wish to return to edu-cation. They should also offer bridges between various levels of edu-cation. In particular, they should promote the use of information technologies to that end.
- Devote special attention to first-year students who are not aware of the university system and its methods. In particular, modern peda-gogical initiatives based on individual and group activities may not be familiar to everyone.

These are general trends that universities could follow, although selective and targeted actions should also be considered. The path to social equality in the education of the elite (as defined in the Introduction) will be long; it is however indispensable as part of the reinvention of the research university.

REFERENCES

Beguin, A (1976). "Une face cachée de l'enseignement. Analyse sociologique d'une cohorte d'étudiants inscrits à l'UCL." Thèse de doctorat en sociologie, Louvain-la-Neuve.

Bourdieu, P. & Passeron, J.C. (1985). Les héritiers: les étudiants et la culture. Editions de minuit (Le sens commun), Paris.

Conference of Ministers responsible for Higher Education (2003). "Realising the European Higher Education Area", Communiqué, 19 September.

De Meulemeester, L (2001). "La démocratisation de l'enseignement universitaire. Mythe ou réalité?" Mémoire de licence en sociologie, Louvain-la-Neuve.

Droesbeke, J. J, Hecquet, I. & Wattelar, Ch. (2001). La population étudiante. Descrip-tion, évolution, perspectives, Editions de l'Université de Bruxelles.

European Council (2000) Lisbon, and (2002) Barcelona.

CHAPTER 12

Globalization of Research and Development in a Federated World

Wayne C. Johnson[1]

INTRODUCTION

During the decade of the 1990s, the interaction between the typical research university and industry underwent a profound and accelerating change. As the economy strengthened it was industry that drove much of the interface with its increasing need for people and ideas. By the end of the decade the need for people in all technical disciplines had become insatiable, whereas the perception of technology as the road to immediate riches had become de rigueur. Both these situations were unsustainable, but they managed to reinforce each other in a very unhealthy way. Certainly, some of the emerging trends which occurred over this period – including the increasingly rapid transfer of new ideas from universities to the marketplace – should be considered to be favourable. While this probably reached a crescendo in the dot-com venture capital bubble which is unlikely to be repeated, time horizons have certainly shortened, awareness of the value of intellectual property has increased, and the need to engage sooner and more collaboratively with corporations has intensified.

Another emerging trend in this space is the increasingly global dimension of activity. From the viewpoint of the true multinational corporation, both the necessity and the desirability of engaging with research universities

1 The author would like to acknowledge, with gratitude, the assistance of Mr. Lou Witkin, of HP's University Relations Worldwide, in the preparation of this chapter.

became a business imperative. This trend is often confused and lumped under the concept of cost reduction outsourcing. In fact the situation is more complex for the large multinational, and involves decisions around the need to invest globally for a variety of reasons. Some of these include the availability of skilled talent, regulatory requirements, closeness to market, offset requirements for R & D investments in exchange for market access, proximity to exceptional academic expertise, tax incentives and many others.

The trend towards business federation also became more pronounced during this period. Again, resources were strained to the breaking point, while at the same time information technology provided new tools for collaboration. This trend included increasing partnership outsourcing between industry and academia. In the research arena this culminated in several high profile industry investments from leading U. S. companies such as Microsoft, HP and IBM in key universities.

The events of the bubble-bursting 1990s with their presumption of wealth creation, and the implicit need for new ideas accompanied by potentially disruptive technology, as well as the opportunities represented in the global marketplace, have resulted in a fundamental change in the relationship between industry and academia. Further, a need exists for substantial reform of the entire U.S. and European ecosystem if long-term damage to the system is to be avoided. Both sides are missing a profound opportunity for strategic partnership resulting from inaccurate perceptions and the lack of a unifying strategic framework coupled with insufficient public policy investment.

EVOLVING U.S. AND GLOBAL R & D ECOSYSTEMS

U.S. investment in the R & D ecosystem after the Second World War, based on the recommendations from Vannevar Bush and the attendant leadership position enjoyed by the U.S. in innovation and the competitive advance in technology, have been well documented. These investments have led to the emergence of a strong U.S. research university ecosystem that has complemented the industry research labs, effectively creating a virtuous cycle of new technology and ideas. At a time when there were few competitors due to the impact from World War II, the National Science Foundation, NASA, DARPA (The Defense Advanced Research Projects Agency) and other government agencies provided the seed funding for R & D expansion and innovation. In the last ten years, these research and development investments have decreased from both the government sector and from within industry. As R. Stanley Williams, a renowned scientist and Hewlett-Packard Fellow engaged in cutting-edge research in nanotechnology, has pointed out in testimony to Congress (2002a): "In the physical sciences and engineering, the support from the U.S. government for academic research has been decreasing in real terms for over a decade."

Figure 1. Trends in Federal Research by Discipline

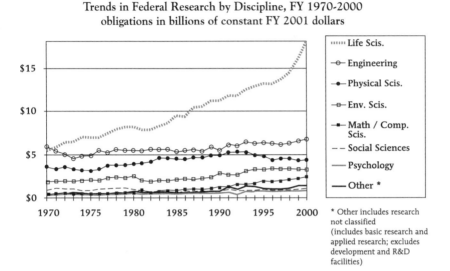

Trends in Federal Research by Discipline, FY 1970-2000
obligations in billions of constant FY 2001 dollars

* Other includes research not classified (includes basic research and applied research; excludes development and R&D facilities)

Source: National Science Foundation, *Federal Funds for Research and Development FY 1999, 2000, and 2001,* 2001. FY 2000 data are preliminary. Constant-dollar-conversions based on OMB's GDP deflators. APRIL '01 © 2001 AAAS

Clearly, corporate research operations steadily declined over the 1990s. This has caused much hand-wringing over the future of corporate research. Famous science and engineering bastions such as Xerox PARC and the old AT&T Bell Labs have gone through painful downsizing. Corporate research and development funding is estimated to be $194 billion in 2003, a modest 0.13 % increase over 2002, and a significant reduction in corporate R&D funding from the 7-8 % above inflation of recent years (Wolff, 2003, p. 8). The old system has been replaced by a new federated model involving collaborative work at various corporate, government and academic labs. As noted previously, the time between new inventions and product roll-outs is collapsing. "Fundamental science breakthroughs now have fairly rapid commercial applications," says Walter W. Powell, a guru in organizational behaviour at Stanford University. (Greene, 2003, p. 74). The impact of globalization has also caused many corporations to conduct research off-shore. The long-term concern, according to Merrilea J. Mayo, director of the Government-University-Industry-Research Roundtable at the National Academy of Science could be the eventual loss of American competitiveness and the permanent loss of higher-skill jobs. "That 'giant sucking sound' that Ross Perot heard [as the result of NAFTA (North American Free Trade Agreement)] is now happening in R & D," according to Mayo. (Greene, 2003, p. 76)

The more substantive issue may be the considerable investments now being made on a worldwide basis that mimic the success of the research investments made by the U.S. government after the Second World War. One example stands out: the enormous investment under way in China in science and technology. Chinese universities granted 465,000 science and engineering degrees in 2001, approaching the total for the U.S. (Einhorn, 2002, p. 80). The bottom line is that the virtuous cycle in the U.S. is being starved, while the rest of the world continues to invest.

CHANGING INTERFACES BETWEEN THE RESEARCH UNIVERSITY AND INDUSTRY

"In the past, internal R & D was a valuable strategic asset, even a formidable barrier to entry by competitors in many markets. Only large corporations like DuPont, IBM and AT&T could compete by doing the most R & D in their respective industries" (Chesbrough, 2003, p. 35). This was the age of "closed innovation", exemplified by corporate research centres like Bell Laboratories and Xerox's Palo Alto Research Centre (PARC). Today, there has been a fundamental shift in how companies generate new ideas and bring them to market. In the new model of "open innovation", a company commercializes both its own ideas as well as innovations from other entities, such as universities. (Chesbrough, 2003, p. 36).

Companies run across the spectrum from closed innovation to open innovation. Even within a large high-tech company like HP, various segments may be closed or fully integrated innovators, while other segments may be open innovators, eagerly embracing collaborations with universities. Also, in the large high-tech companies and IT industry, there may be dozens of patents representing incremental advances associated with a given product, while in other industries, such as pharmaceuticals, there may be a single enabling patent for a given product.

As industry has embraced open innovation, it has come to view the research university both as a source of graduates and applied research. Applied research conducted in universities has replaced a significant portion of the research that had been done in corporate labs such as Bell Labs and IBM research. Researchers in companies have shifted to advanced technology/advanced product development. To take advantage of open innovation, industry and universities need to identify the boundaries and establish effective processes to connect across them.

One of the key boundaries is the cultural differences between industry and universities. "Some boundaries can be addressed through routine, accepted business practices. For example, most sourcing processes use some kind of contractual negotiation to deal with organizations' differing goals, agendas and financial interests. Other boundaries, such as those involving culture and work pace, require more high-touch interventions" (Linder, 2003, p. 48). "Successful innovation partnerships bridge 'like to like' processes: Researchers in one organization work with researchers in another" (Linder, 2003, p. 48). For example, HP often manages research projects with universities through its own closest equivalent, its corporate research laboratory. HP also occasionally improves information flow in strategic partnerships with universities by placing researchers at the partner university. "A company's sourcing approach must ensure enough information flow (another boundary) to keep innovative activities on track" (Linder, 2003, p. 48).

Significant work and personal commitment are necessary on both sides of the boundary to prepare open communication channels and strong working relationships which can result in an effective technology transfer conduit. "Creating a culture in which external contributions are accepted, let alone welcomed, continues to be problematic in many companies that use an ad hoc approach. Overcoming this problem requires a significant investment of management time and effort. For example, a leading high-tech firm recognizes universities as sources of cutting-edge intelligence and research. But to nurture these strategic relationships and take advantage of their benefits, managers have to spend time with the professors while developing internal relationships to ready their own organization to make use of the ideas" (Linder, 2003, p. 44). Another change to the interface between universities and industry is the emergence of functional organizations within companies whose specific responsibility is to manage the external technology and research function. This has been driven by the need to understand the university culture and to have an effective point of contact to ensure that these relationships provide value. HP's University Relations organization is provided strong support from the highest levels of company management, due to a keen awareness that external research relationships are key strategic leverage points for the overall business goals and objectives of the corporation.

Another boundary is work pace and the high expectations corporations hold for their university partners. The corporation is usually very demanding in terms of accountability for dollars spent. The university must provide regular evidence of accomplishments and communication of planned milestones, as well as continuous delivery of research reports and prototype demonstrations which represent the concrete value of the work performed over a specifically identified period of time. In order for universities to speak the same language to their corporate partners, special organizational accommodations on the side of the university have increasingly been implemented. "... private labs usually work more quickly than those at universities. One large organization has specifically established a small-firm channel to take advantage of the speed differential. Some universities are countering by establishing organizations that sit on the boundary between academia and private industry – for example, MIT's Industrial Liaison Program – to manage university research with a mentality in which meeting deadlines, making progress reports and achieving commercially valuable outputs are part of the effort" (Linder, 2003, p. 48).

CHANGES IN INTELLECTUAL PROPERTY POLICIES

The partnership between industry and universities has been weakened over difficulties associated with the negotiation of intellectual property (IP) rights in research contracts in recent times. The issue is driven by the most part from sheer budgetary issues facing research universities. Economic pressures have affected endowments of even the largest and strongest universities. With the decline in the financial markets and the dependence of universities on financial investments to offset rising operations costs, universities have undertaken an aggressive posture with corporations regarding control of IP as a funding mechanism for retaining research superiority, and, in the process, have alienated and frustrated U.S. companies which are increasingly unwilling to be held captive. Attorneys are heavily involved in these negotiations and the lengthy amount of time to set up research agreements has become unwieldy. On the other hand, foreign universities are highly interested in negotiating quickly and effectively with U.S. corporations to set up research agreements. They do not get sidetracked on IP rights, and are taking advantage of the chasm which has opened between U.S. universities and corporations around the IP disagreements.

R. Stanley Williams, HP Fellow, Hewlett-Packard Laboratories, testified on these troubling issues before the Senate Subcommittee on Science, Technology and Space on September 17, 2002. Williams stated that "large U.S. based corporations have become so disheartened and disgusted with the situation [i.e., negotiating intellectual property rights with U.S. universities] they are now working with foreign universities, especially the elite institutions in France, Russia and China, which are more than willing to offer extremely favourable intellectual property terms." (Williams, 2002a, p. 5). What happened that brought the relationship between U.S. companies and U.S. universities to this point? Stan Williams effectively describes the trend: "Largely as a result of the lack of federal funding for research, American Universities have become extremely aggressive in their attempts to raise funding from large corporations. Severe disagreements have arisen because of conflicting interpretations of the Bayh-Dole Act." (Williams, 2002a, p. 5). The great irony surrounding Bayh-Dole was that it was implemented to encourage the commercialization of government-funded academic research. Over time the exact opposite has happened. In his response to questions by Senator Wyden, Williams amplified: "In my opinion, the root of the problem is in the desperate financial situation of most American universities. In the physical sciences and engineering, the support from the U.S. government for academic research has been decreasing in real terms for over a decade." (Williams, 2002b, p. 1). Williams' assertion is supported by the financial data: "From all sources, support for academic R & D grew 77 % (in constant dollars) during the 1980s, but only 49 % in the 1990s. Federal support grew 55 % in the 1980s, 47 % in the 1990s. Even the biomedical area, which captured at least half of all increases (from all sources) in the two decades, grew less rapidly in the 1990s (68 %) than in the 1980s (89 %)" (Schmitt, 2003, p. 25). (see Figure 2 below)

Figure 2 Trends in Nondefense R&D by Function

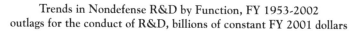

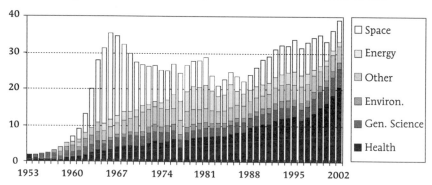

Trends in Nondefense R&D by Function, FY 1953-2002
outlags for the conduct of R&D, billions of constant FY 2001 dollars

Source: AAAS, based on OMB Historical Tables in *Budget of the United States Government FY 2003* Constant dollar conversions based on GDP deflators. FY 2002 is the President's request. *Note:* Some Energy programs shifted to General Science beginning in FY 1998. APRIL '01 © 2001 AAAS

"The prosperity of the 1990s was prepared by the R & D investments of the 1960s, when the U.S. federal government was investing 2 % of GNP on R & D. That R & D investment has paid off many folds over the decades, but because we became wealthy, we forgot that we needed to keep investing to stay wealthy." (Williams, 2002a, p. 6). Williams describes the consequences of this reduction: "This has forced the universities to try to raise funds from other sources. Since a few universities have made a large amount of money from a piece of valuable intellectual property, this has encouraged nearly all universities to attempt to duplicate this success." (Williams, 2002b, p. 1).

In response to questions from the Senate Subcommittee, Williams indicated: "Typically at present, negotiating a contract to perform collaborative research with an American university takes one to two years of exchanging emails by attorneys, punctuated by long telephone conference calls involving the scientists who wish to work together. All too often, the company spends more on attorneys' fees than the value of the contract being negotiated. This situation has driven many large companies away from working with American universities altogether, and they are looking for alternate research partners." (Williams, 2002b, p. 1).

Anecdotal evidence appears to indicate that many large companies such as Motorola, IBM, and Intel have encountered similar problems. Because of the law of unintended consequences, the increasingly aggressive, complex and confusing way that universities are approaching technology transfer is souring the relationship between industry and universities in countries like the U.S. and forcing many companies to look overseas for both research and people. Attractive IP arrangements, faster time-to-market, and lower overhead costs have been factors that have enticed these companies to explore relationships with leading universities in India, China and Europe.

"On the other hand, many high-quality foreign universities are very eager to work with American companies, and by keeping attorneys out of the discussion completely they have streamlined processes to allow a successful negotiation to take place in literally a few minutes over the telephone. It is possible to specify what one wants to a professor at a university in China or Russia and then issue a purchase order to obtain a particular deliverable. The deliverable is received and verified to be satisfactory before the American company pays for it, and in this case the American company owns all rights to the deliverable and the process by which it was created. Often, such transactions can be completed in a few months, a fraction of the time required to just negotiate a contract with an American university, which will insist on owning all rights to whatever is produced. Thus, just as American companies were long ago forced to deal with high-quality and lowpriced foreign competition, American universities will either have to modify their behaviour or lose their industrial customers" (Williams, 2002b, p. 1).

Frank Pita, Semiconductor Research Consortium, cites the example of Taiwan. A company can have a $50,000 research contract in Taiwan, with 15-18 students covered under the agreement (at $200/month/graduate student). The government of Taiwan subsidizes the students' tuition, room and board, so the research contract is primarily providing stipends for the students. Also, indirect cost rates are typically lower outside the U.S., typically 20 % vs. 50 % in the U.S. Further, the Taiwanese government provides incentives for students in key industries – students who go to work in the semiconductor industry are exempted from military service. Experts like Stan Williams and Frank Pita indicate that there is a time-to-market advantage in working with a foreign university. Industry is able to negotiate a contract quicker, often with no changes in the proposed agreement.

GLOBALIZATION OF R & D

Globalization is becoming a fact of life in much of the world. Companies look for the most cost-effective means to operate their business, thereby maximizing shareholder gains and ensuring available resources for expansion and future growth. "Economic evolution is inevitable. Companies will always pursue the lowest-cost structure, which means less skilled work will move out of the U.S. to emerging economies. And that's a good thing, because living standards around the world will rise. Workers in developing nations will get new and higher-paying jobs, and consumers in the U.S. will be able to buy products that are cheaper than if they were made at home. The shift first occurred in textiles and other manufacturing jobs, followed by low-end services such as telemarketing and data entry. Now, it's moving up the labour food chain, leaving white-collar workers increasingly nervous" (Madigan & Mandel, 2003). India and China are premier examples of countries which have seized this opportunity in order to bring a better standard of living to their citizenry.

An important example of this trend is India's software industry, which continues to grow. Although software jobs are well-paying – in some cases salary and bonus exceed $100,000 – code writing is not perceived as glamorous work by American-born tech workers (Ginsberg, 1997).

According to Patrick Scaglia, Vice President and Director, Internet and Computing Platform Research Center at HP Laboratories, there are additional reasons which make global R & D federation so pervasive at this moment. "One is the very nature of software R & D at an industrial scale. Developing Software includes a creative step (understanding requirements, generating ideas and prototypes, defining architectures) and a production step (coding then testing, bug fixing, verifying and shipping). Software products have very long life cycles (software never dies) so this cycle is repeated typically on a yearly or twice a year basis as 'incremental releases'of the same product, with enhancements and bug fixes shipped with that new release. Although both the creative and production steps are generally considered 'R & D', they profoundly differ in style and substance over the life cycle of a software product. It is generally accepted that at least 70 % of R & D resources are spent on the 'bug fixing/testing/ship' part of the process, 30 % or less on the truly creative portion that require the highest skill level. Over the last 15 years, companies have found that there is a high cost in maintain-ing and enhancing the software products (the 70 % portion) and have attempted to distribute the process towards lower skilled lower cost locations. The pervasive use of computer networks and the internet enabled it on a large scale. It is now possible to have software R&D done anywhere in the world, while maintaining tight connection among distributed teams. During that same period of time, many countries/governments invested heavily in building up a highly educated workforce with advanced degrees in computer science and related technology fields and continue to do so. As a result the pool of talent in many regions of the world is now highly skilled and com-petitive and can tackle the most advanced part of software technology."

India's software revenue for the year ending March 2002 was $12.3 billion, and exports rose to $9.6 billion in 2002. More than 60 % of India's software exports are to North America (Rai, 2002a). The rapid evolution of a popula-tion of quality software engineers in nations such as India and China could well lead to the outsourcing of advanced engineering and scientific work to low-cost but high-quality overseas suppliers at the expense of domestic high-tech jobs in the U.S. and Europe.

In its globalization efforts, HP has created an R & D programme to deal with the emerging markets in India and other countries. Through HP's e-inclusion programme, HP is working to provide people in some of the world's poorest communities access to greater social and economic opportu-nities by closing the gap between technology-empowered and technology-excluded communities. HP is partnering with private and public entities to provide technology tools and services, and to create locally sustainable solu-tions. For example, HP Labs in India is conducting R & D to create a scalable, self-sustaining IT solution in Kuppam, India.

Globalization has become a fact of life for other industries. Frank Pita of the Semiconductor Research Corporation indicates that the SRC has been a global consortium since early 2000. Prior to that time, SRC collaborated with 45-50 universities, all in the U.S. Currently, the SRC works with more than 85 universities with at least 15-20 outside the U.S., in countries like Russia and Taiwan. HP also encourages collaborations with and among uni-versities worldwide. An example of this is the Gelato Federation, founded in 2002 by HP and eight international research institutions. This open-source community initiative is dedicated to developing public software solutions to address real-world problems in academic, government, and industrial research worldwide. There are now more than 20 research universities and national labs worldwide that are members of the Gelato Federation (includ-ing Groupe ESIEE in France, National Center for Supercomputing Applica-tions (NCSA) in the U.S., University of Waterloo in Canada, the Bioinfor-matics Institute in Singapore, University of Illinois in the U.S., University of

New South Wales in Australia, Tsinghua University in China, National Center for Atmospheric Research (NCAR) in the U.S., CERN in Switzerland, Pittsburgh Supercomputing Center in the U.S., National Institute for Research in Computer Science and Control (INRIA) in France, Pacific Northwest National Lab in the U.S., Ohio Supercomputer Center in the U.S., University of Karlsruhe in Germany, Russian Academy of Sciences in Russia, San Diego Supercomputer Center in the U.S., KTH (Royal Institute of Technology) in Sweden, Pontifical Catholic University of Rio Grande do Sul in Brazil, University of Puerto Rico at Mayaguez, Puerto Rico, Fudan University in China, Zhejiang University in China, and the Georgia Institute of Technology in the U.S.).

Significant attention is needed to address the issue of whether human capital will be built within the U.S. or outside the U.S. "More attention should be paid to educating the U.S. workforce. America is on the cutting edge of the information and technology economy. But others are catching up. India and China award more natural science and engineering degrees than we do" (Madigan, 2003). Stan Williams has observed that U.S. industries based on physical science and engineering face acute shortages of R & D personnel and new ideas to make significant advances in key fields such as nanotechnology. Research conducted at foreign universities provides a source of highly talented graduates. Currently "hirability" is a barrier for this human capital – immigration issues, significant relocation costs, the desire of students to stay in their home country. It is unsettling to realize that in the future, these people may be competitors armed with the knowledge gained in working with U.S. companies.

If we look at the intellectual property problems with U.S. universities, it appears that U.S. universities have inadvertently "shot themselves in the foot" because their research funding may be reduced, with increased corporate flow to foreign universities. "While many of us on the university side of the equation would disagree on why things seemed to have soured in many of our relationships with industry, most of us would agree that something's not right. And while we encourage greater collaboration between industry and our colleagues in foreign universities around the world, it is definitely not a good thing if industry's motivation for developing collaborations with foreign universities is based on the belief that American companies can't work with American universities" (Killoren, 2003, p. 1).

The disturbing convergence of IP struggles that are pushing U.S. corporations to look abroad for university research partners, coupled with the trend towards off-shore contracts with emerging economies, may cause long-term undermining of the U.S. economy and seriously threaten the continued superiority of U.S. research universities. "During the 1980s, the university was posed as an under-utilized weapon in the battle for industrial competi-

Figure 3 Relative Change in Bachelor's Degrees Awarded Since 1986

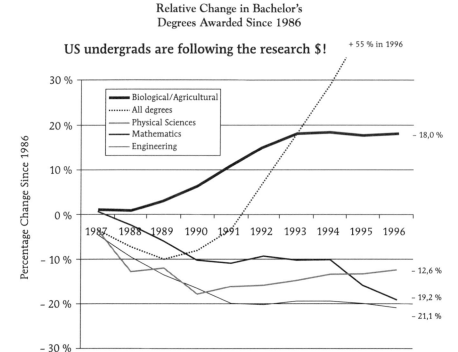

Source: National Science Foundation *Science and Engineering Indicators 2000*.

tiveness and regional economic growth. Academics and university officials are becoming increasingly concerned that greater involvement in university research is causing a shift from fundamental science to more applied work. Industry, meanwhile, is growing upset over universities' increasingly aggressive attempts to profit from industry-funded research, through intellectual property rights. In addition, state and local governments are becoming disillusioned that universities are not sparking the kind of regional growth seen in the classic success stories of Stanford University and Silicon Valley..." (Florida, 1999).

Would companies never have explored building partnerships with foreign universities if they had not encountered the fierce resistance around IP issues? Of course they would have, but it would have taken significantly more time, given the preferences of working with a university partner in the same country, based on time and distance. Unfortunately, universities allowed U.S. industry to experience the benefits of working with foreign universities, and it will take a significant effort to rebalance the equation to place U.S. universities back on a comparable basis.

CHANGING THE ECOSYSTEM: OPPORTUNITY FOR STRATEGIC PARTNERSHIP

U.S. universities and U.S. corporations stand at the edge of opportunity today, with the possibility of renewed partnership and the strategic advantages that can be realized. "Universities are far more important as the nation's primary source of knowledge creation and talent. Smart people are the most critical resource to any economy, and especially to the rapidly growing knowledge-based economy on which the U.S. future rests." (Florida, 1999).

The overriding strategic imperative is the recognition of the importance of the Knowledge Supply Chain (Hanson, 1997). Similar in concept to the material supply chain, the most important aspect of this concept is the need for both parties to view the system in the context of a seamless, end-to-end process of knowledge creation and transfer.

Figure 4. Supply Chain Comparison (Hanson, 1997, p. 159)

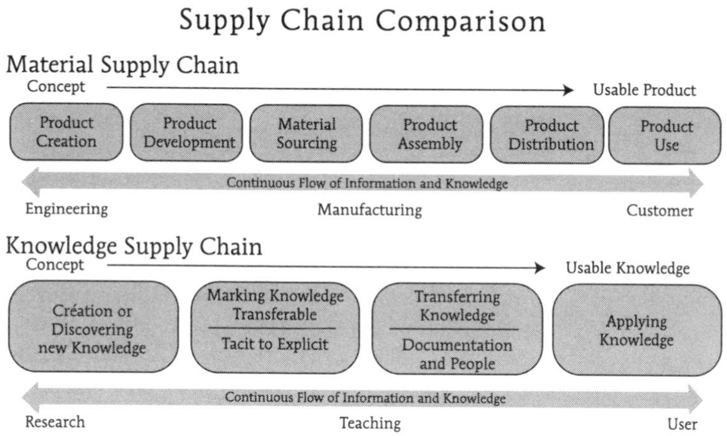

Supply Chain Comparison

Material Supply Chain

Concept ————————————————————→ Usable Product

Product Creation	Product Development	Material Sourcing	Product Assembly	Product Distribution	Product Use

Continuous Flow of Information and Knowledge

Engineering   Manufacturing   Customer

Knowledge Supply Chain

Concept ————————————————————→ Usable Knowledge

Création or Discovering new Knowledge	Marking Knowledge Transferable / Tacit to Explicit	Transferring Knowledge / Documentation and People	Applying Knowledge

Continuous Flow of Information and Knowledge

Research   Teaching   User

Source: Knowledge Supply Chains: A Next-Generation Manufacturing Project.

The Knowledge Process Today

The knowledge process today is stratified between academia and industry. Both institutions generate knowledge and transfer knowledge, but in most cases there are major barriers between the two cultures that impact the ability of both segments to create new knowledge to satisfy society and to improve competence and the ability to learn.

Figure 5 The Knowledge Process Today (Hanson, 1997, p. 161)

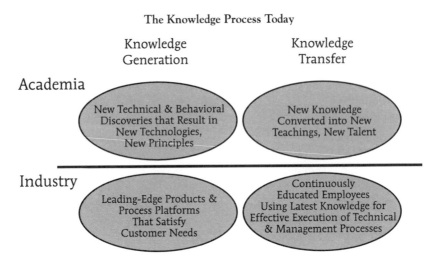

The Knowledge Process Today

Source: Knowledge Supply Chains: A Next-Generation Manufacturing Project

What are the solutions? They include (1) building long-term relationships, moving from sponsorship to real partnership, (2) making a commitment to "live" in each other's environments and (3) learning to trust and capitalize on partnerships to leverage scarce resources.

In order to implement these solutions, partners in the Knowledge Supply Chain must understand how they fit into the larger, integrated knowledge process. They must eliminate ignorance and distrust to capitalize on the different strengths and capabilities of each partner. They must recognize that the ultimate goal is to satisfy the end customer, and the goal can only be achieved when each partner is also satisfied, i.e., that each partner has the responsibility to help others succeed. Lastly, they must be an integral part of the continuous, free flow of information and knowledge, to eliminate time and knowledge gaps that isolate them from users and suppliers.

The Knowledge Process of the Future

What are the potential outcomes? For industry they include a more effective and efficient access to knowledge and reduced technology-development-and-deployment cycles. They also include the potential for improved return-on-investment on corporate expenditures for training and research, to create a better balance between job security and corporate flexibility. For universities, the outcome is increased funds and capacity for continuing and pursuing relevant research, insuring the long-term health of the academic enterprise, and establishing more appropriate and efficient markets for graduates.

Figure 6. The Knowledge Process of the Future (Hanson, 1997, p. 162)

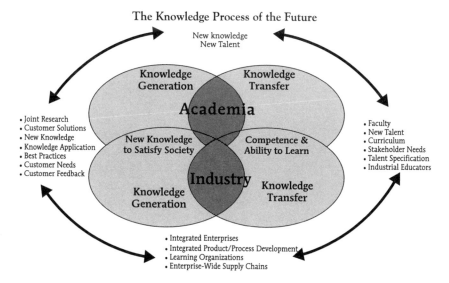

Source: Knowledge Supply Chains: A Next-Generation Manufacturing Project

Partnership Framework

From the university perspective, industry is viewed as the partner who is often missing when hiring needs dry up and who produces technology of increasing complexity with little pay-off to increased teaching efficiency and learning. Understanding the lessons of supply chain management as they apply to the management of university relationships, it can be seen that the development of a strategic partnership proceeds along a continuum.

The other important understanding is that this continuum has many of the same characteristics as Maslow's Need Hierarchy. You must satisfy the early steps in interacting with an institution (i.e., safety and security) before you move toward strategic partnership (i.e., self-actualization).

Accordingly, it is possible to map a series of representative activities of engagement with a university, from the more traditional industrial investments (recruiting, sales, job fairs) to those that may be described as strategic (business development, joint partnership). Moves up the continuum require greater group and leadership involvement. Activities can take place out of order within the first three levels of Awareness, Involvement and Support, but the fourth and fifth levels of activity – Sponsorship and Strategic Partner – will not be successful unless the first three engagement levels are secured. The most important ingredient for success in this paradigm is trust.

Figure 7. The Partnership Continuum

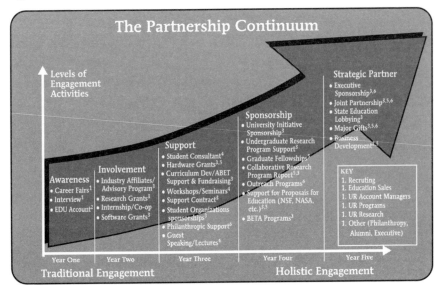

Source: Wayne C. Johonson, Worldwide Director HP, University Relations

Based upon experience in working with universities, this process typically takes up to five years to reach the level of Strategic Partner. Most corporations typically operate at levels 1 and 2 in what can be described as a conditioned-response mode of interaction. These interactions tend to be self-serving for the corporation and, although they satisfy some of the requirements for a successful partnership, the university community will not fully engage.

The execution of an effective university-industry strategy requires engagement across a wide-range of university units and departments, with simultaneous coordination of all the corporate stakeholders. The process must be viewed as holistic for long-term success.

REFERENCES

Chesbrough, H. W. (2003). "The Era of Open Innovation", *MIT Sloan Management Review*, Spring, pp. 35-41.

Einhorn, B. et al. (2002). "High Tech in China; Is it a threat to Silicon Valley?" *Business Week*, October 28, pp. 80-91.

Florida, R. (1999). "The role of the university: leveraging talent, not technology". *Issues in Science and Technology*, Summer, pp. 67-73.

Friedman, T. (2002). "Globalization, Alive and Well", *New York Times*, 22 September, WK13(L) col 1.

Gelato Federation. http://www.gelato.org.

Ginsberg, S. (1997). "A foreign affair: Tech firms vie for émigrés'affections", *San Francisco Business Times*, September 29.

Greene, J. et al. (2003). "Reinventing Corporate R&D", *Business Week*, September 22, pp 74-76.

Hanson, W. C. (1997). "Knowledge Supply Chains: A Next-Generation Manufacturing Project", January, http://www.imti21.org/Documents/ngm.pdf.

Hewlett-Packard Corporate Affairs: e-inclusion; http://ca.corp.hp.com/einclusion/.

Hurt, J. C. (2001). "Partnerships For Innovation", *National Science Foundation*, August 28.

Kantrowitz, B. et al. (2003). "Learning the Hard Way", *Newsweek International*, September 15, p. 50.

Killoren, B. (2003). "The Industry/University Congress From NCURA's President..." *NCURA newsletter, a publication of The National Council of University Research Administrators*, July/August.

Linder, J. C., Jarvenpaa, S. & Davenport, Th. H. (2003). "Toward an Innovation Sourcing Strategy", *MIT Sloan Management Review*, Summer, pp. 43-49.

Madigan, K. & Mandel, M. J. (2003). "Outsourcing Jobs: Is It Bad?", *Business Week*, August 25, p. 36.

Maslow, A. (1970). *Motivation and Personality*, 2nd ed., Harper & Row, New York.

Mayo, M. J. (2003). *Business Week*, September 22, pp. 74-76.

Moore, J. S. (2002). "Industry Sponsored University Research in Information Technology: Some Recommendations Regarding Intellectual Property Agreements", *CRA Snowbird Conference*, October 1.

Rai, S. (2002a) "India: Growth in Software", *New York Times*, 19 July, W1(L) col 2.

Rai, S. (2002b) "Chinese Race to Supplant India in Software", *New York Times*, January 5, C1(L) col 3.

Schmitt, R. W. (2003). "Bolstering Support for Academic R&D", *Issues in Science and Technology*, Summer, pp. 24-26.

Williams, R. S. (2002a). "Testimony on behalf of the Hewlett-Packard Company before the Subcommittee on Science, Technology and Space of the Senate Committee on Commerce, Science and Transportation of the United States Senate", September 17, http://commerce.senate.gov/hearings/091702williams.pdf.

Williams, R. S. (2002b). Senate Committee on Commerce, Science, and Transportation, Subcommittee on Science, Technology, and Space, Post Hearing Questions for Dr. R. Stanley Williams, from Senator Ron Wyden, Hearing on Nanotechnology, Washington, D.C., September 17.

Wolff, M. F. (2003). "See U.S. R & D Spending Up 3.4 % in 2003", *Research Technology Management*, March/April, p. 8.

PART IV

• • • • • • • • • • • • •

Financing and Governing
the Research University

CHAPTER 13

Financing the Research University: A European Perspective

Luc E. Weber

INTRODUCTION

The climate of increasing competition which strongly influences the daily business of universities in their basic missions of research, teaching and service to society is made particularly challenging today as it has become more and more difficult for universities to secure sufficient funding. This is as true in Europe as it is in North America. While in the 1950s, 1960s and, to some extent, in the 1970s, the massive growth of universities was made possible by increasing financial support by the State, different types of sponsors and, almost exclusively in the United States, the students themselves, securing sufficient funding has now become much more difficult. This has serious consequences for universities as they are forced to adapt to their rapidly changing environment with financial resources lagging behind requirements, and, in some cases, even diminishing.

This chapter will begin with a brief analysis of the main reasons why the climate of increased competition is making securing adequate resources more difficult. After this review of the harsh reality of university funding, the chapter will analyse different methods that universities should explore and develop to diversify and increase their funding. This section will focus mainly on the European context as the institutional setting clearly differs from that in the United States. The next chapter (chapter 14) by Marye Anne Fox will look specifically at the American dimension of the question.

THE CHALLENGE OF SECURING ADEQUATE RESOURCES

In order to analyze the sources of difficulties in financing universities today, it is useful to distinguish between the expenditure and income sides of the university budget.

Expenditure side of the budget

The overwhelming cause of financial difficulties on the expenditure side of the university budget is the increasing cost of providing education and doing research. There are many reasons for this. The most important are:

- The massive growth of higher education, with a proportion of 40 to 60 % of class-age population presently studying in higher education institutions, compared with only 10 to 30 % 50 years ago, has brought much higher demands on the budgets of universities as they absorb these rapidly increasing enrolments, while avoiding a drop of education standards due to a lower staff/student ratio.
- The increasing expansion and complexity of knowledge – with more knowledge created by the present generation of scientists than during the entire previous history of science – has created a multiplication of specialization in all disciplines. Therefore, any university department now needs to have 3 to 5 times more academics for teaching and research purposes. Moreover, more and more discoveries are being made in areas where two or more disciplines overlap. Therefore, multidisciplinary approaches are becoming a necessity; however, they are more costly precisely because they require the collaboration of people from different disciplines.

The impact of these two fundamental developments has been reinforced by other factors of a more technical nature.

- *Teaching is and will largely remain labour-intensive.* Though it may seem strange that academics are teaching largely as they have for the past 100 years – with a blackboard and chalk, or at best with an overhead projector – it remains a fact that knowledge is generally transmitted face-to-face between students and teachers. Moreover, even if progress in the transmission of knowledge is greater than is apparent or is in fact accelerating thanks to greater use of the possibilities offered by information and communication technologies (ICTs), preparing the "courseware" for any sort of distance-learning course is itself very labour-intensive and therefore so costly that it is still not clear today whether it will be possible to spread the initial investment cost over a number of students large enough to have significant productivity gains. Furthermore, it is widely accepted that the newly promoted pedagogy – based on guiding the students in their own learning efforts –is, if done correctly, more costly than traditional, *ex cathedra* course delivery. Finally, research universities are more sensitive to these realities as the proportion of their students enrolled in Master or Ph.D. programmes is greater than in higher-education institutions focused mainly on education; therefore, their students– teacher ratio is significantly smaller, contributing to even greater increases in the cost of teaching.

- *Science – "big" science as well as social sciences and humanities – is becoming increasingly costly.* According to Ehrenberg (2003a, 2003b), "... the average research-and-development expenditure per faculty member across 228 major research universities in the U.S.A. more than doubled between the academic years 1970-71 and 1999-2000, paralleling the increases in general expenditure per faculty member that took place at those institutions." Moreover, "... despite the generous external support that universities have received for research during the same period, the average institutional expenditure on research per faculty member more than tripled. As a result, the portion of the average university's research paid for with institutional funds rose from about 11 per cent to almost 21 per cent." The reasons why academic institutions are bearing an increasing share of the costs of their faculty members' research are manifold. "In particular, theoretical scientists, who in previous generations required only pencils and paper, now often need to use supercomputers. Experimental scientists rely on sophisticated laboratory facilities that are increasingly expensive to build and operate. Moreover, research administration now includes stricter monitoring of financial records and environmental-safety regulations, as well as more detailed review and monitoring of research involving human subjects." This phenomenon, characteristic of hard and life sciences, can also be observed within the social sciences and humanities, which today require large-scale monitoring and networks of scientists representing many disciplines, as well as multidisciplinary approaches. In addition to that, the closer relationship between basic and applied research necessary to improve the transfer of technology is also a source of increased costs.

- Efforts to gain economies of scale, in particular through restructuring, greater collaboration or merger with another institution at departmental, faculty or institutional levels also involve, as has been well recognized in the private sector, major start-up costs before producing positive results, if any, on the quality and/or effectiveness of teaching and research. In other words, any effort to become more effective and to save financial resources begins in fact with an increase in costs!

- Moreover, the climate of increased competition also makes it more costly to attract the best faculty members – junior and senior – with attractive salaries and/or better working conditions (scientific equipment, research, technical and administrative staff). The same is true of attracting the best students, crucial for maintaining and improving the level of research and the visibility of the institution.
- Last but not least, the strong presence of the State in the management (administration) of universities – despite their autonomy – does not promote cost-conscious management of the institution.

Income side of the budget: recurrent difficulties

In order to analyze the challenge to financing research universities, I shall distinguish between recurrent (long-term) challenges which will be considered in this section, and short-term difficulties which will be described in the next section.

- As the different ways and means to solve recurrent difficulties will be considered in-depth later in this volume, I shall make only a brief analysis of them here. Basically, the main challenge for universities is to persuade governments and other sponsors, public or private to give higher education greater priority. There are at least two reasons:
- For those resources originating from the public sector, which are by far the most important in public universities and also quite substantial – even though lower – in private, not-for-profit universities, higher education and research institutions are in direct competition with other responsibilities of the State. Whatever priority it wishes to give to higher education, the State is facing increased demands in the areas of social security, health, general education, transport, security, defence and, more recently, the fight against terrorism. It would therefore be a serious mistake to believe that governments and parliaments could attribute an absolute or even a top priority to higher education and research; they obviously also have to consider other societal needs. So, at best, public resources allocated to higher education and research can grow only slightly more rapidly than the average growth of the public budgets – an insufficient increase to cover the rising costs described above. The fact that higher education and research cannot be given an absolute priority has been made clear once again by recent events in the U.S.A. and within the European Union, although both regions consider that knowledge has

become a production factor as important as labour and capital. The U.S.A. demonstrated its changing priorities by allocating for military expenditure many billions of dollars – substantially more than it has ever allocated to higher education and research. The European Union is facing a serious trade-off between respecting its stability pact which limits the public deficit to 3 % of the Gross National Product and, among others, implementing its objective to become by 2010 the world's most competitive region thanks to a knowledge-based economy (see chapter 3). Difficulties in public support for higher education and research may even worsen as there are increasing signs in developed countries that many ambitious government programmes – in particular social welfare programmes – set up in relatively affluent periods over the past 40 years, are no longer sustainable.

• The other basic reason for the limited support to higher education and research is the difficulty the sector has faced in convincing the authorities and the general public that the benefits are worth the costs, in other words that investments in higher education and research yield a high return on investment, along with major cultural benefits. Another way to describe the problem is to stress that society, politicians and entrepreneurs act on the basis of a very short-term viewpoint. Fundamental research is often so abstract that it is impossible for most of the population to understand that sooner or later some of the results will be very beneficial to society at large. This is all the more difficult because the development of science also has consequences which are – in some cases rightly, in some others not – considered undesirable by a large portion of the population. These include nuclear arms and nuclear waste, chemical pollution, some types of genetic manipulation and so on. Similar misunderstandings appear regarding the objectives and methods of teaching in research universities, compared with those in vocational higher education institutions. In particular, many employers complain that the programmes are much too theoretical and that students do not acquire the type of knowledge or skills that would be useful to them in a job. This remark obviously has a grain of truth to it; however, it is clearly a short-term view as it fails to take into account the fact that the best education universities can offer is to "learn how to learn". Finally, the university collectively has a strong tendency to behave like an ivory tower; lack of communication and even arrogance are detrimental to the credibility of academic institutions.

Obviously, the difficulties in financing research and research universities have more concrete reasons. The following seem to be the most important:

- *The competition for research money, for sponsors and for students.* Universities are not alone in their search for financial support by public agencies or private sponsors to finance research projects. Moreover, more students are aware that universities are not all of the same quality in the discipline that is of interest to them, so naturally they try to enrol in one of the best departments. Finally, where tuition fees are paid, differences in fees from one institution to the next affect students' choices of their place of study.
- *The difficulty research universities face in obtaining from agencies supporting their research projects the full cost of the research, rather than just the marginal cost.* Indeed, in most cases, the research subsidies cover the expenditures incurred for additional expenses (research staff, special equipment and current expenses) and only a small proportion of the overhead costs for office or laboratory space, equipment, as well as the salaries of the head of department and support staff, although those are substantial. The best proof of this situation is the criticism of unfair competition that private laboratories often make against university laboratories, as the former have to cover all costs linked with their research activities. The same argument applies for courses set up for lifelong learners. It is in general difficult for universities to charge the full cost of running these programmes.
- Finally, it is more difficult than it appears *to diversify the sources of funding for research and teaching.* The reason is that, as we shall see in the next section, they are interdependent. For example, potential private sponsors are often reluctant to support public universities, arguing that they already pay high sufficient taxes to the State; or the State, and in particular the minister of finance, is reluctant to concede tax exemptions for donations to university activities, complaining that the cost of universities represents an important charge on the expenditure side of their budget.

Income side of the budget: short-term difficulties

The ongoing difficulty in financing research universities mentioned above has recently been made more acute because of the poor economic situation in 2001 to 2003. Most national economies, after having benefited in various degrees from ten years of continuous and, in the United States, rapid growth are now suffering from a very low growth, or have even fallen into recession. Moreover, after reaching spectacular new highs in 2001, the stock markets suffered a very severe crash, which decreased the average value of stock by approximately 50 %. Also, both phenomena are largely interlinked, and this combination has deeply affected the traditional financial sponsors of universities. Due to the slowdown of economic activity and to the activities linked with the stock market, the public sector experienced a strong decrease in growth in revenues or even an absolute decrease. The public sector has therefore been encouraged to reduce the rate of growth of its expenditure and, in some cases, even the level of public expenditure. The impact of such policies has been all the more dramatic where the public bodies are forced by law to balance their budgets, which is often the case at the second or third level of public entities (American states, Swiss cantons, local authorities). The harsh consequences of these budgetary cuts – many American states are prime examples – are perhaps a useful reminder that part of the extraordinary increase in public revenues could have been put aside to prepare for the inevitable arrival of weaker economic conditions at a later stage of the financial cycle.

The poor economic situation affects not only public revenues, but also revenues originating from contracts with private business. In a recession, firms are invariably reluctant to invest; therefore, they tend also to reduce research contracts they pass to universities.

- On another register, in countries like the U.S.A. where firms, trust funds and individuals are encouraged to donate money to charities, culture and education, the falling value of assets now makes people think twice before making donations. Moreover, universities that have been able to accumulate an endowment fund – in a few institutions, these funds are worth many billions of dollars – are directly affected by the drop in the value of assets; they have to reduce support to their own research projects or to gifted students from modest backgrounds studying at the university. This in turn has an impact on expenditures and revenues.

- Although it concerns the expenditure side of the budget, it is important to point out that universities are often too slow in adapting their expenditures to falling revenues and, when they do make the necessary changes, these often have negative consequences on the career development of young scientists. This is due to the fact that universities function on the basis of huge fixed capital in the form of buildings and scientific, as well as IT, equipment and a lot of manpower. As the senior positions have been granted tenure, those most affected by austerity measures are the young scientists employed on limited contracts. Apart from the social cost of laying off staff, such actions have the effect of cancelling years of human investment by universities, as it is often impossible for those affected to return to academia when the situation improves because a new generation, which has just finished their Ph.D.s, is offered any available research positions.

REMINDER OF THE BASIC PRINCIPLES

The position of universities in the economy

As the preceding analysis of difficulties suggests, it is essential, in order to conceive a realistic strategy for improved university financing, to have a very clear idea of the position of universities in the circular flow of revenues and expenditures of the economic system. Figure 1 illustrates this, showing clearly the rigid constraints on university financing (Weber, 1997, p. 363). Just as the resources available to government depend on the taxes paid by households and the business sector, so the financial resources available to students and universities depend on the resources that government, households and businesses agree to set aside for higher education and research. This is a fact that should encourage university leaders and faculty members to be realistic when they request funding.

Figure 1: Position of Universities in the circular flow of revenues and expenditures within any economic system.

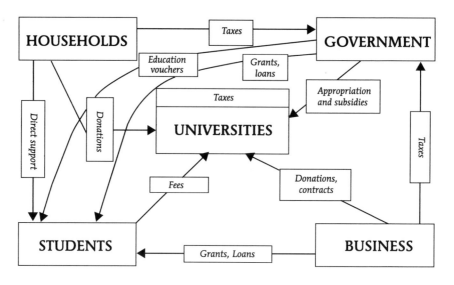

If we look at the respective role of the different agents, we can see that:

- Governments are financed by taxes paid by households and businesses, and give financial support to higher education and research by allocating money to universities (appropriations and subsidies) or to students (grants and loans, or education vouchers),

- Households directly support students, in general their children,
- Business either supports students by giving them loans or grants or directly supports universities with donations and contracts,
- Students may be invited to pay fees; however, in addition to the direct support from their families, they can receive either grants, loans or education vouchers from the State, as well as grants or loans from business.
- Finally, universities are funded through appropriation and subsidies from the State, donations and contracts from the business community, fees paid by students and donations from households. Moreover, they can benefit from the return on investment of their own wealth, if any.

Basically, if we stick to this level of generalization, there is no other way to finance a university. This means two things:

- In a given economic situation, any increase must come from the acceptance by government, business, households and students to assign a higher priority to higher education and research, which means that they have to reduce their priority for other areas, or that, in a situation of economic growth, the different agents must accept that universities take advantage of part of the benefit of that growth.
- If there is no such acceptance for an increased level of priority for higher education and research, the different sources of university financing are obviously narrowly interdependent. In other words, if in a given economic situation, one agent decreases its financial effort in favour of universities, this must be compensated by an increased effort on the part of other agent. For example, if the government reduces its effort, it has to be compensated by a greater effort by students, households or business. Vice versa, if students are invited to pay higher fees, this may induce the government to reduce its own effort.

Main differences between Europe and the U.S.A.

One of the very positive contributions of the Glion Colloquium is that it helps the participants and the readers of the books from both sides of the Atlantic to learn about the situation in the other continent or countries, allowing them to benefit from the experience of others. As it will appear clearly from the contribution in the next chapter from Marye Anne Fox, there are serious differences between the U.S. system and the European sys-

tem and, within Europe, between the British and Irish systems and those
from continental Western and even Eastern and Central European countries.

- The greatest difference is certainly the *coexistence in the U.S.A. of
  public universities* – that is universities supervised by a political body
  and largely financed by it – *and private universities*, which are independent of the State and get the greatest part of their financial
  resources from students fees and donations; the latter nevertheless
  receive public money, principally through their research projects. If
  the private universities are traditionally not-for-profit, we have seen
  in recent years the creation of numerous "for-profit" teaching institutions and the development of trans-border education, by which
  public or private non-profit institutions often set up for-profit
  branches abroad.

- Another important element is the fact that many U.S. universities
  can decide on the quality and quantity of their students, which
  improves the efficiency or their teaching programmes.

- All American students – in private as well as in public universities –
  pay *students' fees* which can reach very high levels in the best private
  universities, whereas, in continental Europe, the fees paid by students
  are generally rather symbolic, that is less than 5 % of the average cost
  of the education they receive. This situation is about to change in
  England where the government is proposing to allow universities to
  charge up to £3,000 a year.

- Unlike the United States, in Europe, in particular in continental
  Europe, *donations* to universities are relatively unimportant. Therefore, European universities, in particular continental institutions, do
  not have an endowment fund or, if they have one, it is very modest.
  The most frequent situation is the creation of specific foundations
  which may then support university research or other university
  activities related to the objectives of the foundation. Many of these
  foundations are in general independent of any university institution
  and tend therefore to finance projects on a competitive basis related
  to their objectives and criteria. The reasons for this unsatisfactory
  situation are complex. One is certainly the long-standing tradition
  that giving to charities does not extend to culture and education.
  Another reason is that in most European countries, donations by
  individuals to educational institutions are not tax-deductible; often,
  only corporations can benefit from such tax deductions. Moreover,
  there is no "alumni" culture in European universities: students come
  and go, and no institutionalized links are set between the institutions
  and their graduates, so that they cannot be invited to contribute to

make donations to their former institution and would probably refuse to do so, as European students do not identify with the institution where they have studied to the same extent as U.S. students do.

• *The relationship of universities with industry* is also less developed in Europe than in the U.S.A. Even if European universities have numerous research contracts with industry, those contracts cover the marginal cost of a research project and only part of the overhead cost; however, it is rare that they contribute to financing the institution. Moreover, in Europe the policy of protecting the intellectual property of university research is at an early stage, which means that no or very few resources accrue to universities through this channel.

• *Research contracts financed by European national governments and the European Union* are certainly important; however they do not reach the level of contracts financed by the U.S. departments of defence or energy, or the National Institute of Health (NIH).

• Finally, the ambition of European countries and the European Union to create a European Higher Education Space and the European Research Area (see chapter 3) will not be financially neutral. It is very probable that the implementation of the Bologna process will contribute to an extension of the duration of studies and the ambition to create the most competitive economy in the world by 2010 will require more resources: the European Commission would like European States and enterprises to allocate one additional percentage point of Gross National Product to research, which implies the training of more than 500,000 additional researchers.

SECURING RESOURCES FOR THE EUROPEAN RESEARCH UNIVERSITY

The above analysis suggests clear ways and means to increase funding of research universities. It is obviously very useful for European universities to search for solutions looking at the American example, without, however, losing sight of the many differences in cultural and institutional backgrounds. We shall therefore now underline ways and means that European research universities should explore and implement to increase their financial resources. I shall consider four areas of action likely to improve the financial situation for European research universities (see also Thyss-Clement, Balling and Weber, 1997). The first one aims at increasing the level of priority given to higher education and research by politicians, business people and the general public. The three others suggest ways for universities to increase their own resources or spend them more efficiently.

Better position research universities politically

The first and principal measure that universities should take is to make all possible efforts to increase the level of priority given to higher education and research and to each institution, by politicians, business people and the general public. In Europe, where public funding dominates, such efforts should be aimed first of all at increasing the political priority given to research and research universities. The strategy should be a general strategy of communication to convey the importance of research and research universities, as well as the strong collective and individual return on investments in human capital and research. This strategy should be adapted to the targeted audience: the general public, politicians, businessmen and women and students.

- *Developing a communications strategy aimed at the general public* implies actions such as organizing open days about science, taking advantage of selected events to inform the public, offering programmes of lectures aimed at the general public, developing "question-and-answer" forums on the Internet, writing specific contributions for the media, etc... The aim is to reduce as much as possible the gap between the university and the general public, and to demonstrate the huge volume of scholarship accumulated by universities, whose staff can make a major contribution to important social issues. It should be explained that the knowledge and methodologies accumulated by academics are highly effective in explaining the world around us and in solving problems. However good they are, ideas and principles will not be sufficient to convince politicians; universities should therefore take the initiative in drawing up and signing agreements of goals with their government, fixing the principal lines of action for the next 4 to 5 years in contractual form. They could also consider persuading the government to guarantee the appropriation to universities in a formula that incorporates indicators of the main sources of expenditures. However, these two methods, which can be used to make the financial contribution of the State to universities transparent and binding, will have a positive impact only if they are well conceived; otherwise, they may be rather counter-productive, reducing the autonomy of university leaders or linking university funding to criteria which are not, or are no longer, relevant.
- Universities should *lobby political parties, members of parliament and of governments,* in particular to make them aware of the importance of knowledge creation and transmission for the competitiveness of the country and of the region, as well as for improving the welfare of the country and its inhabitants. In other words the objective is to con-

vince them that an increase in higher education and research funding will contribute to accelerated economic growth, falls in unemployment, improvements in public policies and, last but not least, a better cultural background for the whole society.

- Finally, universities should also *focus their communications effort on businessmen and women and their associations*. Strangely enough, many – I dare say even the majority of – entrepreneurs are not aware or do not want to know that fundamental research is a necessary precondition for technological progress, or that a university education, compared with a more vocational training in teaching and vocational colleges, is a much better preparation for learning throughout life, and that this has become a necessity for all because of rapid changes in technology and knowledge itself.

- European universities should also make a much greater effort to *attract good students*. This means fighting the tradition of considering students as a burden. The future potential of research at any research university depends largely on its ability to enrol good students in its Master and Ph.D. programmes and to retain the best of them in its research teams.

Such a communications strategy is certainly easier to describe than to implement. Indeed, universities are generally rather self-centred and slightly arrogant, therefore less inclined to approach their present and potential partners in the public and the business sectors in order to convince them of their importance for society at large, as well as potential students to convince the best of them to enrol in their institution. Therefore the first thing to do for the leadership of each institution is to persuade members of institution itself that these actions are necessary.

Although all these actions are needed, we should be realistic. If it was easy to convince political bodies to upgrade the priority given to higher education and research, this would have been done long ago. Moreover, the numerous other responsibilities of the public sector are also represented by their own lobbies, which do everything possible to gain a higher priority for their area of concern. Therefore, it is almost certain that even increased communications efforts will not be sufficient to gain funding for all financial needs and increasing costs at the university. This is why European universities must also take measures to diversify their sources of funding and to try to exploit those potential sources of revenue they have generally ignored until now.

Student tuition fees

Compared with the American situation, the potential source of additional revenues which seems, at least at first sight, the most appropriate for European universities is to introduce or increase significantly students' tuition fees. There are strong arguments in favour of this policy, but also serious difficulties and concerns.

Charging tuition fees has at least three clear advantages:

- On a purely financial basis, it would bring important additional resources to each institution, depending obviously on the level of fees. It seems reasonable to assume that European universities could raise fees up to a level of 10 to 30 % of the average student's annual cost, the latter being computed as the total university cost divided by the number of students. This would obviously be a burden for the students or their parents. However, we should not lose sight of the fact that this sacrifice is small compared with the private rate of return on the individual student's investment. Moreover, the amount paid for tuition represents only part of the total cost paid by a student, which is equal to the sum of the tuition fees, the cost of living during studies and the opportunity cost of forgoing any income or higher income during studies.

- From an economic point of view, charging fees contributes to a better allocation of resources. Students who have to pay for their studies – even if it is only a small part of the costs they generate – are encouraged to be more rigorous with their study choices and to work harder. Reciprocally, students who pay for their studies are in a stronger position to insist upon the relevance and the quality of the programmes offered to them. This means that universities that raise relatively high fees need to make sure that the quality of the education they provide is in line with the individual's investment.

- Moreover, considered from the social justice viewpoint, charging tuition fees eliminates or reduces the regressive impact of free education on income distribution. This means for economists that free higher education creates income redistribution from the "poor" or the "modest" to the "rich", that is contrary to the direction usually aimed at by social policy. Despite political efforts over a number of decades, this undesirable phenomenon continues because the proportion of low-income-class children studying at university remains very much smaller than the proportion of children from better-off families. Now that in Europe higher education is financed mainly by taxes, many citizens on low incomes are paying taxes – even though at low levels – to cover public expenditures, including higher education, although it is unlikely that their children will go to the university, with therefore the likelihood of obtaining higher revenues in the future.

Inversely, students of high-income families are over-represented at universities and can expect higher salaries during their career.

- Finally, charging fees forces foreign students, whose parents do not pay any tax in the country, to contribute to the financing of a public service they consume, which benefits those residents who pay taxes.

As mentioned above, there is a strong political resistance to charging significant tuition fees. One of the reasons is the tendency for politicians and politically sensitive citizens to confuse a political objective, that is (almost) unanimously accepted – that there should be no financial barrier to access in university for all those who have the capacity, in other words no discrimination based on families' financial situations – and the mean to reach this objective, which for many is free higher education. In other words, higher education is wrongly considered politically as a public good, which it is not. For a public economist, the two characteristics of a public good – that is the possibility of excluding those who are ready to pay the price and the absence of any rivalry between users – are not met (Weber, 1997, pp. 42-44). Therefore, there is no necessity to provide it for free, as long as access to all capable students from low-income backgrounds is made possible through targeted support, in particular grants and loans, and that due account is taken that the effort made by those studying has a positive impact even on those who do not (in technical terms, produces some external benefits).

This confusion between the political objective of access without financial discrimination and the belief that this objective requires higher education to be provided free of charge has negative consequences in that the positive contribution of fees for a better allocation of resources, as well as the regressive income distribution impact, are neglected. Consequently, there are very strong arguments for formulating another policy mix in order to satisfy the access objective, without the inconvenience of the means, free higher education. The obvious solution is to charge tuition fees, and simultaneously to take special measures to help those whose access would be prevented because of the fees. The solution is to develop a grant and loan system in favour of deserving students from low-income families in order to cover not only their cost of living during their period of study, but also the fees they have to pay. There are many different ways to develop a grant and loan system, but this is not the place to do it. Moreover, although it has nothing to do with the fee question, it appears that free higher education and/or a generous grant and loan system are not sufficient to induce a significantly higher proportion of low-income students to go to university: proactive measures, which concern in particular primary and secondary school, appear to be indispensable.

Although I consider that introducing or increasing students' fees has become a necessity for European universities, there is one danger which must be resolved before going ahead. This danger, identified by many observers and taken into account very seriously by many rectors' conferences and individual universities, is the likelihood that the State would grasp this opportunity to reduce its own contributions. As appears clearly in the circular flow of income and expenditures in Figure 1, university studies can be paid indirectly by households and business through the taxes paid to the State or directly by the students, as well as by households and business through tuition fees and other support to the university or to students. In a situation of strong competition between different public sector requirements, we cannot exclude the possibility that the State decides to disengage, at least partially, from tasks which can be paid directly by the beneficiaries – especially in this case where it is easy to identify them – and to continue supporting activities whose beneficiaries are much more difficult to identify, such as defence, security and general administration.

Further measures on the income side of the budget

The first two ways to increase university funding developed above – convincing the State, business and the general public that higher education and research are an important public investment and introducing or increasing tuition fees – seem to me to be potentially the two most rewarding measures. However, this does not mean that university leaders should neglect other initiatives (Clark, 1998). On the contrary, it is wise to have an extensive strategy, as additional resources, even if modest, add up, contributing to the finances of the institution. I shall briefly enumerate them without much comment as the lack of these resources has been analysed before when describing the shortcomings of the present system. Furthermore, these other measures speak for themselves.

- Develop an appealing institutional culture covering staff and students and, in particular, create a circle of alumni who should be informed of the development of the institution and, from time to time, invited to make a special contribution for a specific project or to the specially created endowment fund. We should however be aware that increasing student mobility might make this increasingly difficult.

- Lobby parliaments and governments to persuade them to adapt the fiscal system in order to exempt from taxation individual income or company profits donated to universities.

- Promote donations from businesses and foundations to universities, research projects or students; use these donations to finance specific activities or to create an endowment fund.

- Increase revenues from business-like activities, in particular by renting premises (lecture halls, sport facilities) when not used for university activities and by organizing special teaching programmes.
- Intensify the collaboration with industry and governments by taking research contracts.
- Make better use of the accumulated intellectual property by patenting research results and creating start-up enterprises.

Indispensable accompanying measures on the expenditure side of the budget

As mentioned at several points, it would be unwise to believe that these measures to increase the financial resources of the research university will miraculously produce a huge increase in revenue. Even if progress is made, university financing will remain a permanent challenge for university leaders. Therefore, it is essential to make better use of the scarce resources. This means facing many sensitive questions, in particular:

- Fixing clear priorities (and secondary objectives) and better positioning the institution in order to reinforce what is being done well, to search for economies of scale and, whenever possible, an optimal size at each activity level;
- Paying more attention to the selection (whenever possible) and even the recruitment of students, in particular at Master and Ph.D. levels;
- Better governing and managing the institution by improving its organization, the decision-making process and by implementing rigorous management tools;
- Using incentives to encourage and reward – instead of using constraints and hierarchical pressures. In universities, as in no other institution, the innovation potential is to be addressed among the entire staff body, and separated from considerations of hierarchy. It is therefore indispensable that the goals and activities of all concerned should converge. Experience shows that it is extremely difficult to reach this collective effort in imposing decisions hierarchically (Weber, 2000). On the contrary, it appears that a lot more can be achieved by using stimulating measures, for example by offering additional resources to those units or teams working along the line of the objectives set up by the institution. However, these incentives should be used reasonably to avoid creating internal inequalities.

CONCLUSION

Even if the present situation in European universities seems less acute today than in the United States, the financing of research universities on both sides of the Atlantic will become more and more challenging due to increasing costs and competition. Finding new resources requires a change of attitude by politicians, students, business people and the general public, as well as much tougher management, based on clear priorities. All this has been known for ages. In this respect, there is little room for reinventing the way European universities are financed. However, there is a difference: the time has come to transform discourse into action!

REFERENCES

Clark, B. R., (1998). *Creating Entrepreneurial Universities; Organizational Pathways of Transformation*, IAU Press, Issues in Higher Education, Pergamon, Oxford.

Ehrenberg, R. G. (2003a). "Who Pays for the Growing Cost of Science?" http://chronicle.com/weekly/v49/i49/49b02401.htm

Ehrenberg, R. G., Rizzo, M. J. and Jakubson, G. H. (2003b). "Who Bears the Growing Cost of Science at Universities?" Working Paper 35, Cornell Higher Education Research Institute (CHERI), p. 26.

Thyss-Clement, F., Balling, M. and Weber, L. (1977). "Five Ways to Improve University Funding", Cre Doc No. 2, Association of European Universities, Geneva.

Wagner, A. (1996). "Le financement de l'enseignement supérieur: nouvelles méthodes, nouveaux problèmes", *Gestion de l'enseignement supérieur*, vol. 8, No 1, March 1996.

Weber, L. (1977). *L'Etat, acteur économique*, Economica, Paris.

Weber, L. (2000). "Financial Management and Planning: or How to Implement Changes more Smoothly" in *Higher Education Reform for Quality Higher Education Management in the 21st Century*, RIHE International Seminar Reports No. 11, RIHE Hiroshima University, Hiroshima, pp. 71-79.

Williams, G. (1990). *Le financement de l'enseignement supérieur, tendances actuelles*, OCDE, Paris.

CHAPTER 14

Impact of the Marketplace on the Financial Stability of American Public Research Universities

Marye Anne Fox

INTRODUCTION

I n the spirit of the Glion Conferences, this chapter seeks to describe North Carolina State University (NC State) as an exemplar of an American public research university that has accepted the need to develop additional non-traditional sources of revenue. NC State is a century-old institution of higher education with strong traditions and pockets of stubborn resistance to economically driven change. It has, nonetheless, sought actively to diversify revenue sources needed for improved campus operations in an era of financial austerity, increasing enrolment and rising public expectations for leadership in economic development.

North Carolina State University was founded in 1887 as a land-grant university, created to connect practical research and education in agriculture and the "mechanical and practical arts" to the needs of the state's citizens. As a large, public, research-extensive university, NC State focuses on science, engineering and technology, but also offers students a strong general education in the arts and sciences, together with an array of technical disciplines and professions, such as architecture, veterinary medicine, teacher education, etc. NC State faculty have been active for many decades in collaborating and cooperating with the private sector. Historically, they have been inclined to work closely with industry in solving practical problems. NC State can be used therefore as a case study of how market forces impact planning in technically oriented US universities. Its resource flow can illustrate the pressures felt by American public research universities as the result of troubled state economies and of rapidly changing demands in the character and skills of educated graduates. In many ways, NC State can be considered as the almost classic model of a truly public American research university.

DEFINING THE INSTITUTION

The state of North Carolina, the governmental home for NC State, is located at the northern edge of the "South", as defined by the boundaries of the American Civil War in the mid-19th century. As a Southern state, it exhibits a certain gentility of behaviour and strong roots to the land. It has long excelled in traditional industries: cotton (and hence textiles); farming (and hence tobacco and animal agriculture); forest products (and hence furniture). Over the last century, the growing of tobacco created a comfortable middle class, as well as many wealthy philanthropists, including James Duke, who founded nearby Duke University as a private research institution.

With about 29,000 students, NC State is typically ranked in the top 30–40 among public research institutions in the U.S.A. In the Zemsky classification, NC State is a "name-brand" university. Although public, it is quite selective in its admissions, having sufficient space to accommodate only about one of every four students who apply. In addition to supporting its research faculty in Raleigh, NC State also manages a large extension operation, with offices or research centres in each of North Carolina's 100 counties and in an included sovereign state, the Cherokee Indian reservation, located in western North Carolina.

North Carolina has a very long tradition of unquestioned respect and financial support for higher education. As a consequence, its people, acting through the legislature, have been generous in assuming a large fraction of the financial burden associated with higher education, relegating revenue from tuition as a low fraction of operating expenses. Tuition is exceptionally low, specifically because the state constitution states that "higher education, as far as practicable, be extended to the people of the state free of charge". Although a detailed interpretation of this provision is the subject of annual debate, tuition and fees are among the lowest among its national peer universities. Some legislators will describe targets for tuition in the university system as being low enough to permit access to any deserving student, but high enough to keep individual students focused on progress toward their degrees. Establishing that balance is tricky, especially since North Carolina's state appropriation to student financial aid is also among the lowest in the nation.

NC State is one of three research-extensive universities (with Duke University and the University of North Carolina at Chapel Hill) that have defined Research Triangle Park (RTP), one of the first American state-sponsored efforts at attracting and supporting research-based industries. This tract arose when North Carolina's political visionaries teamed with university leaders to look at the relationship between universities and industry in a new way. As early as the first years of the 1950s, state-supported incentives were offered to attract technically demanding industries to an area defined by the roughly 30-mile sides of a triangle defined by imaginary lines drawn from the centre of each campus to the other two. In fact, the industries that have located in the Research Triangle now have a long history of collaborating with the universities and of hiring their graduates.

There is also an additional entrepreneurial analog of RTP on the NC State campus. Noting NC State's tradition as a research-active, land-grant institution, the governor of North Carolina gave to NC State 1,000 acres of land, adjacent to its main Raleigh campus, expressly for the purpose of fostering university-industry collaborations. NC State's Centennial Campus, so named because the land allocation took place in 1987, the university's centennial year, would focus on small firms, start-ups, and focused research units of large corporations that were not yet ready for major plant siting in Research Triangle Park. It has grown rapidly and is recognized widely as one of the most successful of such ventures in the nation.

The chance to build a completely new campus, while advancing the more standard operations of a strong traditional campus, is an irresistible opportunity for many highly independent academics and entrepreneurs. This new campus could focus on intellectual property development, ultimately leading to commercialization, as well as attracting start-up businesses that could collaborate in facilitating this new kind of technology transfer, while providing valuable experience and financial support to our undergraduate and graduate students.

NC State is one of 16 campuses of the University of North Carolina (UNC) System. Two of these, the University of North Carolina at Chapel Hill and NC State University, grant academic and professional degrees at the bachelor, master, and doctoral level, focusing on basic research, broadly defined, and its applications. About one quarter of NC State students are pursuing an advanced degree. The relationship between NC State and UNC-Chapel Hill is strong, in part because the two institutions share a common funding source in the North Carolina legislature. In addition, there is very little programmatic redundancy. Instead of duplicating areas of NC State's expertise, UNC-Chapel Hill offers professional training and advanced degrees in the arts, sciences and humanities (hence, programmes in business, law, medicine, fine arts, journalism, etc). Our intercollegiate collaborations are therefore natural and easy, and, despite our close proximity, our competition is restricted largely to athletic events. For example, a Ph.D. degree in Biomedical Engineering is offered jointly by the two schools, drawing expert faculty from both sites. This is an appreciable advantage compared with many other American states.

The 14 other UNC institutions do not focus on the generation of knowledge per se, with six instead responding to local needs, usually offering degrees at the bachelor's and master's levels and an occasional doctoral degree relevant to regional requirements. Thus, for example, UNC-Wilmington offers a Ph.D. in Marine Science, taking advantage of its location at the edge of the Outer Banks. One institution is a School of the Arts, focusing on film-making, vocal and instrumental performance, theatre, etc; and another is a small liberal arts institution.

There are also six institutions that have historically served under-represented groups in the pre-1960s days of racially segregated schools in the American south. These schools are now integrated, but are targeted for special growth as the demand for a college education is likely to exceed available slots in the research universities in the next several years. (One of them, NC A&T University, also is a land-grant institution, founded later in the 19th century with the intent of supporting the farm needs of African-Americans. Collaborations in extension between NC A&T and NC State are also very productive.) The heritage of the minority-serving institutions is strong in the United States, and these universities have effective legislative advocates who emphasize serving African-American and Native American students. The existence of such sister schools permits the high selectivity in admissions for NC State by providing access to some public institution of higher learning for every interested and qualified student.

A virtually explicit compact with the citizens of North Carolina presupposes active participation of NC State in recruiting, retaining and supporting new and existing businesses, thus creating jobs and fostering economic growth. Only rarely does a week go by in which the NC State Chancellor is not called to assist the NC Department of Commerce in recruiting industries to relocate to or stay within North Carolina. This role is not universal among presidents and chancellors at universities in the United States, but it is becoming much more common at public, land-grant institutions.

UNIVERSITY REVENUE SOURCES

Because each institution has a different support base, the funds derived from endowment, legislative appropriation, tuition and fees vary significantly from one school to another. Even so, an in-depth look at the operating budget of

NC State might serve as the basis for a comparison with other similar schools.

NC State's annual operating budget is about $800 million. Over the past 20-30 years, the funding base of the university has changed appreciably. Whereas as much as 80 % of total funding came from state and federal appropriations and tuition in the 1960s, the most recent budget year (FY 03) includes funding from a much wider set of sources, with the state appropriation reduced to 41.5 % of derived revenue (Table 1).

Table 1. Summary: NC State University Revenue Sources (In Millions)

	1998	1999	2000	2001	2002
Tuition/Fees	$76.0 (11.2 %)	$78.9	$83.7	$91.7	$105.1 (13.3 %)
State Approp.	$302.1 (44.4 %)	$335.5 (45.0 %)	$340.1 (44.2 %)	$352.5 (43.3 %)	$328.2 (41.5 %)
Fed Approp.	$21.9	$24.4	$23.1	$21.8	$20.5 (2.6 %)
State Grant	$18.3	$22.3	$26.1	$33.7	$24.9 (3.1 %)
Fed Grant	$74.0	$73.1	$71.6	$83.4	$89.2 (11.3 %)
Private Grants/Gifts	$61.6	$68.0	$75.4	$79.6	$75.3 (9.5 %)
Sales	$110.4	$123.6	$129.3	$134.3	$135.8 (17.2 %)
Other Sources	$16.6	$19.0	$19.5	$16.0	$11.2 (1.4 %)
Total	$680.9	$744.8	$768.8	$813.0	$790.2
#students	27,529	27,960	28,011	28,619	29,286

Revenue received from enrolled students is listed as "Tuition and fees". Differentiation between these two revenue sources is crucial in North Carolina, where university support levels, including those funds to support enrolment expansion, are set by the legislature. Our elected leaders then establish a specific formula for incremental annual cash flow, and appropriated money is allocated to specific line-item categories. More than two-thirds of the sum shown in Figure 1 is represented by tuition. Tuition is revenue associated with the delivery of instruction, which is set in North Carolina by the state legislature, whereas fees are assessed, with the advice of student representatives and the institution's Board of Trustees. Fees are used to support student life, through recreational sports, athletics events, local transportation, student government, etc.

Revenue derived from tuition at NC State is low, compared with direct state appropriation. Although North Carolina is atypically generous compared with most U.S. states in providing this level of appropriated support, the state government in North Carolina insists that levied tuition also be kept very low and provides very little support through student financial aid. Even within the UNC System, there is a substantial variation in tuition, from about $2,500 per year at NC State to about $1,000 per year at Elizabeth City State University. These numbers are much lower than at private institutions: our neighbour Duke University, for example, set tuition at over $30,000 for the same period, and couples the tuition payments with substantial investments in student financial aid grants.

In addition to state appropriations, NC State receives a substantial federal appropriation, largely from the U.S. Department of Agriculture, to operate the North Carolina Cooperative Extension Service. This service provides professional advice to growers and breeders and maintains support service offices or research centres throughout North Carolina. Substantial support for these efforts requires careful managerial supervision and yearly contractual negotiation with each cooperating county. Annual budgets for each centre range from about $100,000 to several million dollars. This is a responsibility not shared by most European rectors or, indeed, by many US presidents and chancellors.

This work is complementary to a newer Industrial Extension Service (IES) that provides financial or technical advice to small businesses through a fee-for-service agreement. Some IES services are subsidized by the U.S. Department of Commerce. Services provided include, for example, assistance with environmental regulations, collaboration on urban planning or natural resource management, writing effective business plans, or brokering loans for businesses seeking to expand.

Federal grants are funds awarded in response to specific proposals by individual faculty members or small groups. Securing sufficient external sponsorship for their scholarly research is a major commitment of time and effort by nearly all U.S. faculty. This is necessary because state appropriations are almost always directed toward instruction in public universities, rather than to research. Increasingly, federal grants require multi-investigator efforts targeting interdisciplinary problems, and may often include collaborators from other institutions in the U.S. or abroad. Generally, no funds are received from the federal government to manage or promote university inventions or other intellectual property. Instead, technology transfer offices are generally self-supporting.

Lacking a medical school, NC State's focus on physical sciences, technology and engineering has produced slower growth in federal research support than in other comprehensive universities that focus on human health. Growth in NC State's federal research thus mimics growth in those agencies that support basic physical sciences, mathematics and engineering rather than in the National Institutes of Health, which have experienced explosive growth over the last decade. As a result, NC State has relied more heavily on collaborative industrial research as a key component of its sponsored research portfolio. In industrial research, it has ranked consistently among the top ten universities in the nation.

Sales represent income derived from auxiliary enterprises managed by the university. This includes athletics, fees for services provided such as housing and food service, income from the bookstore, parking, and the student health center (Table 2)

Table 2. NC State 2002 Sales Revenues (In millions)

Residential Life	$22.0
Dining	$17.7
Bookstore	$12.7
Athletics	$23.4
Parking	$7.8
Student Center	$4.9
Student Health	$7.8
Other	$11.9
Educational Services	$27.6
Total Sales & Services	$135.8

Notice that the figure for "sales" is larger than many of the other categories that are more traditionally thought of as being a university's responsibility. Other sources include real-estate leases, licensing agreements for trademarks and intellectual property, various marketing efforts, etc.

CAPITAL EXPENSE

Over the last five years, as state appropriations have declined as a share of the NC State budget, the number of enrolled students has continued to grow substantially. This reflects the high premium that U.S. students place on attending, and graduating from, top-quality research universities. This growth in absolute numbers, which is taking place under intense pressure from politicians, is greater at NC State than at any of our sister schools, giving us, for example, a larger student body than at UNC-Chapel Hill. Like most American states, North Carolina is experiencing a demographic bubble, with about 20 % more students now in the 9th grade of our secondary schools than was the case when our current freshman class was in that same grade.

This growth puts additional pressure on space, and for many of our colleges the number of enrolled students now exceeds capacity, especially for teaching laboratories in the basic sciences. As a result, NC State must invest substantially in capital for new buildings and for renovation and repair; that is, for expansion space and to address deferred maintenance. This capital expense is being financed through a referendum passed by popular election by North Carolina voters in Nov. 2000 that provides $3.1 billion for construction for post-secondary public institutions, $2.5 billion of which will fund the 16 campus University system. NC State's share of those funds is $468 million to finance over 100 buildings and major renovation projects on the Raleigh campus. This referendum provides support only for classrooms and teaching laboratories, and the university has been forced to locate private sources for all other building requirements. As a result, about $400 million in other needs (student apartments, a visitor/admissions centre, a conference centre and hotel, athletics facilities, recreational/fitness facilities, an alumni centre, and libraries) will be constructed from donations received from private sources or from usage fees. The state provides only approval for self-liquidating financing of these facilities.

CENTENNIAL CAMPUS FINANCES

NC State's Centennial Campus (CC) is recognized widely as one of the best academic-industrial collaborations in the U.S.A. CC currently houses about 60 private companies and hundreds of University faculty in about 1.5 million square feet of space. Its buildings are of several different types, ranging from academic buildings fully funded by state appropriations, through jointly operated buildings financed as self-liquidating projects deriving from the state's bonding authority, to completely private buildings that provide only land lease revenue. As such, CC represents a complex financial stream that includes a huge investment from the private sector that does not appear in our annual operating budget.

State-appropriated buildings are constructed with funds from a specific allocation and house our academic programmes, thus providing space only for NC State students and faculty. Research buildings are owned by NC State, funded through bonded-indebtedness guaranteed through the state, with monthly lease fees from university research groups being used to retire debt. Partnership buildings are those owned by a private developer, retiring debt through lease agreements approved by the university. Venture buildings are those constructed and financed by a private developer, operating on a long-term land lease after which the land and building improvement revert to the university. All leases are at or above local market rates, although the university can choose to subsidize specific research faculty who need specially configured space for sponsored research projects.

All CC tenants must have either an established research connection with NC State faculty or a fully executed licence agreement to develop NC State intellectual property. As such, partnerships on CC are viewed widely as an important and unique opportunity for providing a unique, competitive advantage to the NC State faculty that is not widely available elsewhere. The university reserves the right to veto any lease agreement in a privately owned building, if the lessee is judged incompatible with the university's teaching, research and service mission. We define programme compatibility in potential private-sector partners through a deliberative process involving a broad campus discussion.

In our campus strategic planning, four areas for research emphasis have been identified to build on university core competencies: biotechnology, with emphasis on genomics and bio-informatics; advanced materials; information technology and networking; and environmental sustainability. Those working in these or closely allied areas would be judged to be appropriate partners, and lease negotiations at current market rates would be initiated. In these discussions, we insist on full compatibility of our co-located partners with our traditional academic values of ethics, scholarly openness and published dissemination after a short review period, normally not to exceed 90 days.

Companies located on our campus range from major international companies, like the corporate offices of Red Hat and a research wing of ABB, to small start-ups whose names are not yet widely recognized. A status report about the size and type of partners on our campus is shown in Table 3.

A recent expansion of role on CC is the construction of a research wing attached to a public middle school that will provide a sound research basis for educational interventions for students of ages 11-13, particularly those that encourage girls and members of racial minorities to consider careers in science, mathematics, engineering, or technology. Support services for Distance Education and for learning in a technology-rich environment are also located on CC. We consider such activities as the logical new extension of our land-grant mission.

Table 3. NC State Centennial Campus Update: May 2003-11-27

	April 2003	May 2003	May 2002
Number of Companies (Total)	**61**	**57**	**59**
By Type:			
Advanced Materials	4	3	3
Biosciences	11	11	9
Education	2	2	1
Environmental	12	12	10
Information/Communication Tech.	17	16	18
Other Partner Organizations	15	13	18
By Size:			
Start-up Companies (Total)	13	12	13
IT	5	4	6
Biosciences	8	8	7
Small Business	12	12	12
Non-Profit	8	7	7
Major Corporations	16	14	16
Government Agencies	8	8	7
Services	4	4	4
Number of Employees (Total)	**1.445**	**1.439**	**1.566**
Information/Communication Tech.	583	577	540
Biosciences	49	49	51
Environmental	259	257	244
Education	79	79	70
Advanced Materials	13	12	15
Other Partner Organizations	470	465	646
Number of NC State students employed with CC companies (to our knowledge)	**142**	**146**	**107**
Number of Faculty Involved with CC companies (to our knowledge)	**244**	**252**	**152**

Reflecting a downturn in the national economy, the vacancy rate for research space at RTP is now about 30 %, while that on CC is below 3 %. While the number of employees on the Centennial Campus decreased by about 10 % over the last year during a national recession, the number of associated faculty and students has grown dramatically (by over 50 %). So while companies are reluctant to take on or maintain permanent employees because of the economy, our students appear to be benefiting in having access to great opportunities for co-ops and internships that support their educational goals. Thus, both the company and our students benefit from these collaborations. The increased participation may also represent a shift in attitude as more faculty seek collaborative opportunities with industrial partners close to their academic homes.

A special category of CC units include those involved in multi-company consortia. For example, a new research consortium on the production of non-woven fabrics for industrial purposes has attracted over 25 large multi-national sponsors to a joint laboratory on the CC. The more comfortable interactions fostered by co-location on CC have also had the effect of speeding up contract negotiations, and thus improving the chances of future collaborations and of faster commercialization. The presence of such companies also has had the effect of attracting entrepreneurial students who enrich the character of our management and engineering schools. Many of the most highly qualified industrial partners are contributing frequently to economic, social and cultural aspects of university life by serving as adjunct professors, sponsoring conferences and workshops, serving as external examiners for dissertation examinations, etc. Their presence provides an invaluable contribution to our students'education.

LESSONS LEARNED: SPECULATION ABOUT THE FUTURE

American public higher education has entered a new era characterized by rapidly increasing enrolment, declining state support, and rising expectations for involvement in wealth creation. In this environment, North Carolina's long-standing philosophy of "free" access to education provides an insufficient revenue stream to maintain quality based on state appropriations and student tuition and fees. The seemingly careless withdrawal of state support from higher education makes it increasingly difficult to extend the benefits of a college education to the ever-larger numbers of American high-school graduates who have historically populated the student bodies of public research universities. The quality of the workforce is then impaired and stable state financing for the university becomes even more elusive. As the management of higher education becomes ever more complex, the reality that such institutions cannot rely solely on the state or on student tuition becomes even more certain.

Given that a continuing erosion of state support seems to be inevitable, public research universities must rely on other sources. Most universities, therefore, seek to diversify their portfolio of revenues and to attract private-sector investment. Although universities plan investments and set priorities at a high level, there is a constant tension among competing units in pursuing fund-raising opportunities. When private support is sought by universities, greatest success is attained at the level of colleges and departments, where faculty have been closest to former students who represent the best pool of willing donors. These units are sometimes low on the university organization chart, and the flow of support from the colleges to the university can be slow. In fact, most funds raised in colleges and departments are restricted to a specific purpose, and support received is not readily fungible from the donor's interests into other high priority projects.

Thus, public research universities have become highly decentralized, with each unit behaving as a tub on its own financial bottom. The central administration is then forced to tax and control the units, billing them for electricity, water, maintenance, accounting services and so forth. This financial reality reinforces faculty loyalty to the discipline or the department, rather than to the university, and the consequent decentralization pushes responsibility to generate support and to control costs to the faculty. Operational efficiencies and a focus on economies of scale become significant factors in research universities, but the enhanced demands of politically-demanded larger numbers of students and of burgeoning unfunded mandates make it impossible to balance most university budgets by restructuring.

The university then must pursue other broader sources of support. It develops auxiliary enterprises, like athletics. It pursues federal and industrial grant and contract support. It commercializes intellectual property and derives income from royalties received and equity interests in start-up companies. It explores new opportunities for market-driven support, like the partnerships working on the NC State Centennial Campus. It moves away from its traditional extension and engagement activities, provided free of charge for many decades through state subsidies, to include instead fee-for-service structures. It seeks to secure endowments for retaining outstanding faculty and for covering operating costs.

In this environment, these alternative funding sources must, and will, be actively sought. The greatest successes in doing so will be achieved by adapting to market forces.

KEY ASSETS IN RESPONDING TO A MARKET-DRIVEN FUTURE

The United States is a country of entrepreneurs. American willingness to take risks and to resist bureaucracy is one of our proudest traits and one of our principal assets in developing innovative, new financial models to support higher education. More and more frequently, public research universities have embraced the priority of wealth creation consequent to research discoveries or the development of new technologies as key core missions. The ease of moving exciting new applications from their conception in basic research through potential commercialization is becoming particularly embraced within the faculties of professional schools of comprehensive universities. It is imperative then that such universities pay due attention to providing a complete understanding and justification of their activities to the state citizenry of this important, evolving university mission. Although we are experiencing a downturn in the economy, it is particularly attractive to invest in capital facilities when interest rates are so very low.

Most public research universities are willing to give up (at least partially) state support in exchange for greater autonomy, as generally expressed through the university's ability to control its own destiny. The availability of flexible resources is much more important to many institutions than is the absolute level of support received from the state. When coupled with multi-year financing options, entrepreneurial universities can invest in long-term needs for space and the range of skilled personnel required for attacking serious, multidisciplinary problems.

As with any business, debt financing capacity for major research units is determined by credit rating, and variation from one year to another, when deficits are encountered, can cause real trouble. Because Americans naturally celebrate risk-taking, it is all the more important that the home universities of active academic entrepreneurs accept the importance of establishing reserves, thus being prepared for unforeseen financial needs and challenges. Reserves are particularly important for institutions with substantial investments in, and cash flow from, health care and athletics, and are particularly important as America becomes an increasingly litigious nation. Some major universities, like the University of Michigan, retain one year's budget as an appropriate reserve. In this environment, secure, long-term, stable funding of sponsored research is essential, and is highly sought and rewarded.

Finally, private philanthropy, both from individuals and from private corporations, provides an invaluable source for investing at the margin in projects that foster excellence, team work and creativity. Most public research universities are able to attract and retain top-quality professors only if they can provide to individual faculty members the financial flexibility associated with income derived annually from large, dedicated endowments.

Endowments now exist in major universities for at least some of nearly every programmatic and individual need, ranging from starting new interdisciplinary degrees to scholarships for financially needy undergraduates.

POSSIBLE THREATS

As university budgets rely less significantly on state appropriations and on tuition and fees, stability in sponsored research across emerging disciplines becomes crucial. In recent years, rapidly expanding funds for the support of the life sciences have stood in sharp contrast with the flat or declining sources of support for the physical and mathematical sciences and engineering. An imbalance in federal and state support over more than a decade has had the extremely worrisome effect of drying up the store of basic discoveries on which future technological breakthroughs depend. The risk created by this imbalance is seen most evidently in the shifting demographics of the various scientific disciplines, where real growth in the American scientific workforce has been concentrated in health sciences. Each university president or chancellor is then forced to expend significant effort in achieving legislative intervention at the state and federal levels to maintain expertise in centrally important disciplines.

The growth in the importance of private donations for university operations can also be a double-edged sword. Despite the importance of philanthropy in the operation of cutting-edge research institutions, it is important to realize that public universities have worked at securing philanthropic support for only about 20 years. It is not the American tax structure alone that leads to substantial private investment. It is more generally the perceived responsibility to "give back" to an institution (and to come to the aid of the next generation of students) that prompts generous private contributions.

The reality is that there are enormous costs associated with profitable development operations and with the pursuit of grants and contracts from private foundations. Trained professionals are required to manage prospect lists, to monitor compliance and donor satisfaction, and to identify special interests compatible with university priorities. Leaders must make convincing cases that their universities have been key in improving the quality of the donor's life, either through the education received or through the extremely positive effect a research university exerts on the local community. In addition, many states strictly forbid state funds to be used for raising money, at the same time that donors wish their entire contributions to be allocated to their identified project or endowment. Often donors rebel at contributing to the costs of raising additional support for other purposes.

University leaders must also guard against the assumption that generous private donations relieve public sources of their responsibility to support higher education. Some enlightened state governments even supply a matching pool to encourage private donations, while promising that established revenue streams would be maintained irrespective of external funding success.

Increased reliance on the private sector for day-to-day operations demands close attention to the real rate of growth of revenue, and real returns lower than about 3 %, adjusted for inflation, mean financial trouble for any institution. American universities that are most financially secure are the private, highly recognized universities that have achieved net return above 5 % for the last decade. It is imperative therefore that if private-sector donations are to provide the margin of excellence that differentiates the best research universities from their peers that excellent financial management be secured for the university.

This requirement, in turn, affects university governance, with financial expertise and the capacity to make personal financial contributions becoming more highly sought characteristics of a good Board member than academic creativity. Management skills among academic leaders become vital, although the academic origins of most university leaders provide little focused training on each of the challenges to be encountered in these complex organizations. These administrators must not only manage day-to-day challenges, but must also resist system bureaucracy and constraints. And as focus moves away from major investment in front-line discovery, it becomes increasingly important for public research universities to resist levelling of complex higher education systems such that institutional mission becomes obscure and university aspirations erode to a common, mediocre level.

CONCLUSIONS

The American public research university faces new challenges characterized by more students, lower levels of state support, and more challenging goals associated with economic development. As is true of the missions they pursue, American public research universities are becoming more decentralized, more complex and more entrepreneurial. Diversification of revenue sources is becoming more important, and it is ever more critical that university administrators guard against loss of evident public purpose. In this environment, it is vitally important to maintain emphasis on the traditional functions of the public land-grant university: teaching and learning as life-long commitments, scholarship as a public trust, and full engagement with societal needs. The public research university must always pursue as its primary goal the formation of the next generation of scholars, leaders and innovators. The search for alternative sources of financial support must be related to these goals, which in turn must continue to reflect public purpose and an enduring commitment from the local or regional citizenry.

REFERENCES

Hearn, J. C. (2003). "Diversifying Campus Revenue Streams: Opportunities and Risks," American Council on Education, No. 309583, Washington D. C.
Duderstadt, J. J. and Womack, F. W. (2003). *The Future of the Public University in America. Beyond the Crossroads*. Johns Hopkins University Press, Baltimore.
North Carolina State University (1998-2002). *Annual Financial Reports*.

CHAPTER 15

Governance of U.S. Universities and Colleges

Frank H. T. Rhodes

THE PRINCIPLE OF INSTITUTIONAL GOVERNANCE

Patterns of governance in U.S. universities and colleges differ substantially in public (that is, state-supported or assisted) and private (that is, independently endowed or financed) institutions. But both patterns are based on a single assumption: universities and colleges are the beneficiaries of an unwritten social contract, under which they enjoy substantial institutional autonomy and broad academic freedom in exchange for social responsibility and public accountability. The role of governing boards is to oversee the balance reflected within that social contract. There are quite different patterns of governance and management in the growing number of "for profit" institutions, but I have not included these in the present paper.

Governing boards govern. They represent the ultimate legal authority of the institution. Their very titles reflect the extent and the dignity of their responsibility: they are variously described in different institutions as overseers, members of the corporation, members of the board of governors, regents or – more modestly, perhaps – members of the board of trustees. Whatever the name or title, there is no mistaking their level in the hierarchy of the institution. Regents, overseers, governors symbolize authority; boards of governors govern. This pattern is, of course, also found in Europe: in many British universities, for example, courts of governors represent the ultimate institutional authority.

In contrast, the academic leaders and administrative bodies of our institutions have inherited more modest titles from the medieval church, their ultimate ancestor. Consider the titles dean, provost, chancellor, council, congregation and, in Europe, rector: these are the titles, not of ultimate, but of intermediate, ecclesiastical authority, subservient to kings, popes, cardinals and bishops. Even the rare but grand title of "Rector magnificus", still used in some European universities, occupies an intermediate level within the traditional hierarchy. Medieval church leaders did not have universal authority; their charge was within the church, limited to the congregation of the faithful, to the community of believers, sharing a common faith and a common commitment and embodying common values. That same pattern persists, not only in ecclesiastical communities, but also in the universities that arose from them. Like churches, universities are seen as communities of shared values and common vocation, in which membership is voluntary.

For all their differences, which are substantial, governing boards of universities and colleges share this common authority of ultimate responsibility. University officers serve at the pleasure and implement the policies of their boards. But the board is not only the overseer of the community; it is also the guardian of the community. It is both the guarantor of the responsibility of the community and the custodian of the values of the community. The responsibilities of its dual role involve tension: its oversight role can be exercised effectively only so long as it is balanced by its fiduciary role. And this seeming paradox is resolved by the recognition that the university can effectively discharge its highest public obligation only to the extent that it is faithful to its own values of integrity, impartiality, rationality, excellence, openness and civility. To the extent that those scholarly virtues are eroded, its public service is reduced and the public's trust is diminished. Effective trusteeship involves this balance: overseer and fiduciary. The effective trustee is both. (Rhodes, 2001a and b.)

But oversight is not management. The overseer, the governor, sets the policy; the manager, the executive, implements the policy. The executive may, and generally does, develop and propose policy, but it is the governor who adopts and approves policy. Confusion between these two roles leads to frustration and mismanagement. The motto of good governance is "noses in; fingers out." Consider the trustee role in oversight. On the advice and with the support of the executive, the board of trustees:

- establishes the institution's mission and goals;
- ensures its effective management in achieving them;
- provides for the financial solvency and accountability of the institution;
- appoints and evaluates the senior leadership of the institution;
- assures appropriate procedure and due process within the institution;
- evaluates and perfects its own performance as a board.

I shall discuss each of these roles in detail below, but even to list them is to be reminded that such high responsibility can be discharged only with an appreciation of the complexity of the institution's mission, broad understanding of the issues it confronts, a familiarity with its life and work, an agreement with its values and an appreciation of its style.

All these are required in the exercise of oversight. But the trustee is more than an overseer; he or she is a fiduciary, a guardian, a protector, not only of the performance and accountability of the institution, but also of the institution itself and of the standards and values it embodies. As such the trustee may be required to defend the institution against external intervention or internal intrusion in the exercise of its scholarly function; may be required to affirm the proper autonomy of the institution or assert the authority of its president and faculty, to safeguard the interests and well-being of all its members and to uphold and nurture the qualities and values on which its continued life depends. And, since effective performance requires effective support, the fiduciary trustee will play an appropriate role in garnering support for the institution and its programmes.

This is a large task. The office of trustee is not a political prize to be gained, not a favour to be bestowed, not a reward to be won, though in practice it may be each of these. It is rather a public function to be performed, a societal obligation to be discharged, a vital trust to be fulfilled. To serve as a trustee is to undertake an essential public service, to facilitate a social compact, to ensure an essential partnership, to nurture a vital process in which knowledge is brought to bear in human affairs.

THE PRACTICE OF INSTITUTIONAL GOVERNANCE

This lofty conception of the role of trusteeship is one thing; its effective performance is another. Complaints about the effectiveness of boards on the one hand, and the role of particular trustees on the other, are common both within the campus community and beyond it. Such complaints, however, are nothing new. What is new is the increasing pressure upon boards of trustees and the added strain that this imposes on the overall governance of institutions.

There is no single factor that accounts for this increase in strain, but collectively a number of trends are adding to existing tensions. Among these are:

- *Increased size, range and complexity of institutions.* The challenges of governing a small liberal arts college are very different from the challenges of governing a complex research university with a range of professional schools, an assortment of health services and hospitals, a variety of outreach functions within the state and region, athletic teams of near-professional performance and other conspicuous elements. Each of these involves a range of institutional and public issues that increasingly demand attention from the university's governors. Though many of the issues are properly the concern of university management, rather than governance, the policies for dealing with them require thoughtful procedures and protocols.

- *Complex new partnerships.* The university's role in public outreach and engagement can be performed effectively only by the development of new partnerships. These will involve research partnerships with industry, service partnerships with various not-for-profit organizations and a variety of distance learning and continuing professional education programmes, which, though the parent institution will remain not-for-profit, may themselves be revenue-generating. The variety of new partnerships increases the complexity of both governance and management of the organization.

- *New demands for accountability* increase the task of governance, especially when they involve responsibilities that have long been the sole function of the board. There is, for example, pending legislation that would empower the U.S. Congress "to determine if colleges are raising their tuition and fees beyond reasonable rates." (McKeon, 2003.)

- *A host of new regulatory requirements,* from occupational safety and health to the Homeland Security Act, now pose operational obligations and responsibilities on the board and its officers. Nor are regulations such as these confined to non-academic aspects of the university. The question of the admission of international students, the pursuit of stem-cell research and the recent Supreme Court decision on affirmative action all require a high level of informed oversight of the university's educational and research practices.

- *Increased public expectations of the role of universities* have been accompanied by declining public confidence in their impartiality and cost-effectiveness. The irony of this situation is not lost on those who see the university primarily as an engine for economic growth and development. This responsibility is likely to influence the pattern of academic development, the balance of faculty appointments, the priority of certain fields of scholarship and the number and nature of university partnerships and affiliations. Each of these is likely to be complex, and some of them are likely to be highly controversial.

- *Commercialization* is becoming an increasing challenge for the universities, given the range of their scholarly products and the growing financial constraints under which they are forced to operate. Whether in athletics, patents, distance learning or professional services, the university inevitably acts in part as a commercial enterprise. Even such things as campus food services and dormitory accommodation raise financial issues. Derek Bok (2003) has recently written persuasively on the hazards of increasing commercialization, and the need for a responsible balance between covering costs and generating income through for-profit ventures. In contrast to those who see the hazards of commercialization, others see a need for the university to be run on more effective business lines and demand performance indicators and business audits (for an example of this in the U.K., see Willmott, 1995.) This issue will require continuing scrutiny and adjustment by board members.

- *New demands.* In addition to the issues raised above, increasing demands are placed on the universities to respond to pressing public issues. To name but one, unionization now involves not only members of the faculty on some campuses but also graduate teaching assistants, research assistants, residents and interns, lecturers, adjunct members of the faculty, and post-doctoral fellows. Traditionally few of these groups have been represented by unions, and the new relationship poses substantial challenges for faculty governance on the campus. Providing a reasonable framework within which discussions of this kind can take place is one of the tasks of the board of trustees.
- *Financial constraint* is likely to be added to other pressures upon the university, and to complicate the formidable task of governance in the light of these other requirements (see, for example, Yudoff, 2003.)

TRUSTEESHIP

Trusteeship in an Oversight Role

The oversight role of the board of trustees represents the fulfilment of its obligations as guardians of the social compact and public trust. In that sense a public board represents the public. Inevitably, its oversight will be limited, but it will be effective only to the extent that all its members have a sensitive understanding of the institution, and an appreciation of its missions, goals and standards.

- Appointment of the president. The oversight role of the trustees in most institutions is carried out primarily in the selection and appointment of the president of the university. This is perhaps the most important single role that the trustees play, for on this appointment depend the management and the effectiveness of many aspects of the institution's life and work. The president appoints the other officers of the university and, with the consent of the faculty, the deans of the several schools and colleges. It is this group of individuals who constitute the senior management of the university, and the success of their work is essential to the functioning of the institution.

- The board is also responsible for the regular evaluation of the president and for providing continuing support and counsel to him or her. Beyond that, the trustees are required to be the ultimate body in confirming the mission and goals of the institution, in approving the broad outlines of its programmes, and in assuring its effective management. This involves the following functions:

- Mission and goals of the university. The modern university is one of the most diffuse and free-ranging institutions of the Western world. It is opportunistic, expansionist, inclusive and entrepreneurial. Because of this, it needs some distinctive statement of mission and goals, not only to distinguish it from the 4,000 or so other institutions of higher education, but also to serve as a benchmark and point of reference against which its performance and future direction are measured. Though the president and faculty will have the major role in framing this statement of mission and goals, it is the trustees who must evaluate and endorse it (Morrill, 2003.)

- Ensuring effective management. The trustees do not manage the institution. But the trustees do assure themselves that the institution is effectively managed by others. This means that typically they have a voice in approving nominations made by the president for senior executive positions and that the executive officers of the university meet regularly with the trustees to provide information on progress within their various fields of responsibility.

- Oversight of the facilities, properties and grounds of the university. One of the significant responsibilities of board members in a major university is the oversight of the university's buildings, properties and facilities. On a large campus these represent a multi-billion dollar investment. The most direct way in which this is exercised is in the planning process for the development of the campus as a whole and in the oversight of the design, construction and maintenance of campus buildings and property. Typically the board will appoint a specialist committee for this task.

- Appropriate procedures. The trustees are responsible for assuring both themselves and the general public that the procedures adopted by the university are legitimate and appropriate. Procedures cover things as different as student admissions, on the one hand, or tenure requirements on the other. In all cases the task of the trustees is to ensure that the procedures are appropriate, are understood, implemented and publicized, and are capable of withstanding public scrutiny.

- Due process. It is the trustees' responsibility to ensure the availability of due process to members of the campus community. Some of the situations in which due process is required may be both visible and controversial. One thinks, for example, of cases involving dismissal for cause, denial of tenure, and similar actions. It is the trustees' responsibility to ensure that there are adequate mechanisms for appeal and review in such cases.

- Financial solvency. The trustees approve each annual budget, and they are responsible for the overall financial solvency of the university in the longer term. For this reason, in private institutions, the trustees may also be responsible for the overall management, rather than oversight, of the university's endowment. For the same reason, the audit committee of the board generally reports directly to the board, and not through the president of the university. In both public and private institutions the board is the final arbiter of budgetary and financial decisions. Though the deliberations of the board will generally involve only review of existing proposals from the president and his or her officers, the ultimate responsibility of the trustees for the financial well-being of the institution is a clearly accepted principle.

- Accountability. It is through the board that the institution is made accountable to the wider public. Although sometimes state legislatures intervene by inserting themselves in this linkage of accountability, it is through board review and oversight that the public is best assured that its investment in higher education is being responsibly managed and effectively used.

- Delegation. The board is clearly limited in the time it can devote to the affairs of the institution, making the delegation of appropriate authority to the president and his or her officers one of the primary tasks of the board. This delegation involves both specific delegation and implied delegation. It is generally understood, for example, without any formal delegation, that teaching is in the hands of faculty members. But occasionally in public universities, boards of trustees may assert a role in determining the curriculum. In one recent instance they intervened to decide whether credit should be given for ROTC – Reserve Officers' Training Corps – courses.

- The delegation in other cases may be more specific. Most boards, for example, on an annual basis delegate to the president of the university the authority to award degrees. Indeed the formula for the awarding of degrees often includes the phrase "By authority of the board of trustees and on the recommendation of the faculty, I do hereby admit you to the degree of...."

- Self-evaluation. Together with the responsibility to evaluate virtually everything connected with the university, the board has the responsibility to evaluate itself. Boards vary greatly in the quality of this evaluation. They are perhaps more likely to exercise it where they are not elected by the public nor appointed by the political process. But no matter how board members are selected, they have an obligation for self-evaluation. This assessment is of primary importance, because it involves not only the effectiveness of the officers and members of the board, but also the effectiveness of its procedures and meetings.

Fiduciary Role of the Trustee

In contrast to the supervisory role of the trustee, the fiduciary role involves the responsibility not only to oversee, but also to nurture and support the institution. In broad terms this means defending the autonomy of the institution against both external intrusion or assault and improper internal erosion; to nurture the community itself; to defend its values and standards; to support the president and uphold his or her authority; and to assist in garnering resources that make possible the appropriate pursuit of the university's activities.

The fiduciary role, though important, is far from automatic. It does not mean providing uncritical support for every activity, but rather ensuring, by understanding, questioning, challenge and inquiry, that the university enjoys the support and the freedom required to pursue its stated goals.

In private universities the importance of trustees in garnering financial support is greater than it is in public universities, although in both sectors trustees may play a useful role in relationships with local, state and federal authorities. The balance here is a delicate one, however; joint leadership of the president and the board chairman is essential in guaranteeing the success of this part of the board's responsibility, and in ensuring that it does not overwhelm the other responsibilities described above.

The Individual Trustee

Trusteeship is a public obligation. The ideal trustee will not only be informed, challenging, candid and inquiring but also committed to the institution and its values, disciplined in his or her role as a trustee, and – once persuaded that their performance is appropriate – supportive of the president and his or her officers.

In theory, a board made up of such individuals will function effectively, but much depends on the working partnership between the chairman of the board and the president of the university. Candour, frequent contact and personal trust between the president and the board chair are essential to ensure that there are no surprises, no secrets, no end runs, no short cuts, no inappropriate leaks, no sacred cows and no second-guessing by members of the board or the administration. The responsibility of board membership is a heavy one, and the demanding nature of the office can bring out both the best and the worst in those who serve.

PUBLIC AND PRIVATE UNIVERSITIES

Private universities account for some 70 % of the 2,173 non-profit, four-year institutions of higher education in the United States, but they enrol fewer than 40 % of all the students. They include a large number of small institutions, most of which are classified as colleges of one kind or another, rather than universities. A half-century ago, enrolment was more evenly divided between public and private universities.

But private universities occupy a position of special significance in the scheme of American higher education, not only because of their numbers, but also because of their influence. The Ivy League, MIT, Caltech, Stanford, Chicago and a handful of other comparable universities, exercise an authority out of all proportion to their size by providing benchmarks for programme quality to which all universities, both public and private, can aspire. The great flagship public universities – California, Michigan, Wisconsin and Illinois, for example – are institutions of broadly comparable stature, but the role of a small group of private universities as pacesetters for all universities should not be underestimated. Private universities also play a valuable role as a bulwark against the intrusion of others, whether from local, state or federal government or from industry, professional groups, unions or others, in the autonomy and work of higher education. It is more difficult for state government, for example, to exercise undue or improper influence on the affairs of public universities than it would be if private universities did not exist.

Perhaps the biggest practical difference between public and private universities is in their method of governance. The differences here are so significant that some critics see them as affecting the future of the institutions themselves. Private universities enjoy the leadership of boards whose members are generally self-appointed, though some may be elected by alumni, faculty or other groups, are typically large and generally have a majority of members who are alumni. A board of 60 or so would not be unusual in a major private university. The proceedings of these boards are generally private and their business is conducted in a strikingly apolitical atmosphere. Many such boards now deliberately build in membership so as to reflect the international nature of the alumni and faculty body and the professional breadth of the institution itself. These boards are generally very supportive of the institution and its officers and are broadly seen as very effective. They include respected leaders from every area of public life.

Public boards of trustees, in contrast, are generally appointed by the governor and/or the legislature of the state. In a few cases, they may be elected by the state's citizens. These boards are generally small, containing from eight to 12 members. They are not all dominated by alumni, though many of them tend to be. Their meetings are held in public, and they sometimes become very political in their activities. They vary greatly in their effectiveness, but they are broadly supportive of the institution and its constituencies. In some states individual universities are governed by their own governing boards; in others several campuses of a single university are grouped together under a single governing board. In still other cases, there is a statewide system of higher education, represented by a single board, and in still other cases, for example the University of California system, there are multiple universities within a single statewide system. This leads to great variety in the performance and effectiveness of boards, as well as in the autonomy of the institutions involved.

Two converging trends are likely to diminish the differences between the great flagship public research universities and their independent sister institutions, which Robert Zemsky has helpfully identified collectively as "medallion institutions". One of these trends is the pressure of the market, which will increasingly drive both public and private medallion institutions towards broadly similar ventures. The second trend is the steady diminution of the level of state support for public institutions, and especially for public medallion institutions.

As the state contribution declines, one might suppose that the level of state influence would also decline. Already at some of the medallion universities, more than half the buildings on campus have been constructed with private funding. Many of the leading public universities receive rather less than 20 % of their funding from the state government. In light of the declining state contribution, it may be asked whether the present pattern of governance for public universities is appropriate for the future. This question was faced in the mid-19th century by the founders of Cornell who, in exchange for some limited state support at what was created as, and still remains, a private institution, agreed to the inclusion on its board of a number of representatives of the state. These people include the governor of the State of New York, the temporary president of the Senate, and the Speaker of the Assembly, three trustees appointed by the governor, one trustee from the field of agriculture and two from the field of labour. The total board size is over 60, but arrangements such as this give the state an informed and influential voice on the board. The levels of tuition in the four contract colleges at Cornell, for example, are determined by the Cornell board of trustees, but are subject to formal approval by the State Legislature.

The situation at Cornell is unique and so is not likely to provide a precise model for other universities. Ezra Cornell, for example, agreed to give his endowment to create the university, only if the state would declare it the land grant institution. There was no public state university of New York in existence until 1948. Nor is the organizational balance within Cornell an appropriate model for the great public universities. There are 12 colleges at Cornell of which only four – Agricultural and Life Sciences, Human Ecology, Industrial and Labor Relations and Veterinary Medicine – are contract colleges, run with financial support from the state. The annual level of state support is some $134 million out of a total university annual operating budget of $2.1 billion. Students receive Cornell degrees, and faculty appointments, salaries, financial aid, and other matters are determined by the university. Although faculty members at other state university campuses are represented by faculty unions, there is no such union at Cornell.

The Cornell model, while not appropriate for every public university, does suggest a way in which states may choose to limit their present total authority over the governance of major public universities, while still retaining a major influence upon that governance. The recent decision of Miami University of Ohio to charge "private level tuition" and provide generous financial aid suggests another complementary direction of adjustment in the face of declining state support.

Because private boards of trustees are generally large, they typically meet only quarterly for one or two days, with much of the detailed work of the board delegated to committees. These generally include, for example, an executive committee and committees for state and federal relations, campus life, academic affairs, finance, investment, buildings and properties, development, nominating and governance, campus relations, compensation and other matters. Much of the work of the board between meetings is carried out by the executive committee, which typically holds monthly meetings.

In addition to this formal board structure, most of the constituent colleges of private universities and of some public universities have their own advisory boards and councils. The medical college at Cornell, for example, has a board of overseers of some 30 to 35 people, including some of the leading citizens of New York City. Most of these members are not graduates of the institution, but they play an increasingly important role in the life of the institution. Advisory committees for other colleges and in some cases for departments play corresponding roles.

CAMPUS GOVERNANCE

Effective governance within major American universities is not limited to the central governing board. It also extends down into the institution, with a variety of structures. The most significant of these is the governance system established by the faculty, with authority delegated by the board and/or the president. Generally speaking, faculty governance is based on the assumption of shared goals, values and interests and with the recognition that membership of the university carries both rights and responsibilities. Faculty participation in governance varies widely from place to place, from college to college and from institution to institution. Almost everywhere, however, there is a faculty governing body, typically referred to as a faculty senate or faculty council. This represents faculty members at large, and deals with the major policy questions. Typically it might be concerned with teaching terms, grading policies, and similar matters. Election to this central council or senate is generally conducted on a departmental or collegiate basis, so that it is broadly representative of faculty members across the institution.

Faculty governance is exercised at multiple levels. Each department, centre, school or college, for example, will have its own faculty governance structure, typically consisting of an executive committee responsible, under the dean, chair or director, for overall policy and performance. A principle of subsidiarity generally applies, so that decisions are most appropriately made at the lowest possible level. Thus decisions about the teaching strategy and programme in chemistry are properly made by the department rather than by the college or the university councils. Faculty governance is rarely simple, is frequently ponderous and is sometimes frustratingly ineffective. The degree of faculty participation may be low and variable. Overall, however, it has served the universities well, and it remains an essential factor in the vigour of university life. It is made more effective by the recognition that on various matters, faculty members and governing councils will have differing degrees of responsibility. Some items, for example, may be referred to the governing faculty simply for information, while others may involve more formal consultation and review. Still others may require approval. In each case it is important to recognize the division of responsibility.

Some matters involve multiple levels of faculty and broad responsibility. Thus a faculty appointment or tenure decision in, say, classics, will be developed within the classics department, but will typically be subject to confirmation by a college committee, a university-wide review committee, the president and the board of trustees.

Some recent writers have suggested that both faculty governance and faculty performance would be improved by the development of a Socratic oath, similar to the Hippocratic oath taken by members of the medical teaching faculty. (Rhodes, 2001c.) Others have urged that a social contract be developed. (Rosovsky, 2001.) This has proved to be a controversial and difficult question, but it is one that is not likely to go away and is one that may give some assurance of accountability, even as it improves teaching performance on campus.

On most campuses, university staff will also have a governing structure. This typically takes the form of a staff assembly, elected by staff members of the university so as to be broadly representative of the range of interests and concerns of the staff. Because a typical major university may have thousands of staff members, the pattern of governance is important. The staff assembly will typically elect its own chair and that person generally has access to the president. In the same way, the faculty will generally elect a dean of the faculty or a chair of the faculty senate who will also have access to the president. The issues discussed by the staff assembly might include benefits, security issues, parking and transportation, facilities and campus life. Again participation tends to be spotty, and some of the responsibilities of the staff assembly will be influenced or diminished to the extent that members of staff are unionized.

Student governance. Student governance typically involves the election of a university-wide student assembly. There may be separate assemblies for graduate and professional students. The range of issues typically reviewed by such assemblies includes such things as housing, campus life, athletics, student societies, health and safety, security, financial aid and comparable items. As in the case of faculty and staff governance, the leaders of the student assembly typically enjoy access to the president. The president or his or her representatives will generally address the assembly on an annual basis and be available for questioning. Representatives of the president's office will typically join the assembly at most of its meetings to provide whatever background information may be required.

CONCLUSION

All in all, university governance is complex, cumbersome and slow. Its results would rarely please an expert in efficiency, but the very nature of universities and the historical origins of faculty and student guilds indicate that a representative pattern of governance has served institutions well. While the present participatory system can undoubtedly be refined and improved, it is unlikely to be replaced soon by a more hierarchical corporate model, as some have advocated.

Yet university governance is unlikely to remain frozen in its present form. Its current variety suggests otherwise, as do the various trends and pressures described above. Indeed, it seems likely that these trends and pressures will require leadership and management at every level within the university to become more nimble, creative and effective. That itself will impinge on governance and will require new organizational arrangements. But the best universities are likely to remain communities of scholars whose members recognize common interests and shared concerns. That implies a high degree of both academic freedom and institutional autonomy, but the price of that is public accountability. It is the genius of the pattern of American university governance that, with all its imperfections, it has served to ensure and balance both.

REFERENCES

Bok, Derek (2003). *Universities in the Market Place*, Princeton University Press, Princeton and Oxford.

McKeon, Howard P. (2003). "Controlling the Price of College," *Chronicle of Higher Education*, July 11, p. B 20.

Morrill, Richard L. (2003). "The Overlapping Worlds of Academic Governance", *Trusteeship*, Vol. ll, No. 1, pp. 29-32.

Rhodes, Frank H.T. (2001a). "The University at the Millennium: Missions and Responsibilities of Research Universities," in Hirsch, W.Z. & Weber, L.E. (eds), *Governance in Higher Education, The University in a State of Flux*, Economica, London, Paris, pp. 3-14.

Rhodes, Frank H.T. (2001b). "The Glion Declaration 2000: University Governance at the Crossroads," in. Hirsch, W.Z. & Weber, L.E. (eds), *Governance in Higher Education, The University in a State of Flux*, Economica, London, pp. 195-204.

Rhodes, Frank H.T. (2001c). *The Creation of the Future*, Cornell University Press, Ithaca.

Rosovsky, Henry (2001). "Some Thoughts About University Governance," in Hirsch, W.Z. and Weber, L.E. (eds), *Governance in Higher Education, The University in a State of Flux*, Economica, London, pp. 94-104.

Hirsch, Werner Z. & Weber, Luc E. (eds), (2001). *Governance in Higher Education, The University in a State of Flux*, Economica, London, Paris.

Willmott, H. (1995). "Managing the Academics: commodification and control in the development of university education in the U.K.", *Human Relations*, 48, pp. 993-1027.

Yudoff, Mark G. (2003). "The Purgatory of Public Universities," *Trusteeship*, Vol. ll, No. 2, pp. 8-12.

CHAPTER 16

Governance in European Universities

Marcel Crochet

INTRODUCTION

The purpose of the present chapter is simply to suggest ideas about university governance in a time of change; it is a follow-up to that of Frank Rhodes (chapter 15) within the European context. There is no unique or ideal system of governance in higher education; it would otherwise have been discovered a long time ago. Still, one may evoke a number of guidelines which constitute the backbone of leadership in modern universities. In the first section, we state that change in a time of crisis requires management. In the second section, we list areas where it seems indispensable. In the third section, we put forward a common structure in which leadership may be efficiently exercised. Finally, we discuss some problems and challenges which such a structure might be confronted with in European universities.

UNIVERSITIES AND CHANGE

Today's European universities have little in common with those of the 1950s. While their central missions of teaching and research have undergone considerable change, they are also concerned about their social impact and their role as an agent of influence and progress. It is generally agreed that most universities have chosen Whitehead's thoughts as a vision for today's higher education. In his 1929 book entitled *The aims of education* (1929), he proposed ideas which today constitute the backbone of our university system. For Whitehead, the future of a nation lies in the narrow bond between its progressive elements of all kinds, in such a way that education influences the public place and vice versa. Imagination is at the core of Whitehead's vision of the university. "The university imparts information, but it imparts it imaginatively. At least, this is the function which it should perform for society. A university which fails in this respect has no reason for existence." Imagination loses its meaning when it is not accompanied by realization and thus transformation.

Some of the major transformations universities have been going through were well summarized in Frank Rhodes' paper on "The university at the millennium" (2001).

- Quite fortunately, the number of students increased considerably over the last 50 years. The level of education is definitely recognized as a key to personal development and to qualified employment. It is a major victory, but only part of the battle has been won. Investigations show, in fact, that the student population in universities does not reflect the social structure of society; sons and daughters of poorly educated people tend to reproduce the same family pattern. Innovative strategies are needed to solve such a crucial problem and to confirm the role of universities as a fantastic instrument of social mobility.

- "Universities have become the essential gateway to and foundation of every major profession" (Rhodes, 2001). Universities must be attentive to new needs of commercial, non-commercial and social enterprises, offer new programmes, promote adult education and reorientation. They should, in that respect, avoid Peter Drucker's reflection that "when a subject becomes totally obsolete, we make it a required course". In particular, universities must realize that students' expectations have also changed over the years: active learning, information technologies, multidisciplinary vision, connection with contemporary questions are today's ingredients of teaching.

- In Europe, universities are the major providers of fundamental research while modern technology and applied science rely on its discoveries. Since the mid-80s, European programmes, research contracts with companies, spin-off incubators have become efficient actors of economic recovery. Some regional applied research centres are presently financed by European programs.

- "The university and its stakeholders" has become a most appropriate expression for describing the new association between its environment and the university which opens the doors of its ivory tower and its environment. Quite a number of institutions have created new campuses in Europe over the last decades. In order to be supported by the surrounding regions (whose citizens, after all, pay taxes to finance the university), they need to invent with them new links and to become a source of imagination for a better society. Universities are also more and more concerned with social services. Typical examples are health networks associated with university hospitals, continuing education for schoolteachers, orientation centres for secondary schools.

- Over the last five years, the challenge for European universities has gained in intensity due to its own collective momentum: the Bologna process requires a major commitment in untraditional matters. The emerging student and academic mobility, systematic evaluations, accreditation procedures will reveal their quality. While competing for the best students and the best professors, universities will need to cooperate and make difficult choices, because they cannot be good at everything. Simultaneously, research trends proper to the 6th European Framework programme require new associations.

Initiative, analysis, imagination: such are the keywords for the moving university today. How is it going to cope in the long run with such transformations? Frank Rhodes rightly observes that "in spite of these major changes in responsibility, membership and complexity, the university has shown almost no change in its organization, management and governance, and only modest change in its teaching style". The matter is complicated, because one should simultaneously remember Whitehead's (1929) warning that "the combination of imagination and learning normally requires some leisure, freedom from restraint, freedom from harassing worry, some variety of experiences, and the stimulation of other minds diverse in opinion and diverse in equipment".

CHANGE, PROGRESS AND MANAGEMENT

Quite clearly, the university is a world of increasing complexity; this perception is confirmed by a number of qualified staff who have been serving the university for several decades. Year after year a faster rate is imposed in order to meet new requirements. The Bologna process is not going to make things any easier: deans and department heads are at present elaborating future programmes, promoting mobility, preparing joint degrees. Enterprises under such pressure would undoubtedly request the help of business consultants, but everyone knows the distance between their culture and that of the university, which faces a number of challenges proper to higher education. Still, it is worthwhile to itemize a number of topics which should undoubtedly require special attention from large research university managers.

- *Human resources.* Most European universities expanded rapidly in the late 60s and early 70s. Thirty tears later, they suffer a major personnel rotation with its advantages (lower age range, new ideas, new disciplines) and the associated disadvantages (discontinuity, loss of expertise). Universities compete for the best academics, with the new and welcome dimension of European mobility. Recruitment within the present decade undoubtedly constitutes the major factor that will determine the future of the university. Young candidates are eager to know about career and promotion policies, salary scales, quality evaluation and incentives of various sorts. Simultaneously, information technologies have deeply modified the structure of administrative staff; in particular, its expected managerial ability increases year after year.

- *Change.* The last 50 years have been marked by major scientific discoveries, interdisciplinary approaches, new competence. The university needs to adapt its response to these demands: new degrees, continuing education, creation and deletion of departments. The management of change is difficult in universities where quality and scholarship are often associated with secular traditions. Traditional departments are not keen to depart from established structures or to accept personnel and funding reallocations for emerging disciplines or for new degrees. Change is unproductive unless it is accepted by all; its implementation is difficult and requires the highest care from university managers.

- *Strategic vision.* Change should not be the fruit of impulse. On the contrary, it should result from a strategic vision which has become indispensable over recent decades. While the promotion of such a vision belongs to the university leaders, it should be conceived by an appropriate reflection group; it should also be shared by the entire community. Today, the context is changing so fast that the university needs permanent study groups to evaluate the environment, to perceive developments in other countries, to be sensitive to social needs, to measure evolving employment structures and requirements. A good example is pedagogy: for centuries many European universities have relied on passive learning, which does not meet contemporary educational needs; lifelong education requires students to learn how to learn while they attend the university. The transformation of pedagogy in the university system precisely requires a shared strategic vision of its future. Another example concerns research: multidisciplinary work, work in large teams, international cooperation are relatively recent trends which need to be firmly implemented in the university system. Within the new context of the Bologna process, institutions must adopt new strategies if they wish to remain research universities.

- *Long-term budgeting and fund-raising.* It is true, however, that financial constraints make it very difficult for universities to implement their strategic vision which should lean on available resources. Long-term financial predictions are difficult to elaborate; in most European (public) universities, revenue depends upon government allocation which varies with time, with the economy and with the political situation. University managers need to constantly evaluate financial perspectives in order to frame their projects within an accessible perimeter. Additionally, as in the United States, universities will not be able to go past basic government expectations and show a difference unless they can count on the support of private and industrial sponsors. Such support is impossible to raise unless university management adopts a fund-raising policy and establishes a relationship with potential donors.

- *Communication.* Large universities are communities of several thousand people who should ideally share the vision adopted by the management. It is a considerable challenge: the percentage of executives is higher than in any commercial enterprise (academics versus total), while most of them have their own ideas regarding the future of the university. It is recognized that faculty adhesion to our objectives is indispensable, but, according to James Duderstadt (2001), "faculty loyalties are generally first to their scholarly discipline, then to their academic unit, and only last to their institution". He correctly observes that "while faculty members are – and should always remain – the cornerstone of the university's academic activities, they rarely have deep understanding or will accept the accountability necessary for the many other missions of the university in modern society". University management needs to organize communication with the various components of the university: professors, researchers, staff, unions and students. Inappropriate communication may be the cause of failure of a well-designed strategy while "victory will be given to the one whose troops are gathered around a common objective" (Sun Tzu, 1972).

- *Administration.* The administrative staff is the keystone of university management. Amateurish administrative practices are incompatible with the development of modern universities that manage the careers of several thousand people and deal with considerable amounts of money. A primary task of management is to organize the administration, to recruit the best staff and to control quality. A university is indeed a very intricate mechanism which cannot possibly function without smooth and accountable procedures.

GOVERNANCE AND LEADERSHIP

We have just evoked a number of items which require special care at a time of change. While the natural trend in large human enterprises is to reproduce traditional patterns, including quality, a lack of consideration for these items means a lack of response to new demands in a changing environment. The only response is leadership; it must however be practised with care and adapted to the specific world of higher education: the exercise of authority without a shared vision is indeed generally disastrous. The wealth of a university is measured in terms of values and not capital; any progress contributing to values is equivalent to capital gains in a commercial enterprise. Leadership requires a simple and efficient system of governance. While a variety of systems exist, depending upon the country as well as the university, it is worth mentioning a few simple and maybe idealized trends proper to European universities which may lead to efficient leadership.

- *The Administrative Board (Board of Directors, Board)* is the supreme body of the university; it holds the final responsibility with respect to the State and other stakeholders. The Board appoints and dismisses the upper executives of the university, possibly at the suggestion of the Rector (or President), the Executive Board or the Academic Senate. The Board is primarily concerned with the strategic vision of the university which it defines with the help of the Rector and its Executive Board. It accepts investments and annual budgets based on long-term budgeting capabilities. In particular, the Board exercises control over the execution of the budget and its allocation to various items. The Board is in charge of salary policies although, in many European countries, they are defined by the State. It is responsible for quality control and is kept informed about its results. The number of Directors should not be too large. In addition to a limited number of top executives of the university, the Board should be made of representatives of stakeholders: region and State, social organizations, companies (future employers) and also some experts in educational development. Students are members of the Administrative Board in a number of countries; we will discuss that matter in the next section.
- *The Rector (President, Vice-chancellor)* is the upper executive of the university. He or she reports to the Board for the execution of its strategic vision and its decisions. By analogy with commercial enter-

prises, some consider the Rector as the Chief Executive Officer of the university who assumes the link between the university as a whole and the Administrative Board. It is preferable however to view him as the prime minister who enjoys a large independence and an ample delegation for the execution of his tasks. He chairs the Executive Board and chooses his collaborators. He is responsible for the interface between the university and the State and other institutions of higher education. Among his many duties, the Rector keeps permanently informed about the evolution of higher education and proposes strategic visions to the Administrative Board. He promotes innovation in the university, generates new ideas and evaluates the possibility of their materialization. He keeps up a permanent contact with Faculty Deans and Department Chairmen regarding the implementation of the strategic vision and university policies.

- *The Executive Board (Rectorate, Presidency)* supports the Rector, who is its chairman, and helps him to achieve his task. It is composed of a number of close collaborators (vice-rectors, vice-presidents ...) with special assignments: budget, finances and staff; student affairs; academic affairs; research and other matters that deserve delegation and special care, such as communication or pedagogy. The Executive Board, which should not be too large, has an essential role and needs to show full solidarity with the Rector. Most (if not all) of its members should be selected by the Rector who, in a way, makes up his government. The Executive Board prepares new policies while staying in touch with Faculties and Departments.

- *The Academic Senate (Academic Council)* is the legislative body of the university for academic and student affairs. Depending upon the institution, it is composed of professors, students, representatives of personnel and possibly deans or representatives of the Executive Board. The role of the Academic Senate is essential as its approval is needed for the implementation of university policies. Once again, no step forward is possible without a shared vision of the future. To that effect, links need to be maintained between the Administrative Board and the Senate, either through the Rector or the Chairman of the Board.

- *Faculties and Departments* constitute the core of the university. Being responsible for the primary missions of the university, i.e. teaching and research, they need to act with a large degree of autonomy. It is not easy to propose limits between centralization and decentralization, which vary from country to country. The best approach seems to implement the principle of subsidiarity (see e.g. Weber, 2001): upper bodies should not intervene as long as Faculties and Departments can perform their mission and be loyal to the vision proposed by the Administrative Board and the Rector. Decisions which engage the future, such as the designation of new professors, the enlargement of staff or the opening of new study programmes must remain in the hands of the Rector or of the Administrative Board.

PROBLEMS AND CHALLENGES

In principle at least, such a simple system of governance should allow universities to evolve and to be responsive to change in society. However university administrators know that nothing is simple in higher education: any change creates difficulties, problems to solve or, more positively, challenges to overcome. Let us briefly consider a few of these challenges, each of which would require a deeper analysis.

- *The university and the State.* Most European universities are financed by the State; even those that enjoy "private" status are often subsidized. The State of course does not limit its intervention to finances: it determines the educational structures, the range of degrees and sometimes the contents of the programmes. In some universities, the State appoints the members of the Administrative Board and even the professors (proposed by the Board or the Rector). Major reforms such as the implementation of the Bologna process require fundamental legal modifications which may not leave to universities the degree of independence they need to meet new demands. In a recent article, the French newspaper *Le Monde* (2003) quotes a university president claiming that "our autonomy only exists on paper. In fact, we live within a complicated system of guardianship by the government", while another says that "the State should have a regulating role, which means that it should not manage decisions of every university." Quite clearly, "the lack of flexibility in the management of budgetary resources, legal constraints or else the absence of human resource management limit the room for manœuvre of universities." The implementation of new ideas in large universities is incompatible with intrusive legal systems which seriously limit their degree of autonomy. Still, the government pays the bill. It will be essential in the future to define the type of freedom and independence which governments should leave to universities as long as they comply with global perspectives and accept financial and quality control.
- *Students and management.* Students are the major stakeholders of the university; as such, they have been members for many years of a

number of committees which are directly concerned with student life: course evaluation, transformation and creation of study programmes, social subsidies, organization of academic life. A more recent trend, which is a legal requirement in several countries, is to include student representatives in organs at all levels of the university, such as the Administrative Board. It is *a priori* difficult to accept that young and often inexperienced students will, within the Administrative Board, appoint higher executives or new professors, or else decide on the budget of the various faculties. However, once they respect the necessary discretion on personal, financial or strategic matters, it is positive for the university to display to students the clarity of its decisional process and to explain the meaning of its decisions. Students need to be trained to exercise management: a good practice would be to introduce new student-partners of the Board to the workings of the university and its challenges. A potential danger is for the Board to deviate from its core business and to be involved in political confrontations which are proper to the student movement. Student participation seems to be very efficient in a number of countries (in Scandinavia, in particular); they should inspire universities which are new to such policies.

- *Election vs. appointment.* It is generally recognized that modern universities need to adopt forms of governance that allow its executives to assume true leadership. Prevailing theories of management do not favour, however, the election of executives at essentially all levels of the university, from basic research units up to the Rector. Still, the election system, which was adopted in universities when they were born, is alive and well. It is doubtful that those who favour appointment against election will soon prevail, although they have a point: in hard times affected by change, how can one possibly govern along a strong political line assumed by the Administrative Board or other upper levels, while being indebted to the electoral basis and meeting them daily? Proponents of the election system claim however that being elected is an essential guarantee of credibility within the university system. It is obvious that change is not for tomorrow, but that clarity would help. An elaborate list of duties, responsibilities and power in the hands of the elected person, together with a description of the stakes would undoubtedly lead voters to choose the right person for an appropriate leadership at times of crisis.

- *Clash of visions.* Universities have gained the conviction that they should open up to their stakeholders, with particular attention to the world of companies and potential employers of its students. The presence of their representatives on the Administrative Board is extremely useful, bringing together a new approach to management and the wish of well defined objectives which may sometimes be lacking in higher education. However, while enterprises have their own approach to management, universities cultivate secular and well respected views on teaching and research which may not be in line with the former. Once again, the only way to join forces that have ignored each other for so long seems to be to explain the university, its vision and its values.

CONCLUSION

There is no unique way to govern a large research university. It obviously needs professional management with the help of rather simple structures, if it wishes to meet new demands and future challenges. However management is not incompatible with the values of humanism and education for all, a concept which higher education has cultivated for so many centuries. On the contrary, it should be considered as an efficient instrument of leadership and progress.

REFERENCES

Crochet, M. (this book). "Social Diversity in Research Universities", in Duderstadt, J.J. & Weber, L.E. (eds), *Reinventing the Research University*, Economica, London.

Duderstadt, J. J. (2001). "Fire, ready, aim!", in Hirsch, W.Z. & Weber, L.E. (eds), *Governance in higher education, the university in a state of flux*, Economica, London, pp. 26-51.

Le Monde (2003). "A la veille de la rentrée, les universités réclament plus d'autonomie", October 10.

Rhodes, F. H. T. (2001). "The University at the Millennium", in Hirsch, W.Z. & Weber, L.E. (eds), *Governance in higher education, the university in a state of flux*, Economica, London, pp. 3-14.

Rhodes, F. H. T. (this book). "Governance of U.S. Universities and Colleges", in Duderstadt, J.J. & Weber, L.E. (eds), *Reinventing the Research University*, Economica, London.

Sun Tzu (1972). *L'art de la guerre*, Flammarion, Paris

Weber, L.E. (2001). "Critical University Decisions and their appropriate makers: some lessons from the economic theory of federalism", in Hirsch, W.Z. & Weber, L.E. (eds), *Governance in higher education, the university in a state of flux*, Economica, London, pp. 79-93.

Whitehead, A. N. (1929). *The aims of education*, Williams and Norgate, London.

PART V

• • • • • • • • • • • • •

Conclusion

CHAPTER 17

Challenges and Possible Strategies for Research Universities in Europe and the United States

Luc E. Weber and James J. Duderstadt[1]

The Glion IV Colloquium brought together university leaders from Europe and the United States to share their perspectives concerning the future of the research university. Although originally proposed as a workshop to "reinvent the university", there was general agreement that, as social institutions, universities have been quite remarkable in both their resilience and their capacity to adapt to changing social conditions in the past, and that there was every reason to expect that they will continue to do so in the future. Hence the discussion focused more on the reaffirmation of those traditional values and roles that have made the university such an enduring force in western culture and understanding the challenges, opportunities and responsibilities that would demand further change in the years ahead. While recognizing the unique geopolitical circumstances that would shape the strategies of particular institutions, there were several common themes that emerged from the conversations, as well as a number of suggested approaches to developing institutional strategies and action agendas.

1 We wish to thank Professor J. F. Grin, from the University of Geneva, and Mr. Gerry Taggart, from the Higher Education Funding Council for England, who took extensive notes of the debates and made useful proposals for the issues addressed in this conclusion. We are also grateful to our colleagues Frank Rhodes, Robert Zemsky, Howard Newby, and Jakob Nuesch, who made valuable comments on an early draft of the conclusion. However it is also important to note that the ideas developed in this conclusion, although largely derived from the presentations and discussions of the Glion IV Colloquium, are the responsibility of the authors.

THREATS AND CHALLENGES, OPPORTUNITIES AND RESPONSIBILITIES

As social institutions, universities are subject to the same powerful economic, social and technological forces driving change in the rest of our world. The emergence of a global, knowledge-driven economy has intensified the need for nations to provide advanced educational opportunities for a substantial proportion of their workforce, thereby adding the burdens of massification to a public funding base already stressed by the rapidly escalating costs of quality education and scholarship. The learning characteristics of the digital generation of young students, coupled with the higher education needs of adults forced to adapt to the ever-changing demands of the high-performance workplace, are compelling universities to explore new learning paradigms such as inquiry-based, interactive learning and lifelong educational opportunities.

Demographic change is also driving a major transformation in the need for and character of higher education. The increasing mobility of populations is changing radically the ethnic composition of regions (e.g., the growth of Latina and Asian populations in the southwestern United States or the immigration of east and central Europeans, as well as Africans, into the European workforce) as well as creating new minority concentrations that are all too frequently under-served with educational opportunities. Despite the growing needs for advanced education, an ageing population in both the United States and Europe seems increasingly reluctant to spend tax funds on the necessary investment in higher education in preference to other priorities such as health care, personal security, and tax relief.

The exponential evolution of information and communications technologies has become another disruptive force, driving rapid, profound and unpredictable change in social institutions such as universities. Digital technology is transforming all aspects of the university: its activities (teaching, research, service), its organization (academic structure, faculty culture, financing and management), and its environment. Although most Glion IV participants believe the research university will continue to exist in much its present form in the near term, meeting the challenge of emerging competitors in the marketplace will likely demand significant changes in how we teach, how we conduct research and how our institutions are financed. Over the longer term, Moore's Law promises a more radical transformation of the university.

Intellectual change is also an important force, as information-rich disciplines such as biomedical sciences and earth systems science compete with reductionist disciplines such as physics and mathematics for priority and support. Both the complexity of contemporary research problems and the expense of experimental facilities are driving scholarship increasingly toward interdisciplinary teams of investigators supported by international scientific facilities (e.g., the Large Hadron Collider at CERN and the South Pole station).

These social, technological and intellectual forces are creating powerful market forces, both challenging the traditional models of the university and stimulating the appearance of new competitors such as for-profit and cyber-space universities. The emergence of global markets is creating more transparency and increasing competition among both institutions and national systems. Today universities are challenged to better position themselves in this marketplace by becoming more visible and competitive, focusing on their core competencies while outsourcing other activities through alliances, similar to the strategies adopted in the business sector. This profiling of institutions raises a number of strategic issues for university leaders, such as the type of research (basic or applied), the focus of research (physical sciences, life sciences, social sciences), the relative priority given research relative to teaching, the priorities among various levels of education (bachelor, doctoral, professional), the pedagogical philosophy (teaching pushed or learning pulled), the character of the curriculum (traditional liberal arts or career-focused), and the method of delivery (campus-based or distance learning).

Research universities face a particular challenge in acquiring the resources necessary for quality teaching and scholarship. Public budgets are increasingly strained by priorities such as the health-care requirements of an ageing population, the burden of increasingly unsustainable social services, the need to replace ageing transportation and urban infrastructure, and the new security demands of an increasingly dangerous world. Many citizens are becoming increasingly individualistic, stressing the priorities of private needs of a market-driven economy rather than addressing the public needs of the general population. As a consequence, the resources available to most universities simply cannot keep pace with the rising costs of excellence in higher education or the rising expectations of the societies they serve.

Perhaps even more fundamentally, there has been an erosion in the sense of trust that has existed among public authorities, the general population, and the university. Rather than viewing higher education as an investment one generation makes to benefit the next, governments are increasingly holding universities accountable for addressing utilitarian objectives such as workforce skills or economic development. The climate of increased competition in the private sector, induced by tight public budgets, the lack of transparency of decisions made by universities, their great difficulty in communication with the public, all undermine a sense of societal trust of the university, thereby eroding the autonomy so necessary to adapt to change and perform its fundamental roles by challenging existing premises and creating knowledge for the future.

SUGGESTIONS, SCENARIOS AND STRATEGIES

History has shown that procrastination and inaction are dangerous approaches to an era of change. Burying one's head in the sand and hoping threats will disappear can lead to disaster. How, then, should the research university respond? How should it plan for the future? What actions should it take? The Glion IV Colloquium established that while there is considerable agreement about the forces driving change in higher education both in the United States and Europe, there are as many different approaches to developing strategies and actions as there are participants in the conversation.

Yet some strategies seem universally compelling. For example, the climate of increased competition will demand that universities specialize more in what they can do best, striving to excellence in more specific niches. The days of the truly comprehensive research university, the effort to be all things to all people, may be coming to an end. Yet the character of research universities demands they maintain a certain breadth in basic and applied research as well as in postgraduate education. Research universities face the threat of losing students to those institutions that focus more on serving the short-term requirements of the labour market or losing research funding to specialized institutes that focus on a particular area.

Beginning with the Basics: Values, Roles and Missions

It is during a time of challenge and transformation that it is most essential for universities to reconsider and reaffirm those key values, roles, and missions that should be protected and preserved even while other characteristics may change. For example, how should research universities set priorities among their various roles such as education of the young, the preservation of culture, scholarship and basic research, serving as a social critic, and applying knowledge to serve society? Which values and principles of the university should be reconsidered? While most would regard values such as academic freedom, openness, critical thinking and a commitment to excellence as invariant, what about other practices such as the guild character of faculty governance or the unassailable security provided by academic tenure?

In particular, universities should reconsider their most important roles of producing and transmitting knowledge, that is research and teaching, in terms of service to society. For example, what is the right balance between curiosity-driven research, driven by the interest of the faculty, and more applied research addressing key social priorities? To be sure, there is ample evidence to suggest that much of curiosity-driven research builds the knowledge base that later leads to practical applications. Yet in the short term, it is sometimes difficult to make the case for basic research in appealing for public support. Similarly, the value of the liberal education that universities provide in the academic disciplines is sometimes at odds with the career-oriented education sought by students, parents and governments. Public demands for accountability are increasing, tending to push towards applied research and workforce education. Yet the unique value of the research university arises from a balance between basic and applied research, just as it does between a liberal education and professional training.

Here the capacity of research universities to position themselves in the evolving global market for students, faculty, resources and prestige by focus-ing on where they can achieve true excellence becomes important. The mis-sions of the top research universities such as Oxford, Cambridge, the Federal Institutes of Technology in Zurich and Lausanne, the Catholic Universities of Leuven and Louvain-la-Neuve, the Universities of Geneva, Leiden, Stras-bourg, Twente or the Karolininska Institute in Europe, or Harvard, MIT, Stanford, and the Universities of California, Michigan, and Wisconsin in the United States tend to be determined primarily by tradition, grass-roots faculty interests or the serendipity of opportunity, rather than by any general institution-wide strategy. Their success can be attributed to a comparatively favourable environment regarding funding, relative autonomy from govern-ment intrusion and the ability to compete successfully for the best students and faculty. These factors allowed them to compete effectively for research funding, thereby reinforcing their established excellence and benefiting from a "virtuous cycle".

The challenging question today is whether such a laissez-faire approach at the level of leadership of the institution will be sufficient in the years ahead to sustain quality in the face of the more intense competition arising from other institutions that seek to better profile and position themselves to respond to the changing marketplace. Clearly the rising costs of excellence in teaching and scholarship will pose formidable challenges to most research universities. It was the sense of the Glion IV participants that most research universities will be compelled to think and act more strategically, to rigo-rously analyse their strengths and weaknesses, as well as the threats and opportunities before them.

For example, in Europe, since the Bologna process will result in a clearer separation between general studies and more advanced studies at the post-graduate level, research universities should consider whether they should concentrate more of their resources on research-led teaching at the masters and Ph.D. level, reducing their activities at the bachelor-degree level to those necessary to meet regional needs. Such a strategy would result in a decrease in total enrolments, but it would also free faculty resources to increase the number of specialized or interdisciplinary programmes and improve the quality of teaching. Other universities might choose instead to emphasize more undergraduate or professional education.

Research universities should also assess whether they can achieve a critical mass of intellectual resources in the disciplines they offer, since this is both a necessary condition for quality and for an efficient use of resources. If this is not the case in certain disciplines, they should consider other alternatives such as discontinuing academic programmes, developing alliances with other institutions to achieve the necessary critical mass in other areas (as is happening in the French-speaking part of Switzerland), merging with or perhaps taking over other institutions. In other words, the competitive forces on higher education may drive the same phenomenon of restructuring we have seen in other economic sectors such as banking and transportation, complete with mergers and acquisitions and the appearance of new competitors and possibly even the demise of some established institutions.

Institutional vs. System Strategies

Here it is important to distinguish between the challenges and options available to a single institution and those facing a higher-education system at the regional, national (state), or continental (E.U. or U.S.) level. As an increasingly competitive marketplace demands mission profiling and positioning at the institution level, governments should demand greater diversification and hierarchy of their system of universities. Clearly all universities should not aspire to become world-class research universities, although many will continue to do so. A robust national system will require regional institutions providing undergraduate and professional education to regional workforces, an array of specialized institutions addressing particular needs (teacher preparation, workforce training, lifelong learning), in addition to research universities with competitive capabilities in research and graduate education. While such hierarchies may conflict with the egalitarian views of many societies (not to mention the political ambitions of local government officials), the reality is that both the available resource base and regional/nation needs can justify only a limited number of research universities.

In the United States, different regions (states) rely on different mechanisms to encourage and enforce differentiation. In some, such as California North Carolina, and Ohio, there are well-defined "master plans" that determine the missions of various institutions. Perhaps the best known is the California Master Plan, which dictates that the top 12.5 % of secondary school graduates will have the opportunity to attend the University of California with its nine (soon to be ten) research university campuses, while the next third attend the campuses of the California State University system, which has thus far been discouraged from launching Ph.D. programmes or major research efforts. The rest of the population is served by local two-year community colleges, with the opportunity to transfer into four-year institutions. Although now challenged by changing demographics and economic base, the California system has been remarkable over the past half-century in building perhaps the world's greatest public research university, while providing educational opportunities on a mass scale for Californian citizens.

In sharp contrast are those regions, such as Michigan and Texas, that rely almost entirely on the marketplace to drive differentiation. Here individual institutions are coordinated only very loosely by state-wide policies or governance and instead encouraged to compete vigorously for student, faculty, resources and political favour. Institutional ambitions to expand missions in inappropriate directions are constrained by the marketplace and the availability of additional resources. Interestingly enough, this entirely market-driven approach has proven to be just as capable as the centralized planning models in other states, and perhaps even more cost-effective.

One final characteristic of the United States system is important to note: the strong role played by private universities, those with limited public support and independent of government authority. In part because of historical factors, the United States has been fortunate in the growth of a large number of elite private research universities, including several that rank among the finest universities in the world (e.g., Harvard, Yale, Princeton, Stanford, MIT, Caltech). Although these receive only modest direct support from public tax dollars (e.g., through research grants, student financial aid, or subsidy of professional programmes such as medical education), they do benefit enormously from generous tax policies that encourage strong private giving and the growth of assets such as endowments. These private universities not only provide strong and usually beneficial competition with public institutions, but they also provide a resilience to American higher education unmatched in other nations.

Clearly an important part of the strategy in building competitive research university systems in Europe will involve some consideration of stimulating similar private, largely government-independent, research universities. There is a sense that, at some level, the privatization of higher education in Europe is already occurring, but current cultural resistance to student fees and existing tax policies keep this at a low level. Indeed, one of our participants suggested that perhaps the best way to drive rapid change in European higher education would be to encourage several of the leading American private universities (e.g., Harvard, Stanford, or MIT) to open satellite campuses in Europe, charging the same fees, but delivering the same high quality and reputation of academic programmes as they offer in the United States!

While the successful implementation of the Bologna process and the rightly envisaged creation of a European Research Council will lead to greater market mobility and competitiveness within Europe, there were concerns expressed by Glion IV participants that these could also create forces driving homogenization of institutions. Some even suspected the Bologna process might be a Trojan horse for the larger agenda of European political integration. To many, the concept of institutional "diversity" is a euphemism for "hierarchy" that still represents a taboo for many faculty members and political leaders. Yet there was a sense that in an environment characterized by limited public resources, increasing demands for accountability in addressing social priorities (e.g., massification, workforce training), and intense market competition, research universities could survive only in highly diverse and hierarchical university systems. While it may be difficult politically to achieve a planned differentiation of university missions, market forces will continue to demand institutional diversity.

The Changing Nature of Education and Scholarship

The changes in the nature of scholarship, from disciplinary to multi/inter-trans/cross-disciplinary, from specialization and reductionism to information-rich sciences and complexity, from basic to applied scholarship, will likely reshape the intellectual architecture of the university as well as its organizational structure. Perhaps it is time that research universities reconsider the key themes of the Enlightenment in which social progress is related to new knowledge, yet within a new paradigm such as a 21st-century version of the land-grant acts that created the public research universities in America.

Of particular note here is the increasingly rapid and non-linear nature of the transfer of knowledge from the library and laboratory into practical application. Although the academic disciplines are likely to continue to influence key institutional characteristics such as faculty recruitment and academic programme quality, the changing nature of scholarship will likely demand a more intimate integration of basic research with professional programmes (e.g., molecular biology in the clinical sciences or social sciences in business administration). This will pose a particular challenge to universities without appreciable activity in those professional disciplines that connect directly with society.

Similarly the changing nature of education demands a reconsideration of the teaching mission of the research university. Young, media-savvy students increasingly demand interactive, collaborative learning experiences and will take more control of their learning environment. Adults seeking lifelong learning opportunities will approach universities as consumers of educational services rather than students.

The Glion IV participants learned of many important experiments both in Europe and American involving both student-centred learning and research-led curricula. Yet, to date, the high cost of such paradigm shifts left traditional classroom teaching (e.g., lectures) as the most cost-effective method, particularly in the context of massification. Furthermore, the faculty reward system and the importance of grantsmanship for institutional finances are likely to continue to maintain the balance in favour of research over teaching, at least for faculty members heavily involved in research and graduate education. The likely consequence will be an increasing separation of roles in which faculty increasingly focus on the design of learning resources and objectives, while others (part-time lecturers, adjuncts, practitioners, or student peers) assume primary responsibility for delivery of learning experiences to students.

Students and Faculty

Paradoxically, the most important strategic action that research universities should take is one that has been the key to success thus far: a determined effort to seek the very best faculty and students. Of course, the key to the reputation of a research university is the quality of its faculty, since this determines not simply the quality of academic programmes but the ability to attract outstanding undergraduate and graduate students, gather external support – particularly research grants – and perform cutting-edge research. The effort to attract, develop, and retain outstanding faculty requires the capacity to offer competitive salaries – a particular challenge to public universities with limited resources or overly constrained by government compensation policies. But, just as important, it demands the capacity to build high-quality research environments (laboratory facilities, equipment, research assistants, graduate students, research policies). Furthermore, it requires rigorous recruitment, promotion and retirement policies.

Similarly, the quality of the student body, particularly at the graduate and postdoctoral level, is key both to the quality of research programmes and the ability to attract the best faculty. Those institutions constrained by public policy, practice or culture in adopting selective admissions policies are at some risk, since mediocre students can pull down the general level of academic programmes at both the undergraduate and graduate level.

Here it is important to recognize that the marketplace for the best faculty and students has become an increasingly global one, breaking loose from the constraints of national borders or institutional policies. The long-standing mobility of faculty and students in the United States has created an intensely competitive marketplace in which universities compete aggressively for the best people, and faculty loyalties are less to a particular institution than to their discipline or research group. In effect, the U.S. marketplace for talent has become a Darwinian ecosystem, in which the wealthy elite universities act as predators feeding on the faculties of their less well-endowed prey, luring away their top faculty. This has been particularly true of those elite private universities such as Harvard that tend to build their senior faculty by recruiting established scholars from other institutions that have invested heavily in their development from the junior ranks.

Although this competition is currently most intense in the United States, there has been a long-standing trend for American universities to also attract many of the best graduate students and faculty from Europe and Asia. From this perspective, the Bologna process, coupled with the effort to build a European-wide competitive grants system through the European Research Council, might be interpreted as an effort to respond to the reality of this intensely competitive international marketplace for academic talent by building a European market comparable in quality and bigger in size than that in America. Yet, beyond investment and policies, a key difference remains the vast difference in the mobility of students and faculty in Europe, where both local policies and cultures tend to bind faculty to particular institutions, and the United States, where a truly free market for the best students and faculty exists, with sometimes ruthless efficiency.

Resources

The rising costs of excellence and the increasing competitiveness of the marketplace for the academic talent pose formidable challenges to research universities in acquiring the necessary financial resources. It has become increasingly clear that few governments will have the capacity or the will, in the face of other compelling social priorities, to provide the funding necessary to build and sustain world-class research universities. Hence a key element of institutional strategies must be to build more diversified and robust funding portfolios. Here we find a very considerable difference between American and European practice and strategies.

In the United States, there has not only been a long-standing mix of public universities, supported by state tax dollars, and private institutions supported primarily by student fees (tuition) and private philanthropy, but as well a several-decade-long trend for both public and private research universities to build resource portfolios with a balance of public tax support (direct appropriations, research grants, student financial aid), student fees (where many public universities now charge tuition comparable to private universities, at least for students from other states), and private philanthropy (both through direct gifts and the income earned on the endowment funds accumulated through earlier giving). In fact, there is an increasing similarity in the mix of financial resources characterizing public and private research universities, with direct government support now comprising only about 10 % to 20 % of the support of the leading public research universities. This not only expands greatly the resource base available to American research universities, but it gives them a financial resilience against the inevitable ebb and flow of various sources of public and private support. It has also allowed a real rate of growth of 4 % to 6 % in revenues, providing the capacity to innovate and adapt to a changing environment.

In sharp contrast, most European universities continue to rely heavily on government support, with relatively modest contributions from student fees and philanthropy. In part this is due to cultural traditions such as the resistance to student fees. But it is also due to the fact that the capacity of universities to access alternative financial resources such as student fees or private gifts are strongly dependent upon government decisions and policies. The challenge for European universities is to develop the capacity to augment government support with additional funds raised essentially on a contractual basis. In a sense, universities can sell their teaching (student fees), research services (research contracts and intellectual property), services (health care, economic development), and, in a sense, reputation (private giving from loyal donors). Beyond this, they must develop the capacity to accumulate, manage and benefit from the income on assets (endowment). But in pursuing such strategies, European research universities should be aware that the effort to broaden resource portfolios will be quite difficult in the early stages and could pose risks to traditional funding sources such as government support.

The introduction or increase of student fees is probably the most promising approach to increasing revenues. However throughout Europe there is a strong resistance to fees, with a few exceptions in Spain and England. This may be due in part to a confusion between the perspectives of higher education as a "public responsibility" and as a "public good". Higher education is certainly not, at least in an economic sense, a public good implying that it should be provided free, even if it produces external benefits for those not participating directly as students or clients of a university. However, Europeans largely agree that higher education is a public responsibility which means that it must be provided or at least regulated by the State.

The consequences of this confusion are far-reaching, particularly with respect to the resistance to raising fees such that students contribute more directly to the funding of their studies. First, the payment of fees by students actually yields a better allocation of resources (on both the supply and demand sides of higher education). Second, free access to higher education produces a regressive impact on the income distribution of a country. These are two strong arguments in favour of raising student fees, provided that sufficient need-based financial aid is provided to prevent fees from becoming a barrier to low-income students, and provided as well that governments do not simply offset the additional income from rising student fees by reducing their public funding of higher education.

Contract research represents a second important revenue possibility. European universities have already become quite active in contract research, and the key here is to develop even more effective strategies both at the institutional level and at the national or European Union level to build competitive research grants programmes. The increasing commercial value of the

intellectual property resulting from research (and perhaps eventually instructional) efforts also has considerable revenue potential, albeit accompanied by
some risk to the research environment if universities become overly protec-
tive and bureaucratic.

Philanthropy could also be an important source of additional funds, but
only if governments develop and implement tax policies that provide strong
incentives for private giving, such as allowing individuals and corporations to
exclude from taxes the amounts given to universities or the income universities generate on accumulated assets (endowment). Although some European
institutions (Oxford and Cambridge) have launched major private fund-
raising campaigns in the United States where such tax policies have existed
for decades, philanthropy will only become an important revenue source if
such tax policies are adopted directly by the host nation.

The services provided by research universities can also provide significant
revenue streams. Those universities with medical schools can tap the income
generated by the clinical activities of their faculty and students. Executive
management education provided to corporate executives by business schools
has also proven to be a lucrative income source for American universities.
Many professional disciplines such as engineering, business administration
and health sciences can build profitable consulting services. Again, however,
tax policies are key to the effectiveness of such efforts.

One of the major differences between American and European universities
involves endowments, the accumulation, investment and benefit from the
assets acquired through private gifts or services (research, clinical income).
This has been key to the vitality of private higher education in the United
States, with several of the elite private universities accumulating many billions of dollars of endowment assets. But even public universities have
moved aggressively to build endowments, with some accumulating assets
comparable to those of private universities (e.g., U. Texas at $10 billion or U.
Michigan at $4 billion). Income from these endowments not only provides
the additional funds necessary for excellence and innovation, but in many
institutions provides a substantial portion of the base support for academic
programmes. (Harvard's $18 billion endowment yields an annual payout of
roughly $700 million a year.)

Yet once again it is clear that without favourable tax policies, such strategies are clearly impractical. There are currently no tax incentives in Europe
(or most of the rest of the world) for individuals to make donations to universities or for corporations to fund research projects, since these are not deduc-
tible from their income. Although universities can lobby their national
governments, in particular their ministries of finance, to change the tax laws,
they will face major challenges. After all, most European universities are
already seen as a tax burden, and hence ministers of finance will not be keen

to accept new loopholes in the tax laws. Beyond this, there is in European universities practically no culture of alumni loyalty that could be tapped for private gifts.

Leadership, Management and Governance

Better profiling or positioning an institution to respond to market forces can only occur if universities can initiate strategic planning and, more importantly, make and implement decisions, which usually implies making structural changes that affect people. Yet the majority of European universities and still many in the United States are characterized by a cumbersome and extremely slow decision process. Furthermore many are limited by burdensome governance constraints, whether due to intrusive relationships with governments (both U.S. and E.U.), the political character of their governing boards (U.S.), the guild culture in their faculty governance (E.U.), or the weak authority given university leaders (both U.S. and E.U.).

Yet, addressing this challenge of leadership is complex. Simply providing greater authority to the rector or president is insufficient because in universities there is considerable institutional knowledge among the faculty. There is a very serious trade-off between the creation of a streamlined administrative hierarchy and relying on a more democratic system of shared governance, which is necessarily cumbersome, but allows for the participation of all those who can make a contribution to the improvement of the institution. Hence leadership strategies should involve three often conflicting objectives: strong leadership, light decision and control structures, and broad consultation of all stakeholders.

As universities become more complex, good management becomes more important. Since over 80 % of the expenditures of universities involves human resources, the effective management of people and their activities becomes paramount. Yet the long tradition of selecting academic leaders from among the faculty poses a challenge, since the best scholars and teachers may not be the most effective leaders and managers. Clearly additional training in management methods, including the use of modern management tools in supporting decision-making, has become critical. Furthermore, the presence of talented and experienced administrative staff becomes ever more critical for the efficient and effective operation of the contemporary research university.

In Europe, there is increasing recognition of the need to reconsider the mechanism of control and influence over the research university by government, since this tends to limit or threaten the autonomy of institutions at a time when more flexibility is necessary to adapt to a rapidly changing world. One solution being explored by both public authorities and universities is to create an administrative board with real power that sits between the state and the institution. This would allow for a clear separation between the bodies that prepare a solution and those that make and control it. The leader of the institution, a rector or president, is either in a position to make a decision, which must be confirmed by another body, or in a position to propose a decision that should be made by the board and confirmed by the state. The delicate question here is whether members of the institution, e.g., the faculty, can be members of the board or if the latter should be composed exclusively of external members. Obviously there are good arguments for either solution, but a pure system of decision and control argues for a board composed only of external members.

Beyond leadership, there are important management issues that need to be addressed. In the face of limited resources and increasing public accountability, universities need to be more aggressive in adopting the cost containment and quality assurance practices proven so effective in the business sector. This generally demands the decentralization of authority over both human and financial resources, along with an appropriate system of accountability. A continuous system of quality audits of academic departments that focuses more on outputs, e.g., the quality of student learning or research productivity, than inputs, such as student selectivity or faculty reputation, has become a must. The methodology is organized around the drafting of self-evaluation reports, review committees comprised of external peers, and the consideration of these reports by the university leadership (president, deans, government bodies). Experience demonstrates that a serious effort at quality evaluation can frequently reveal shortcomings, making transparent what was often suspected but hidden. In other words, good universities can improve still further with such a quality culture. Yet here faculty opposition can be strong, since many faculty members will resist efforts to apply such quality controls, arguing that the academic community is simply too different from the corporate setting.

CONCLUDING REMARKS

There seems general agreement among the participants in the Glion IV Colloquium that the research university faces a period of significant challenge and change, driven by an array of powerful economic, social and technological forces. Key in transforming this era from a threat to an opportunity is institutional flexibility (particularly that arising from a more robust and diversified funding model) and institutional autonomy (allowing universities more control over their destinies during a time of change). Strong evidence for this is provided by the great success of private research universities and "privately-financed" public universities in the United States, and this enhanced flexibility and autonomy should clearly be an objective of European research universities if they are to compete in the global marketplace.

There are currently many contrasts between the characteristics of the research university in Europe and the United States. European institutions function in a highly fragmented marketplace, still controlled by nation-states (although many of their faculties compete globally); most European universities are still almost entirely dependent upon government support, without the benefit of significant student fee income, private giving, or endowments; student and faculty mobility is still highly constrained, at least compared to the United States; private (government-independent) higher education is still modest; institutional leadership is relatively weak (frequently elected by the faculty); and true institutional autonomy is limited.

The most immediate objectives for research universities in Europe are:

- Control over tuition policies
- More favourable tax policies (to encourage philanthropy and build endowments)
- More institutional autonomy
- Stronger institutional leadership
- Stronger differentiation and stratification of institution mission (likely determined more by market forces driven by competitive research grants and faculty and student mobility than by government policy)

Perhaps the ongoing Bologna process and the effort to build an EU-wide competitive research grants system by the European Research Council will provide a useful political umbrella under which such issues can be explored both by universities and governments. But here a caution is warranted. The big, bad wolf of the marketplace can be a useful device to elevate the political visibility of the need to change. But crying wolf too often, without taking aggressive internal actions to address the changing demands on the research university, could lead to disaster. Markets are inexorable and global in extent. They are likely to dominate higher education – and public policy – for several decades, and represent a reality that must be addressed in a strategic fashion through aggressive internal decisions and actions as well as external persuasion and influence.

American research universities also face some unique challenges, not the least of which are the attitudes of an ageing society (the "baby boomers") who increasingly seek the gratification of personal needs (e.g., health care, security, tax relief, and personal consumption) over social priorities (e.g., investing in schools, reducing poverty, integrating minority populations). The same extraordinary and growing gap between rich and poor in the

United States also appears in the decoupling of the wealthy "medallion" universities from the rest of the higher education enterprise, driving predatory practices in which the rich institutions feed on the poor (raiding their best faculty and students). American universities continue to be relatively insular, with inadequate priority given to developing stronger international character in their instructional and research programmes (particularly in the area of social sciences and languages). The absence of any true higher-education policy at the federal level has eroded the public purpose of American higher education, abandoning traditional objectives such as broad student access and academic excellence in favour of responding to the near term rewards of the marketplace. Here American universities may have much to learn from the deeper historical and cultural ties of their European counterparts.

Yet it is important for research universities in both Europe and America to recognize that the competitive forces driving change in higher education are truly global in extent. The mobility of capital, people and ideas leads to a global, knowledge-driven economy, which not only links more tightly the economic welfare and security of nation-states, but immerses their social institutions such as the research university in a global marketplace. While the strategies for addressing the future of individual research universities will be determined by unique historical, cultural and environmental factors, the imperatives for change will be universal.

Imprimé en France
Composé et Imprimé par Jouve
11, bd de Sébastopol, 75001 PARIS - FRANCE
N° 337081N. Dépôt légal : Janvier 2004